Y0-CBD-779

TENSIONS IN POLITICAL ECONOMY

BUCHAN AN'S TENSIONS

REEXAMINING the POLITICAL ECONOMY and PHILOSOPHY of JAMES M. BUCHANAN

EDITED by PETER J. BOETTKE and SOLOMON STEIN

MERCATUS CENTER
George Mason University
Arlington, Virginia

ABOUT THE MERCATUS CENTER AT GEORGE MASON UNIVERSITY

The Mercatus Center at George Mason University is the world's premier university source for market-oriented ideas—bridging the gap between academic ideas and real-world problems.

As a university-based research center, the Mercatus Center trains students, conducts research of consequence, and persuasively communicates economic ideas to solve society's most pressing problems and advance knowledge about how markets work to improve people's lives.

Our mission is to generate knowledge and understanding of the institutions that affect the freedom to prosper and to find sustainable solutions that overcome the barriers preventing individuals from living free, prosperous, and peaceful lives.

Since 1980, the Mercatus Center has been a part of George Mason University, located on the Arlington and Fairfax campuses.

© 2018 by the Mercatus Center at George Mason University
All rights reserved.
Printed in the United States of America.

The Mercatus Center at George Mason University
3434 Washington Blvd., 4th Floor
Arlington, Virginia 22201
www.mercatus.org
703-993-4930

Cover design by Studio Gearbox, Sisters, Oregon
Editing and composition by Publications Professionals, Fairfax, Virginia
Index by MWIndexing, Washington, DC

ISBN 978-1-942951-41-4 (hardcover)
ISBN 978-1-942951-42-1 (paper)
ISBN 978-1-942951-43-8 (ebook)

Library of Congress Cataloging-in-Publication Data are available for this publication.

CONTENTS

INTRODUCTION

PETER J. BOETTKE AND SOLOMON STEIN

James M. Buchanan was one of the premiere political economists of the 20th century. Intellectually, he served as a cofounder of the Virginia School of political economy identified with him and the work of his colleagues and students. Organizationally, he directed the academic centers[1] through which the interdisciplinary strands composing the field were woven together. Indeed, Buchanan was at the heart of the emergence of public choice and the reintroduction of politics to academic economic analysis. His contributions extend to many of the other research programs contributing to the gradual rediscovery of political economy in the post–World War II economics profession, including experimental economics, law and economics, the UCLA property rights tradition, his defense of pre-Keynesian public finance, the radical subjectivist post-Keynesianism of G. L. S. Shackle, and Austrian economics. This may seem like a disjointed portfolio given contemporary disciplinary boundaries, but it reflects the continuity between Buchanan and the Old Chicago School of his mentor, Frank Knight. The contribution most distinctively Buchanan's own, *constitutional political economy*, was recognized by his receipt of the Nobel Prize in Economics in 1986. This constitutional project emerges from Buchanan's scholarship in public finance, constitutional economics, and contractarian political philosophy.

Buchanan's early works on public finance, as contributor to this volume Richard E. Wagner has recently explored in detail (Wagner 2017), already contain the components from which his later constitutional project would be assembled. Inspired by the work of Swedish economist Knut Wicksell, Buchanan criticized the prevailing approaches to public finance for their implicit assumption of a benevolent autocrat, effortlessly and flawlessly willing and able to implement whatever scheme of taxation or regulation was determined to be socially optimal within a model. Such a construction not only led to policy recommendations based on comparison of the costs associated with actual economic activity against a fictitious alternative, but it also obscured why and how a group of individuals not already subject to an autocratic political order would ever engage in political action. In the alternative, Buchanan argued for a view of politics as exchange, understanding the provision of public services as determined via agreement among the political community. Buchanan's vision was that rather than provide technical implementations imposed upon individuals, political economists would offer potential proposals whose desirability would (and could) be known only when deliberated upon and chosen or rejected (see Buchanan 1959). It was also necessary to understand the operation of democratic processes as they, in fact, occur, populated by individuals with their own interests, which do not vanish upon entrance into political life. Understanding the operation of political institutions when populated entirely by self-interested actors is critical to assessing the robustness of such institutions when confronted with the frailties of humanity.[2]

Study of the pathologies that result from the institutional incentives at play in political institutions forms one prong of the research program of public choice economics, providing the omitted theory of government failure required to engage in comparative institutional analysis and lacking in conventional welfare economics. The constitutional project that is associated distinctively with work done by Buchanan and numerous coauthors, however, attempts to step back from the opportunism associated with individuals acting within relatively known institutional environments and looks at how the rules governing those environments might best prevent those undesirable results internal to the system. Constitutions, in creating procedural constraints on later political behavior-as-usual, take center stage in Buchanan's work. Constitutional political economy's explanatory component rests in Buchanan's project alongside its justificatory, normative elements. The project of constitutional political economy looked to understand the products of the constitutional environment and the outcomes that result from various constitutional implementations. Constitutional economics provides a crucial input into Buchanan's program of classical liberal contractarianism, an understanding of how best to promote, justify, and protect a social order of free and responsible individuals. The program of constitutional political economy Buchanan articulated and contributed to for over a half-century remains ongoing and incomplete, as Buchanan recognized. The essays in this volume engage with that program by exploring tensions within Buchanan's project.

What, however, does it even mean to identify and explore a tension within a scholar's work? The range of explanations for the presence of tensions, and the consequences that might (or might not) flow from those different types, is covered by the preliminary remarks to Wagner's essay. Tensions may be unrecognized problems, incoherence, or inconsistency problematic for an argument; but this does not exhaust the possibilities. They could reflect shifts in thought or, more fundamentally, dialectical elements, by nature refractory to treatment through simple, definitive assertions. Wagner discusses the use of aggregates in Buchanan's treatment of the burden of public debt as an instance of a contradictory, problematic tension in Buchanan's work. A contrasting, dialectic tension arises between two opposing visions of political society, one "sentimental," resting on the productive potential of mutually coordinated individuals, and one "muscular," in which strife plays a dominant role in human affairs. Buchanan's ebb and flow between these two visions is a reflection of the liberal project's uncertain relationship with the political more generally.

Roger D. Congleton's chapter considers an additional category of tensions that one often confronts when faced with work of the scope and depth of Buchanan's constitutional economics: the apparently problematic tension that, when given a more extensive critical analysis, is not in tension at all. Understanding the resolution to such superficially inconsistent issues ultimately offers insight into the structure of the arguments as a whole. Congleton considers Buchanan's seemingly disparate assumptions regarding the importance of individual ethical norms as precisely such an apparent, but merely apparent, tension. Although Buchanan's view of political behavior as dominated by rational opportunism on the part of self-interested actors is what we would expect from the founder of public choice economics, in his study of individual behavior in general Buchanan sees individual ethical commitments as significant. Buchanan, a champion of behavioral symmetry in modeling the conduct of private and public actors, thus appears to be in violation of his own precept. A closer inspection of Buchanan's model of individuals and their moral aspects, Congleton argues, reveals the amorality of politics to be a consequence of Buchanan's picture of ethics rather than of problematic arbitrary assumptions.

For Buchanan, the individual adoption of ethical norms resides within their creative and open-ended capacities; but, particularly with respect to interpersonal ethical commitments, their adoption is grounded on the expected benefits of reciprocal cooperation. Ethical norms, once adopted by individuals as internal rules of conduct, tend to be followed even where opportunistic violations would be advantageous, reinforced by communal sanctions for norm violations. Buchanan's perspective on individual ethical commitment is, as Congleton points out, one in which the adoption and adherence to norms of civil conduct largely stem from internalized ethical beliefs but remain contingent on the institutional environment. The institutional differences between one's immediate social context, the large-scale interactions of post-constitutional politics, and the quasi-anonymity of the constitutional moment are the basis for the differences in the importance of individual ethical norms between those settings.

Buchanan's divergent attitudes toward constitutional and post-constitutional politics create a tension considered in Peter J. Boettke and Jayme S. Lemke's chapter as well. Both constitutional craftsmanship and post-constitutional political activity confront what is, in Wagner's terms, certainly a dialectical tension between the capacity to design rules to facilitate certain outcomes and the recognition that all rules will result in unintended and unforeseen consequences. Why, Boettke and Lemke ask, was Buchanan cautiously optimistic regarding the potential for constitutional design to generate rules that effectively structure political interaction, in contrast to the pessimism with which he viewed post-constitutional political designs? They conclude that there is less tension between Buchanan's reflections on the prospects for design at these two levels than initially thought. Boettke and Lemke examine Buchanan's efforts to negotiate those underlying tensions confronted by rational designs within complex, evolutionary orders in relation to similar efforts by F.A. Hayek and Elinor and Vincent Ostrom. The reconstructed project of constitutional political economy drawing on all three of those perspectives resolves one additional bonus tension, showing that Buchanan was not as incompatible with Hayek's evolutionary thinking as Buchanan's own comments often suggested.

Randall G. Holcombe's chapter concerns tensions between Buchanan as a constitutional theorist and Buchanan's constitutional project for a classical liberal social order. The project of constitutional political economy within the context of Buchanan's classical liberalism is instrumental, searching for those rules that prevent the dynamics of political interaction from generating an unchecked expansion of governments at the expense of individual citizens. This differs in uncomfortable ways, for Holcombe, from when Buchanan describes his project of constitutional analysis in terms of its contractarian, justificatory elements. The creation of constitutional rules within the contractarian side of Buchanan's thinking emerges from the agreement on the rules through which those engaged in the constitutional bargaining process are able to exit the perpetual conflict of the Hobbesian state of nature. The outcomes of this bargaining are those procedures for making particular subsequent rules on which the individuals involved are able to agree. Individuals consent to a given set of rules for political decision-making that result in benefits that warrant adherence to the outcomes of the post-constitutional politics, just as individuals choose to suffer costs that result in some cases of application of a particular rule to acquire the benefits of the rule in general. These two perspectives are often in tension when assessing post-constitutional developments: as a contractarian, Buchanan must view the adoption of illiberal policy within a constitutional system whose procedural rules for policy making were the product of agreement as a justified result of the contractual process.

Other tensions between these two programs emerge, Holcombe argues, when Buchanan's justificatory framework makes the necessary move from explicit agreement to a social contract to understanding why nonparties can be seen as having offered such consent. The justifications for the conceptual abstraction of bargaining between rational equals escaping the state of nature also has troubling implications regarding assessing proposals for subsequent constitutional reforms, which are never proposed under the conditions of uncertainty assumed for the initial contract. The justification may also prove too much: as Holcombe points out, Buchanan suggests the contractual order is justified so long as it is preferred to renegotiation from the state of nature. Buchanan-as-contractarian seems thereby reduced to silence regarding nearly all of the concerns involving political and economic liberty expressed by Buchanan-as-classical-liberal.

The limitations Buchanan places by his own admission on the project of constitutional political economy are what concern Stefanie Haeffele and Virgil Henry Storr. Along with abstracting to the relative uncertainty of interests of the constitutional moment, Buchanan proposes the ability to restrict the contract's agreement to unanimity among the "reasonable" and suggests that excessive heterogeneity among the contracting agents could frustrate the attempt to find a mutually acceptable social order. As limiting circumstances for the applicability of constitutional political economy, these restrictions curtail its value in what, as Haeffele and Storr point out, are precisely those circumstances (intractable disagreement among diverse individuals) in the real world where the need to find livable rules to structure political activity is most pressing. These caveats also threaten to subvert the normative and justificatory effort to constrain the scope of political activity to what can attain constitutional consent. Absent a non–post hoc unambiguous notion of when disagreement becomes not only unreasonable but also excludible-unreasonable, or in the case of a proposed social and political community that possesses too few commonalities to share a single political order—neither of which they find provided by Buchanan—Haeffele and Storr see these as ready-made facades for political tyranny.

Gerald Gaus's contribution highlights the internal tension faced in the accounts of Buchanan and others of the contractual exit of rational opportunists from the state of nature. Although the gains from exiting the perpetual war of all against all and forming a society provide a motivation for a contractual bargain, the actual implementation of a political order presupposes regularities in other spheres of interpersonal conduct, such as the norms that compose the "moral order." Buchanan's contractarian vision attempts to address this problem, Gaus argues, through a program he refers to as "comprehensive Hobbesianism," in which the underlying moral orders are, themselves, the result of opportunistic agents rationally choosing to constrain their behavior to capture gains from cooperation. Gaus's evaluation of both Buchanan's version of this recursively rational account of social order's emergence and the literature on the moral order in actual human activity leads Gaus to conclude that comprehensive Hobbesianism is ultimately an untenable project, and he offers some avenues through which constitutional political economy can be loosened from its initial Hobbesian moorings.

The perceived severity of the tension for Buchanan's constitutional project increased incrementally from Roger Congelton's tension—revealed to be apparent rather than substantial—to Gerald Gaus's reassurances that Buchanan's constitutional project can survive the amputation of its original Hobbesian origins.[3] And then there is Christopher J. Coyne's essay on the protective state, which offers a distressingly severe challenge to the viability of the constitutional project itself. The *protective state*—Buchanan's term for the provision of law enforcement and territorial defense from which derives the legitimacy of the government's monopoly on coercive force—is prior even to the productive state's Wicksellian politics as exchange. For some classical liberals, the protective state is the exclusive duty within which constitutional rules should contain political decision-making. If, as Coyne argues, the erosion of constraints on government power is an inherent consequence of the performance of those protective functions, the project of constitutional political economy might offer at most the possibility of postponing, rather than averting, the erosion of liberal societies within the context of nation-states.

David M. Levy and Sandra J. Peart's chapter examines a tension within Buchanan's project that emerges within the context of the underlying methodological and analytical ideas that give the project its unifying characteristics, more than its internal fault lines, and that connect Buchanan's project with his colleagues composing the Virginia School. The four points that define the research space of the Virginia School—the endogenous nature of group goals, analytical egalitarianism, reciprocity as the basic feature of group compromises, and the importance of trade—resulted in a basis upon which to examine social interaction at odds with the prevailing matrix of institutional attitudes in the rest of academia. As the experiences of the Thomas Jefferson Center documented by Levy and Peart here show, the Virginia School's distinctive character was explained by many external observers as having one, somewhat more mundane, cause: ideology. Levy and Peart push back on this interpretation of the Virginia School and, in developing their four aspects, illuminate the tension between the application of analytical egalitarianism to the agents in the explanatory framework and the resistance to the reflexive application of that same framework to explanation of the political economists themselves.

Exploration of tensions within James Buchanan's political economy, where they are amenable to some resolution but even more so where efforts to do so have as of yet failed, is a constructive and critical endeavor. The essays in this volume, and more broadly the scholarly careers of the contributors, illustrate Buchanan's presence in political economy's extended present, that long conversational moment extending back at least to Adam Smith and oriented toward the open-ended future. As Buchanan would say: onward and upward!

NOTES

1. Both the Thomas Jefferson Center at the University of Virginia as well as its successor organization, the Center for the Study of Public Choice at Virginia Polytechnic Institute and State University and, after 1983, George Mason University.

2. F. A. Hayek's description in "Individualism: True and False" of Adam Smith and the classical political economists could apply equally well to Buchanan—thinkers whose "chief concern was not so much with what man might occasionally achieve when he was at his best but that he should have as little opportunity as possible to do harm when he was at his worst" (Hayek 1948, 11).

3. Amadae (2016), in a volume critiquing the logic of game theory in political economy, also explores similar tensions in Buchanan's project.

REFERENCES

Amadae, S. M. 2016. *Prisoners of Reason: Game Theory and Neoliberal Political Economy*. New York: Cambridge University Press.

Buchanan, James M. 1959. "Positive Economics, Welfare Economics, and Political Economy." *Journal of Law and Economics* 2: 124–238.

Hayek, F. A. 1948. "Individualism: True and False." In *Individualism and Economic Order*, 1–32. Chicago: University of Chicago Press.

Wagner, Richard E. 2017. *James M. Buchanan and Liberal Political Economy: A Rational Reconstruction*. New York: Lexington Books.

CHAPTER ONE

BUCHANAN'S LIBERAL THEORY OF POLITICAL ECONOMY

A VALIANT BUT FAILED EFFORT TO SQUARE THE CIRCLE

RICHARD E. WAGNER

James M. Buchanan's contributions to political economy occupy 20 volumes in Liberty Fund's collection of his works; most but not all of his oeuvre appears there, and I have, separately, presented a rational reconstruction of his works (Wagner 2017). It is obvious from reading those volumes that Buchanan located himself within the classical tradition of liberal political economy. It is also obvious that he injected new strands of thought into that tradition. Equally obvious are points of incoherence within his oeuvre. To speak of a tension in someone's body of work, by identifying incongruent elements within that body, is to accept the logic of noncontradiction as a principle to which a coherent body of work should conform. Noncontradiction is suitable for closed schemes of thought, in which Buchanan sometimes engaged. For open schemes of thought, which Buchanan also pursued, thought must be dialectical, where what appears to be tension is instead an interaction among the various parts of some whole that generates the phenomena being examined. Buchanan's political economy reflects both forms of tension, two instances of which this essay explores.

In short, I think Buchanan wanted to develop a political economy for an open and creative system of liberal political economy but could never escape the hold of closed-form theorizing. In this respect, he resembles John Maynard Keynes (1936) who in the preface to his *General Theory* expresses his desire to escape the gravitational pull of equilibrium theory, which he fails to do. Similarly, Buchanan did not generally think of societies in equilibrium terms, but sometimes he did, with the result being a body of work that reveals tensions of a mixed-metaphor quality. The first third of this chapter examines some methodological matters that unavoidably confront any effort to explore tensions within a scholar's oeuvre. The rest of the essay examines two themes within Buchanan's scholarly work that illustrate the two different forms of tension.

PRELIMINARY REMARKS REGARDING TENSIONS WITHIN A SCHOLAR'S OEUVRE

Typically, when someone speaks of a tension within some scholar's body of work, the speaker has detected points of incoherence within that body. That body of scholarship contains incongruent parts that do not form a coherent whole. In rendering this judgment, the speaker is presuming that the various parts of a scholar's oeuvre should be congruent, with congruence entailing harmony among the parts. In contrast to harmonization within a scholar's oeuvre, incongruity denotes discord among strands, as when one piece of a scholar's work conflicts with another piece. To speak of tensions, then, is to speak of something as being not quite right within a scholar's body of thought. Having arrived at this notion of tensions as incongruities within an overall body of thought, it is necessary to ask "So what?" What does it matter if we can identify tensions within a scholar's oeuvre? There seem to be three possible responses, only one of which represents a problematical feature of that oeuvre.

First, those tensions might point to confusion. When a scholar makes contradictory statements in different pieces of work, most likely, those contradictions will be subtle and not obvious. It is easy to point to instances of apparent contradiction within Buchanan's oeuvre, which I shall do later and which many of the other contributors of this book do as well. A student in a class on classical logic would most likely receive a failing grade for submitting a paper with clearly contradictory statements. Should those contradictions be matters of subtle inference, that student might earn a modestly higher grade, depending on the grader's standard of judgment. Still, exhibiting those contradictory statements in the same piece of work would be a negative indictment of a scholar's reasoning. Should those contradictions appear in different pieces separated by the passing of time, a new problem arises with respect to the assessment of tensions in a scholar's oeuvre.

Second, the tensions might indicate scholarly growth. We should not expect that a scholar who has created a large body of work over many years to have had all those thoughts from the start. To embrace this treatment would entail the presumption that a scholar who burst on the intellectual scene on the scholar's day one then simply required a lifetime to articulate what he or she already knew on that first day. Although Buchanan (1949) entered the scholarly scene with a theme that stayed with him to his end, as Marianne Johnson (2014) explains in tracing the origins of his approach to public finance, Buchanan also exhibited huge lines of development that were nowhere in sight on his day one. It is quite reasonable to expect that a scholar's insights would expand and deepen as the years pass and that some of this learning might be incongruent with earlier pieces of thought. This allowance for learning points toward the third possible response to tension in a scholar's oeuvre.

Third, then, contradiction might be desirable, or possibly necessary, regardless of how strongly professors of classical logic might claim otherwise. The law of the excluded middle is one way, but not the only way, of approaching logic. The postulate of noncontradiction is fine in some settings, but it is not the only logical option in play. Dialectical thinking recognizes that the contradiction of yin and yang can be part of a scheme of thought in which the whole requires interaction among elements, each of which seems to contradict the other. For example, it is impossible to ride a bicycle by remaining perpendicular to the pavement: the cyclist must shift continually to the left and then the right to keep the bicycle upright. To lean left a bit and then to lean right does not involve contradiction. On the contrary, it illustrates the dialectic of riding a bicycle.

Classical logic was formulated long before the logic of undecidability appeared on the scene, with the latter expounded delightfully and lucidly in Gregory Chaitin, Newton da Costa, and Francisco Doria's (2012) exposition of *Gödel's Way*. Most problems in classical choice theory appear decidable only because unknowable knowledge is presumed to exist. Any answer to a question rests upon a bed of presumptions that are themselves open to challenge. A simple problem of maximizing expected value illustrates undecidability in spades. All action must entail choices made today with outcomes not appearing until tomorrow. Here, one must distinguish between an observer's language and an actor's language. An observer observes actions and must impose an answer regarding what was observed; however, the observer has not observed tomorrow, only history. If maximizing expected utility is a formulation that eases the observer's mind, that is a fine answer for the observer even if it is delusional: it can't truly represent the mentality of the actor because consequence cannot be experienced at the moment of choice (Shackle 1961).

For the actor, there is no option but some form of resort to animal spirits, as George Shackle (1961, 1972) recognizes with especial lucidity. One of the many unfortunate monstrosities Keynes injected into economics was his conversion of animal spirits into some form of irrational exuberance. It is nothing of the sort; it is simple recognition that all action bridges time by crossing from present—when action is taken—into future—when consequences of action manifest. In many cases, the span of time and the stakes are both small, as when someone vows one evening to go to the store tomorrow to buy bread and milk. No one thinks that any spirit is involved in taking that kind of action. Yet the form of the action is no different from that of someone who stands at the base of a thousand-foot face of granite and vows to climb it free style. Or, again, when someone invests one's fortune in establishing a commercial or manufacturing enterprise. All action spans time and so entails adventures of different qualities from present to future. Process-oriented theories place individual action in the theoretical foreground. In contrast, equilibrium theories eliminate action, save for so-called policymaking interventions into equilibrium systems.

In other words, tension comes in two forms that present different problems of appraisal. On the one hand, it can refer to making inconsistent claims or statements, possibly separated by some period that might excuse the different utterances in response to learning in conjunction with the passing of time. Tensions can reflect confusion, but they can also reflect a scholar's intellectual development. On the other hand, tension can reflect a dialectical effort to characterize some complexities of a phenomenon that cannot be conveyed with closed-form modeling. Even more, what is viewed as a tension from the perspective of the principle of noncontradiction can be an instantiation of a dialectical scheme of thought that seeks to locate some harmony within a tensional relationship between opposites. In this instance, a social theory would not think in terms of locating some point of harmony on which everyone would agree. To the contrary, it would think in terms of keeping the antagonism of opposition within bounds, as Martin Currie and Ian Steedman (1990), Douglas Vickers (1994), and Donald Katzner (1998) illustrate in their treatments of time in economics. In this respect, dialectics pertains to open systems and not to closed systems, for the latter are equilibrium systems. In his scholarly work, Buchanan vacillated between thinking in terms of closed, equilibrium systems and open systems in which equilibrium stood outside that scheme of analysis.

NONCONTRADICTION VS. DIALECTICS IN THINKING ABOUT POLITICAL ECONOMY

An economy is a system of agents and connections among those agents. On this there is no controversy. Where controversy arises is over the theoretical conceptualization of that system. The predominant conceptualization is of a mechanical system. The agents are locked together within an equilibrium, possibly Pareto efficient, but an equilibrium that will persist all the same until external data are introduced into the system, in which case a new equilibrium will be established that again will persist until disrupted by new data. Within the postulated mechanical system, the relationship of parts to whole is synchronic because the presumption of systemic equilibrium has those parts acting in unison, which in turn allows appraisal against a vision of perfection. Arthur Lovejoy's (1936) distinction between this-worldly and otherworldly theorizing maps well onto the distinction between diachronic and synchronic theorizing. A diachronic theoretical schema (Shackle 1972) inverts the standard theoretical framework by conceptualizing societies as creative systems along the lines that Ludwig von Bertalanffy (1968) sketches. A society is conceptualized as containing numerous interacting and creative agents, with the passing of historical time being central to the theoretical effort. This society is an ecology of agents, with ecology taken substantively to denote a locus of interaction among nonidentical entities (Scheiner and Willig 2011). This ecological formulation entails an emergent rather than a stipulated or equilibrated mode of inquiry (Wagner 2012). This simple change in analytical orientation ramifies throughout the domain of inquiry because aggregation becomes theoretically incoherent (Stoker 1993). To be sure, one could always claim that the standard aggregates are typically "good enough" systemic indicators in a world where perfection is impossible. The ecological concept used here is a form of measurement without theory that proceeds by probing for goodness of fit. My interest, however, is not in pursuing a program of measurement without theory because that most certainly does not pertain to Buchanan's oeuvre.

Any reasonable theory that entails a relationship of the parts of some object to the whole must surely recognize that theorizing about the whole of the object entails a higher level of complexity then does theorizing about its parts. At this point, we must face the problem of theoretical reductionism by addressing questions regarding how far any reduction from complexity toward simplicity should proceed. Economists often reduce their models to representative agents or systemic averages, with the latter also reducing a social system to a single agent. Doing this, however, eliminates all phenomena that emerge through interaction among agents, leaving only phenomena that reside within an agent's mind. Should a social system be constituted of numerous Robinson Crusoes, it would not be appropriate to reduce that system to a single Crusoe: interaction among the Crusoes generates emergent phenomena that are products of interaction and that exert causal force upon individual Crusoes. For example, interaction will generate principles of property and contract, along with the associated institutions and conventions that will govern the operation of those principles. Furthermore, from the reverse causal direction, the presence of those principles will influence the substance of the economizing actions that individuals undertake.

With synchronic schemes of thought, there are no outliers. By contrast, outliers do significant work within diachronic schemes of thought, some illustrations of which are provided by Albert-László Barabási (2002) and Malcolm Gladwell (2008). After the style of Thomas Schelling (1978), suppose 100 people are distributed across squares on a plain. Private property is in play, which I interpret to mean that no one moves adjacent to an occupied square. But the persons also constitute a society, which I interpret to mean that no one allows more than three squares to separate that occupant from the nearest neighbor. Now, suppose five of those occupants change locations by moving toward unoccupied territory. This movement will induce shifts of location throughout the society. Suppose that 5 percent movement continues each period. The society will be in continual motion, with the direction of motion supplied by the five outliers. By standard statistical conventions, the society is one of static equilibrium disturbed by exogenous shocks. Yet, by the logic of constructivist mathematics (Bishop 1967), the society is continually in motion, with the direction of movement determined by outliers. In this respect, Joseph Schumpeter (1934) describes entrepreneurship as providing the locus of leadership for a capitalist society.

A parade illustrates synchronous action among its participants. Parades vary in such observed qualities as marching and musical skills; nonetheless, the parade is a synchronized object that reasonably can be reduced to a massed point whose progress can be followed on a map. In contrast, a crowd of pedestrians leaving a stadium, for example, is diachronic and cannot be reduced to a massed point. The pedestrians don't travel toward the same destination, nor do they travel at the same speed. They don't even exit the stadium at the same time. Some leave a bit early if the outcome is no longer in question, whereas others linger after the event is over, possibly for some food and conversation while letting the congestion subside. For a systems-level theory, which was always central to Buchanan's oeuvre, the choice between synchronic and diachronic analytical motifs is of central significance.

A diachronic social theory stands in an antipodal relationship to a synchronic theory. To be sure, the distinction between diachronic and synchronic theories is not just that the latter is static and the former is evolutionary. By itself, that distinction would leave us pretty much where we are now, working with closed schemes of thought. The difference between the pedestrian crowd and the parade convey the intuition behind the distinction I have in mind. Crowds and parades are both orderly social configurations. One would not be mistaken for the other, yet both are orderly in that their participants can function effectively within them. The parade is a closed system; the crowd is an open system. Schemes of thought suitable for thinking about closed systems are not suitable for thinking about open systems.

To function well within a parade calls for different skills and actions than does functioning well within a pedestrian crowd. The parade is reasonably characterized as synchronic. All members of a parade act as a single entity as an instance of an equilibrated object in which relationships among the participants remain unchanged without new data being inserted somewhere in the parade. The pedestrian crowd is diachronic. That crowd could be treated as if it were synchronic, but this would be possible only by freezing all participants in their present positions, much as chess pieces might be frozen in position on a chessboard. To do this, however, would be to violate the very notion of synchronicity, which entails motion over some duration of time.

The relation between the individual and systemic levels within an economic theory is a relation between the parts of that economic society and the whole of it. Any effort at diachronic theoretical construction must start at the level of parts, with the whole being something to be assembled and with the process of assembly being the object of theoretical inquiry, similar to Bruno Latour's (2005) analysis of how social phenomena are assembled through interaction among nonsocial phenomena. Within this alternative analytical framework, system variables do not act directly on one another because those variables emerge through interaction among microlevel entities within the system, as I shall illustrate momentarily.

For the most part, economic theories are formulated within the logical framework of noncontradiction, in which propositions are either true or false. This principle pertains to both the individual and the social levels of analysis. At the individual level, it requires a presumption that individuals choose as they are constrained by given and invariant preference orderings. Without subsequent changes in prices or income, people will repeat the same choices forever, maintaining a synchronic equilibrium in the process. Stated inversely, synchronic macro must impose the requirement that individuals operate with invariant utility functions because this scheme of analysis renders congruent individual optimization and systemic equilibrium.

Without doubt, there are domains in which the principle of noncontradiction pertains. But there are also domains in which it does not. At the individual level, this is the world of creative experimentation where utility functions would be described as only partially ordered. This dialectical setting contrasts with noncontradiction along the lines that Ross Emmett (2006) portrays Frank Knight's critique of the Stigler–Becker claim on behalf of invariant utility functions. For Knight, a significant part of individual action entails reflection-induced change. This type of theoretical framework, moreover, must entail continual movement through time, in contrast to equilibrium theories in which time must vanish. When the dialectical framework is applied at the social level, what shows itself as contradiction appears. At any moment, the mass of people might well act as price takers. At the same moment, however, there will be outliers who are inserting new data into the society. It is, however, impossible for everyone to insert new data at the same time. The very ability to insert new data requires that other people accept data. To think dialectically requires the theorist to think in terms of distributed populations and not in terms of averages or representative agents.

CONTRADICTORY AND DIALECTICAL TENSIONS IN BUCHANAN'S POLITICAL ECONOMY

In the remainder of this essay, I shall examine two types of tension within Buchanan's scheme of liberal political economy. One type of tension pertains to Buchanan's treatment of public debt as shifting forward in time the cost of state activity. This tension entails violation of the principle of noncontradiction when violation does not serve to advance some dialectical scheme of thought. Here, Buchanan's treatment of how debt transfers cost from a present to a future generation, especially in *Public Principles of Public Debt* (1958), is inconsistent with other parts of his thought. Buchanan supported the classical approach to public debt but sought to bring that classical approach into the Keynesian framework that dominated his time. What resulted was a scheme of aggregative thinking that contradicted other parts of his body of work.

The second type of tension points to some challenging issues of dialectical theorizing. Perhaps most significantly, it appears in Buchanan's distinction between constitutional and postconstitutional politics. This distinction, central to both *The Calculus of Consent* ([1962] 1999, with Gordon Tullock) and *The Limits of Liberty* ([1975] 2000), is the dominant theme within his body of work. It appears clearly in *The Calculus of Consent* and continues in his various subsequent efforts to use parlor games as a useful framework for thinking about problems pertaining to the organization of human affairs. This scheme of thought is closed and deterministic rather than open and creative. Yet there can surely be no doubt that, despite his flirtations with closed schemes of thought, the Buchanan (1982) who asserted that order could be defined only through some emergent process was someone who necessarily embraced open schemes of thought that are not reducible to a few people deciding what kind of parlor game to play.

This tension within Buchanan's scheme of thought points toward a distinction between sentimental and muscular versions of liberalism. Perhaps nowhere is this distinction illustrated in sharper relief than in comparing John Stuart Mill's *On Liberty* (1863) with James Fitzjames Stephen's *Liberty, Equality, Fraternity* ([1873] 1993). For Mill, a liberal order is easy to achieve and maintain because personal liberty, equality before the law, and humanity are universal values—so human nature provides a bedding ground within which liberalism can flourish. Stephen agreed with Mill about liberty and equality but not about the fraternal imperative being resident within human nature. Hence, Stephen thought that force would always be part of a well-ordered society, though he recognized that force could be used to subvert a liberal order as well as to support it. For the sentimental version of liberalism conveyed by Mill and later John Rawls (1971), human governance could be reduced to ethics, law, and commerce, leaving no room for the political insertion of force into society. For the muscular version of liberalism, free societies are not self-sustaining and can degenerate without the proper use of force. Whereas Stephen illustrates the muscular version of liberalism luminously, James Burnham (1943) traces that muscular version back to Niccolò Machiavelli and also associates it with such figures from the early 20th century as Vilfredo Pareto, Gaetano Mosca, and Roberto Michels. Burnham could very well have added Carl Schmitt ([1932] 1996) and his recognition of the autonomy of the political to his menagerie of thinkers in the spirit of muscular liberalism.

Buchanan's position relative to the divide between sentimental and muscular liberalism is ambiguous. Much of this thinking reflected an "end of history" style of thinking whereby political force could be abolished through the creation of the proper constitutional rules. Yet Buchanan never fully embraced this style of thinking. Sentimental liberalism treats liberty as a universal value. If it is, people should readily embrace the challenge of living as free persons. But, if a good part of the population is thought to be afraid of living freely (Buchanan 2005), either sentimental expressions of liberalism will transform liberty into servility (Belloc 1912) or political power will be marshaled to lead protesters into accepting the liberal order.

Some of Buchanan's ambiguity is apparent in his embrace of Knut Wicksell's largely sentimental liberalism and the muscular liberalism of the Italian theorists whom Buchanan also regarded highly. Pareto's liberalism is thoroughly muscular, but Buchanan did not often cite Pareto. Throughout his career he did, however, cite Antonio de Viti de Marco. Although de Viti de Marco's (1936) formulation of a cooperative state reflects a relatively sentimental version of liberalism, de Viti de Marco also formulated a vision of a monopolistic state that would elicit a more muscular vision of liberalism wherein a properly active state would be necessary to maintain a liberal order. Indeed, de Viti de Marco's (1930) chronicle of three decades of political struggle shows him operating within a muscular vision of liberalism. Moreover, Buchanan's (1960) presentation of Italian public finance, which did much to present those Italian theorists to English readers, congratulates the Italian theorists for their absence of romanticism toward politics. Yet Buchanan largely sidesteps especially nonromantic works including de Viti de Marco's 1930 volume and works by Pareto (1935), Michels (1915), and Mosca (1939), along with Friedrich Wieser's (1926) explanation of how power is inescapably manifest in society.

CONTRADICTORY TENSION WITHIN BUCHANAN'S THEORY OF PUBLIC DEBT

In his *Public Principles of Public Debt*, Buchanan (1958) claims that public debt is a method of public finance that shifts the cost of public programs from present to future generations. This book was published only 12 years after enactment of the Employment Act of 1946, which had created a national framework for using public debt as an instrument for maintaining economic stability, and with that stability conceptualized as constancy in the volume of aggregate expenditure. If Buchanan's claim was correct, Keynesian-style propositions about using fiscal policy to expand output in times of underemployment would run afoul of some widely held ethical precepts about people's responsibility for the consequences of their actions.

At the surface, *Public Principles* is about the ability of public debt to transfer cost away from people in the present, and it is on this point that the controversy centered. Lost amid this controversy was a deeper point that challenged progressivism far more thoroughly and vigorously than any claims about fiscal policy could have done. Prior to the advent of Keynesian claims on behalf of fiscal policy, American fiscal history was one of deficits during wars and recessions, with surpluses during ordinary times used to retire public debt. In following this pattern, public debt illustrated the principle of what was once known as extraordinary public finance, whereas public debt has been part of ordinary public finance for the past half-century or so. Buchanan (1958) offers some economic reasoning in support of what had been common practice before the 1930s, as Buchanan and Wagner (1977) explain.

Where *Public Principles* really stands sharply in opposition to the progressivist program of domination of the political by self-anointed elites is in Buchanan's presumption that government should be the province of interaction among equals and not an arena where elite shepherds tend to the sheep-like masses. *Public Principles* embraces the analytical egalitarianism that David Levy and Sandra Peart (2008) articulate in their collection of essays on *The Street Porter and the Philosopher*. *Pub-*

lic Principles was written after Buchanan's year in Italy, where he studied deeply de Vito de Marco and other Italian economists. De Viti de Marco and the other Italian writers over roughly 1880–1940 sought to bring economic principles to bear on the actual conduct of government, in sharp contrast to treating government as some kind of perfecting instrument. Besides being a professor in Rome, de Viti de Marco was a member of the Italian Parliament for 20 years. As Giuseppe Eusepi and Wagner (2013) explain, the concepts and categories that de Viti de Marco used in his theoretical work were recognizable to him in his parliamentary work, bearing the relation of a theory of public finance to a practice of public finance. To be sure, the essays collected in de Viti de Marco (1930) explain that fiscal practice is far removed from what de Viti de Marco had envisioned in his model of a cooperative state and indeed reflected more of what he described as a monopolistic state. In any case, a key feature of that Italian tradition was recognition of how different institutional arrangements of collective activity can exert significant influence over collective outcomes. This scheme of thought was far removed from the progressivist scheme in which all would be well if only the right people occupied positions of political domination.

Since publication of *Public Principles* in 1958, Buchanan has been associated with the proposition that the financing of government programs through borrowing rather than taxing is a method that transfers the cost of those programs from present taxpayers to future taxpayers, which might include future instances of now-present taxpayers. In staking out this position, Buchanan voiced support for the presuppositions of classical public finance against the new economic thinking associated with Keynes (1936). Such thinking claimed that public debt should create no particular concern because "we owe it to ourselves," in which case public debt could be eliminated simply by burning the bonds in an incinerator (Schumpeter [1918] 1954).

To be sure, the prime opponent in Buchanan's analysis was probably Abba Lerner (1944), who argued that governments should tax only to forestall inflation; otherwise, they should borrow. But Keynes was well known, and well beyond any circle of economists. Lerner was more narrowly known; moreover, Lerner regarded himself as amplifying Keynes. So Buchanan's selection of his target was a sensible choice. Buchanan regarded the Keynesian claims as inverting the classical precepts that taxation should be the normal way that governments finance their activities, with debt used only in such extraordinary circumstances as fighting wars or providing services during depressions.

Buchanan could have reiterated the classical formulation, but I imagine he suspected that such reformulation was insufficient to counter the Keynesian thinking in support of public debt and activist fiscal policy. He therefore added a moral dimension, though without calling it that. Where the Keynesian claim was that public debt had no moral significance because public debt was just something that we owed to ourselves, Buchanan countered that public debt enabled current taxpayers to provide services to themselves paid by higher taxes imposed on people in future years. Buchanan thus claimed that public debt was redistributive at a time when most governmental activity still entailed the supply of real goods and services.

To claim that public debt entails shifting the burden of public expenditure from one generation to another requires treating generations as acting entities. This is a treatment that Buchanan would have abhorred in other contexts. For one thing, it entails reduction of some set of people who span roughly a third of a century to a single, representative person, and with that person facing a choice between taxing and borrowing. Within this framework of a representative agent, however, it is puzzling how internal public debt could be created because there is no space for a representative agent to engage in transactions. Yet Buchanan viewed internal public debt as the norm and external debt as the exception, arguing, moreover, that no difference exists between the two forms of debt.

Two things seem clear about Buchanan's treatment of public debt, as I explain in my reconstruction of Buchanan's theory of public debt (Wagner 2014); and these two things conflict with one another. First, Buchanan was attracted to public debt in response to practical problems of public finance. The immediate issue was the financing of the interstate highway system that was begun in the mid-1950s. One central issue that arose at that time was whether construction of that system should be financed by issuing bonds that would be amortized in later years or by collecting proceeds from a tax on gasoline. One point of controversy was whether debt could be a means of charging the future users of interstate highways.

Buchanan went to Italy in 1956 with a project on highway finance underway and planned to examine the Italian literature on public debt during his year in Italy. He produced *Public Principles* after his return. Somewhat ironically, *Public Principles* emerged as a more macro-centric book than one would have thought he would write, given both his initial interest in highway finance and the strongly micro-centric thrust of Italian scholarship on public debt. That *Public Principles* was greeted as a macro-centric book is evidenced by the preponderance of the book's reviewers who were macro theorists. This list includes James Tobin and Franco Modigliani, among others. Only Richard Musgrave was a public finance theorist, and he embraced the Keynesian calls for an activist fiscal policy to replace classical claims on behalf of balanced budgets in normal times.

Had Buchanan maintained contact with methodological individualism, as conveyed in both his initial paper on the theory of government finance (Buchanan

1949) and his subsequent explanation (Buchanan 1969) that cost is a concept pertaining only to and inseparable from making a choice among options, he most surely would have avoided using generations as action-taking entities. Public debt, like all credit transactions, creates obligations that bridge present and future. Those obligations, however, are established among the people alive at the time the debt is created. Hence, someone would support debt over taxation only because that person perceived debt to entail lower cost compared with taxation. Here, it is necessary to be clear that lower cost refers to the perception of an action-taking entity and not to some such artifactual construction as a nation.

The Italian literature held the same view. Pareto, for example, considered it obvious that someone who supported public debt over taxation must perceive debt finance to be less costly than tax finance. Both Pareto and Buchanan held that people, when faced with a choice between options, would choose what they perceived to be the lower-cost option. It was the same for de Viti de Marco. These theorists, along with most of the classical Italian theorists of public finance, theorized in a bottom-up or emergent fashion. In their thinking, the amount of public debt relative to taxation emerged out of individual perceptions of alternatives because these were intermediated through some political process in which the best method of public finance was always one that placed burdens on someone else to the extent possible.

This recognition should have shifted Buchanan's attention away from generations as acting entities to interactions and relationships among the individuals present at any slice of time. It is possible to imagine an approach to public debt in which debt finance would be identical to tax finance, as Eusepi and Wagner (2017) explore. In this arrangement, liability for public debt would be assigned to individual taxpayers at the time the debt was created, in contrast to the contingent liability under which public debt is issued. Issuing public debt in this alternative manner would increase the interest rate on political loans because failure by some taxpayers to pay their assigned liabilities would not be offset by higher taxes on remaining taxpayers. Hence, bondholders would bear a higher risk of default when liability was assigned to individual taxpayers rather than being left for future assignment.

In this regard, it is often claimed that the lower interest rate at which governments can borrow indicates a genuine cost saving from organizing political loans under contingent liability as against doing so under explicit liability. This common claim is surely wrong because it assumes that liability rules are irrelevant for managerial conduct. No economist would make this claim under other circumstances. A well-known motif of political action is to accompany projects with cost estimates that are lower than the cost turns out to be, surely part of the public relations strategy of gaining support for the project. A project that gains support when projected to cost $1 billion might not get support if cost were projected at $2 billion. So the project secures sufficient support when projected to cost $1 billion, with continuation of that project accepted despite its being accompanied by an additional tax charge of $1 billion. The lower interest rate on public loans is an illusion that reflects a shift of the risk of default away from bondholders onto taxpayers.

Although Buchanan wrote "Keynesian Follies" in 1987, my classroom remembrance was that he recognized those follies in his teaching in 1963–64, with that recognition reinforced by his invitation to William Hutt, who had just completed *Keynesianism: Retrospect and Prospect,* to visit and teach during 1964–65, or possibly 1965–66. My personal assessment of this particular tension in Buchanan's oeuvre is that it originates in his perception that the Employment Act of 1946 gave political validation to the practice of Keynesian follies. During his Italian visit, he encountered a treatment of public debt that accorded with classical visions of sound finance for governments being the same as those for individuals. Within this classical vision, full employment was a property of a market system with openly competitive labor markets and money based on a commodity rather than on a fiat standard. In *Public Principles,* however, Buchanan wanted to do more than offer a restatement of classical public finance, probably because he sensed that restatement alone would not reverse the Keynesian surge. He responded by giving *Public Principles* more of a macro-theoretic look than it otherwise would have had. In consequence, Buchanan treated the cost-shifting associated with public debt as being between generations, whereas his methodological individualism would have treated that shifting as occurring among individuals in the present; that shifting would lead to changes in future conditions, as I explain in offering a reconstruction of Buchanan's public debt theory (Wagner 2014).

DIALECTICAL TENSION WITHIN BUCHANAN'S THEORY OF CONSTITUTIONAL ORDER

Where Buchanan's approach to public debt clashed with other aspects of his body of work, his approach to constitutional order illustrates the confounding of schemes of thought suitable for open and for closed frameworks. Buchanan often illustrated arguments with closed schemes of thought, yet his interests primarily dealt with open systems. Buchanan did not theorize explicitly in dialectical fashion, and probably did not think of himself as theorizing in this fashion. Should his constitutional thinking be held to the standard of noncontradiction, it would be rife with contradiction. Yet Buchanan was a deep and subtle thinker, recognition of which surely renders it reasonable to treat apparent contradictions as pertaining to simple parts within an argumentative framework aimed at illuminating the complex phenomena that emerge through interaction among those parts. I shall illustrate this claim mostly with respect to Buchanan and Tullock's *The Calculus of Consent* ([1962] 1999), but I could have done so as well for *The Limits of Liberty* ([1975] 2000).

The Calculus of Consent emphasizes the constitutional analysis of systems of order, and it carries the subtitle "The Logical Foundations of Constitutional Democracy." The thrust of *The Calculus of Consent* is to explain how the complex constitutional structure of the American republic reflects both an underlying economizing logic brought to bear on the problem of maintaining liberty and the recognition that some modicum of government is necessary to keep civil peace. Both *Calculus* and *Limits* were written long before the development of computer technology led to the creation of schemes of thought where complex patterns emerged out of interaction among simple parts of that emergent constitutional entity. Mitchel Resnick (1994) crisply conveys that distinction in his examination of how systemic order can arise without action by some ordering agent. Had such tools of thought been more generally available in 1962 or 1975, it is likely that Buchanan would have developed his constitutional themes in a manner that reflected such complexity-based theorizing. The parts that together constituted his theme might well have been portrayed in the same manner, but the systemic qualities of interaction among those parts would have been integrated to different effect.

In numerous places, Buchanan remarked that he regarded the central theme of *The Calculus of Consent*, as well as his constitutional thought in general, as giving economic-theoretic insight into the logic of the complex constitutional construction associated especially with James Madison. In doing that, Buchanan and Tullock ([1962] 1999) and Buchanan ([1975] 2000) developed several simple models that taken together illustrate the systemic quality of Buchanan's argument—a system of analysis constructed through assembling a variety of parts. Relatively recent work on emergence and systems theory has led to recognition that the systems level generally cannot be acquired simply by adding the parts together. Similarly, the behavior of the system cannot be reduced to the behavioral properties of one of the parts. To proceed with such a reduction is to commit what Resnick (1994) describes as the "centralized mindset," which attributes order at the societal level to the actions of some ordering agent at the agent level, when that order is an emergent quality of interaction among the agents.

In contemporary public choice theory, this centralized mindset is illustrated by the median voter model, wherein collective outcomes are ascribed as the optimizing choices of a median voter (see the widely cited treatise on political economy by Persson and Tabellini [2000]). Buchanan clearly worked with median voter models in numerous places, and that model reflects widely held observations about centers of mass. More recent works on computational modeling and theories of emergent phenomena have peered beneath the surface of mass phenomena to reveal the significance of outliers. In this respect, emergent phenomena don't just emerge as a pile of rotting grass that might catch fire. To the contrary, emergence generally reflects the operation of leadership inside the mass, with massed phenomena becoming a recognizable phenomenon only after leadership has been at work. To speak of a median voter, therefore, is to refer to something that stands at the end of a train of activity that results in a vote being taken. The autonomy of the political (Schmitt [1932] 1996) resides in the process leading to the vote, which mostly validates the preceding train of action rather than having produced it.

At the level of a political system, as distinct from the level of the parts that constitute the system, *The Calculus* seeks to give an economic-theoretic gloss on James Madison's constitutional craftsmanship of divided and fragmented government. In doing this, Buchanan and Tullock run strongly contrary to the progressivist strand of political economy that took shape early in the 20th century and that is represented succinctly in Torsten Persson and Guido Tabellini (2000). Progressivist thought reacted against the compound republic established by the 1787 Constitution and sought to convert the compound republic into a simple republic with some point of final authority that could be denoted as a median voter. Other potential formulations could fit the rule by right-thinking experts that the progressives, then and now, envision.

Within the spirit of the compound republic and *The Calculus of Consent* ([1962] 1999), what are described as collective outcomes are not properly described as choices because they are emergent products of interaction among the various parts that together form the system of the compound republic (Wagner 2013). Politics entails processes of complex interaction and not simple matters of choice. Certainly, there is a reasonable domain to which propositions about median voters pertain, but the corpus of political economy is not reducible to some singular act of electoral choice. Buchanan and Tullock affirmed the constitutional foundation of a social system based on a strictly limited ability of governments to intrude into people's freely chosen activities, but with that limited ability based not on personal preferences but on structural features of the compound republic. Vincent Ostrom (1987, 1997) provides a valuable and substantive flying buttress to Buchanan's constitutional thought. Buchanan, both individually and with Tullock, worked at the relatively formal level of economic theory. In contrast, Ostrom engages more deeply in substantive matters regarding the operation of a compound republic (Ostrom 1987) and the difficulties a compound republic faces if it is to be self-sustaining (Ostrom 1997).

A tension exists between Buchanan's constitutional thought and Ostrom's, but that tension is surely more superficial than deep. At the deep level, their liberal orientation led both Buchanan and Ostrom to treat the creation of a polity as a Faustian bargain, with the natural predations of the political being impossible to stop within a simple republic. Even within a compound republic, those predations could not be stopped but might be limited (Buchanan 1975). Such limitation, however, was not a simple matter of desire as reflected in constitutional design because it also required some cultivation of what once were described as republican virtues, which stand in contrast to modern democratic sentimentality in which democracy has become a synonym for goodness.

Early in the 20th century, Pareto responded to Edgeworth-inspired claims about maximizing well-being within a polity: How can one speak of maximizing well-being when well-being for the wolf requires eating the lamb and well-being for the lamb requires the avoidance of being eaten? For Pareto, as for Schmitt, humans are dangerous creatures. Buchanan and Tullock sidestepped addressing the dangerous quality of humans by postulating the existence of some common point of agreement, although Buchanan later voiced doubt about such agreement. The difference between whether people are tame or dangerous creatures is the difference, within a generally liberal framework, between sentimental and muscular varieties of liberalism. For sentimental liberalism, good government can be achieved by well-intentioned people acting through discussion and consensus. For the muscular form of liberalism, reason responds to sentiment and nonlogical action. And, although approbation is often presented as a pro-social sentiment, it is also a close cousin of envy, as Lovejoy (1961) explains and regarding which Helmut Schoeck (1969) sets forth a theory of social process. In contrast to Pareto, John Hobbes, and Machiavelli, all of whom embraced a muscular liberalism, Buchanan seemed to vacillate between the two forms of liberalism.

Buchanan's (1975) articulation of the Samaritan's dilemma sharply illustrates this vacillation. In the original biblical story, the Samaritan came across a beaten traveler and supplied aid. The generalization of that situation, however, leads to a reduction in the care travelers take, leading in turn to an increasing demand for support from Samaritans, and with that growth of support reducing the amount of care travelers take. Should there always be Samaritans willing to offer aid, there will always be travelers who substitute aid for care, so long as that aid renders the travelers whole, whatever that might entail. In contrast to the sentimental species of liberalism, the muscular variety would recognize that the very offering of aid can undermine the requisites of responsible action on which liberalism rests, and so will often refuse to offer aid.

Buchanan worked with a scheme of thought that was suitable for tame creatures, but in doing so he incompletely reflected the Italian tradition he did much to promote. Buchanan's constitutional project starts from a simple analogy with playing poker and carries that analogy forward a great distance to set forth a sharp distinction between choosing the rules by which people will play a game and the outcomes of subsequent plays of that game. Without doubt, this distinction is a helpful mental model for thinking about contemporary affairs in their various manifestations. Yet Buchanan's employment of that analogy entails tensions with other parts of his oeuvre, such as his recognition that the knowledge pertinent to societal operation is never assembled in one place or mind. It comes instead from what can only be emergent processes and, moreover, with constitutional order being a systemic feature not reducible to any individual's direct action. It also is an analytical point of departure that the presence of ultimate harmony among participants works against leaving any degree of harmony as some emergent quality of some interactive process, as Shruti Rajagopalan and Wagner (2013) pursue in explaining the tenuous and fragile quality of notions of rule of law.

STRUCTURE, PROCESS, AND CONSTITUTIONAL ORDER: WHAT DO THEY MATTER?

I contrast Virginia political economy with progressivist political economy in terms of six elements of their respective hard cores (Wagner 2015), presented in table 1. First, Virginia political economy stems from a desire to pursue a political economy of liberty rather than a political economy of control. Second, a program of liberty requires interaction among equals, whereas a program of control entails relationships of domination and subordination. Expertise is present in either case and rendered necessary by the division of knowledge; however, people choose experts under liberalism, and governing cadres impose experts under progressivism. Third, all societies entail practices and institutions of societal control; however, that control emerges mostly through voluntary associations under liberalism, whereas political domination is part of the progressivist program. Fourth, Virginia political economy treats societies as networks of interaction rather than as fields of rulers and masses, which entails a population-based style of thinking in contrast to reducing societies to representative agents or averages; Jason Potts (2000) presents an illuminating contrast between field-based and network-based thinking. Fifth, Virginia political economy portrays societies as processes of emergent interaction

TABLE 1: HARD CORES OF VIRGINIA AND PROGRESSIVIST POLITICAL ECONOMY

	Virginia Political Economy	Progressivist Political Economy
1.	Political economy of liberty	Political economy of control
2.	Self-governance among moral equals via spontaneous ordering	Expert governance of rulers over the ruled through elite control
3.	Robust civil society with private ordering (law)	Anemic civil society dominated by public ordering (legislation)
4.	Societies as networks of interacting agents	Societies as fields of rulers and masses
5.	Societies as reasonably orderly pedestrian crowds	Societies as parades that require parade marshals
6.	Process-based analysis with generative mode of thought	Equilibrium-based analysis with stipulated mode of thought

that are not reducible to some equilibrated structure. Sixth, Virginia political economy pursues a process-based rather than an equilibrium-based mode of thought. It includes both schemes of thought, but in a relationship of foreground to background and with emergent processes occupying the analytical foreground.

This contrast between the two schemes of thought ramifies throughout the domain of social theory. Virginia political economy is a scheme of thought conveyed in the active voice. Any process-based theory has people doing things because it is the doing of things that generates the emergent phenomena that make up societal motion. In contrast, equilibrium theories must be rendered in the passive voice. There can be no action within equilibrium theories because those theories describe states at the end of action: states of being simply exist but are not themselves generated through action and interaction. Indeed, within the framework of equilibrium theory all that can be accomplished is to show sets of conditions consistent with some postulated state of equilibrium. What is hidden from view, necessarily, is the continual transformation of one state into another through creative action and interaction among participants.

To develop a scheme of thought designed to explore the qualities of self-ordering under different circumstances, some scheme of thought bearing some family resemblance to Virginia political economy is necessary. Progressivist political economy, with its postulated state of equilibrium in conjunction with expert-induced shifts from one state of equilibrium to another, is analytically incapable of addressing systems of self-organization. At the same time, however, one of the central implications of undecidability is that experts are truly incapable of acting to bring about some articulated future state. Any expert intervention in this respect will unavoidably generate unanticipated consequences, meaning that experts are no better than ordinary people, save that experts typically are not constrained by property rights and the responsibility for their actions that residual claimancy creates.

MOVING FORWARD WITH THE VIRGINIA TRADITION IN POLITICAL ECONOMY

Peter Boettke (2012) explains that Buchanan, like Knight and Henry Simons, regarded economics as a relatively simple science of great public significance. That science, moreover, can be easily manipulated and distorted in the service of special pleadings of all sorts, and with proper economics serving mostly to explain why the political promises and speeches of the day are mostly sources of problems and not solutions. Knight's generational neighbor, Pareto (1935), turned from economic theory in the 1890s and 1900s to sociology to understand why what he regarded as the compelling logic of economic theory and free completion found such small favor. To do this, Pareto distinguished between logical and nonlogical action. Logical action is the domain of markets, where prices allow direct comparison between magnitudes. Outside of markets, such direct comparisons are not possible, and Pareto designated this area as the sphere of nonlogical action. In light of the current interest in behavioral economics, I should note that Pareto had nothing like irrationality in mind in referring to nonlogical action. Pareto regarded all action as rational within its context, recognizing that people act within different contexts, and with Rosolino Candela and Wagner (2016) contrasting Pareto's approach to rationality in action with that associated with behavioral economics.

In the market context, options can be reduced to a common denominator because of the existence of market prices. In other contexts, no such reduction is possible. Outside the market, Pareto saw competition as occurring between members of elites in society who use techniques of wit and power to gain and hold power. Success in this competitive process depends significantly on the ability of ruling elites to articulate ideological images that resonate with sentiments that are resident within the population and that lead the population to suspend any disbelief it might have. The population can't check those ideological options anyway because the options have no prices and choices associated with them.

Although Buchanan did yeoman's work in bringing to general attention the classical work in Italian public finance over roughly 1800 to 1940, he left aside a vibrant Italian literature on sociology and elites that arose around the same time as the fiscal scholarship. This literature included such figures as Mosca and Michels, and Pareto was part of both groups. Thinking of those sociologists recalls the German political theorist from the early 20th century, Schmitt, and how such muscular theorists as Schmitt, Mosca, and Pareto might have influenced the Virginia tradition of political economy.

Schmitt is a controversial figure, with much of that controversy stemming from a three-year flirtation with the Nazis, although earlier he had tried to defend Weimar against the forces of disintegration of its liberal constitution that he saw underway. F. A. Hayek, for example, excoriates Schmitt in both *The Road to Serfdom* and the third volume of *Law, Legislation, and Liberty*. Yet, as Renato Cristi (1998) explains, Hayek and Schmitt were quite close analytically if the Nazi period is ignored. Indeed, Schmitt's call for a strong state so as to have a free economy is reminiscent of Walter Eucken's ([1952] 1990) call for a strong state, which is based on his similar analysis that the disintegration of the Weimar constitution was due to weakness that left it unable to resist predation by various interest groups.

The problem at issue is the relation between liberalism and things political. For the most part, liberalism treats the political as ephemeral and not as autonomous (Bolsinger 2001). In other words, the political can in principle be tamed by ethics, by law, and by economics. This taming is the task of constitutional construction. In contrast, Schmitt claims autonomy for the political, for he regards the domain of politics as turning on the dichotomy of friend–enemy. It is not that enemies besiege friends, with the political coming into play to sponsor the public goods that would help the friends overcome the enemies. It is rather that the political is itself the situs where the friend–enemy dichotomy is generated, as Ion Sterpan and I explain in our effort to locate the political within a theory of political economy (Sterpan and Wagner 2017). Basically, politics is nonviolent war whereas war is but violent politics. Politics is replaced by ethics and economics within the sentimental form of liberal mentality for the most part. Politics doesn't go away, however, so liberal societal configurations erode without the appropriate application of liberal muscularity. For the normal liberal sentiments that are prone to think of a peaceable kingdom image of a societal end state, Schmitt's brand of liberalism is disquieting in its cold realism. In my judgment, the scheme of Virginia political economy would profit by a further injection of the muscular style of liberalism, which is also something that Buchanan seemed to embrace increasingly as the years passed.

Without doubt, James Buchanan's oeuvre is the fountainhead of what is now recognized as the Virginia tradition in political economy. That tradition did not start from zero with Buchanan's entry onto the scholarly stage; it is an extension of the classical British political economy set forth in Lionel Robbins (1952) and Warren Samuels (1966), and with the widely varying contributions of Knight (see, for example, Knight [1960]) on the problem of combining intelligence with democratic action) serving as a way-station on the road from British political economy to Virginia political economy. Buchanan's oeuvre contains numerous tensions, two forms of which I have explored here. To find tensions in a research program that was developed over more than six decades and contained hundreds of items is not surprising. Furthermore, the existence of tensions points to opportunities for advancing the tradition. The main direction of potential progress, in my judgment, lies in moving ever further in the direction of subjectivism because this direction brings us ever more fully into the domain of emergent and creative social systems in which open-ended human action is the vehicle for injecting change continually into society. To be sure, the continual injection of novelty along with reactions of adaptation takes place against a formal background of eternal verities. In this regard, there is truly nothing new under the sun; however, we don't experience life as eternal verities but only as shadowy reflections and manifestations of those verities.

REFERENCES

Barabási, Albert-László. 2002. *Linked: The New Science of Networks*. Cambridge, MA: Perseus.

Belloc, Hilaire. 1912. *The Servile State*. London: T. N. Foulis.

Bertalanffy, Ludwig von. 1968. *General System Theory*. New York: George Braziller.

Bishop, Errett. 1967. *Foundations of Constructive Analysis*. New York: McGraw-Hill.

Boettke, Peter J. 2012. *Living Economics*. Oakland, CA: Independent Institute.

Bolsinger, Eckard. 2001. *The Autonomy of the Political: Carl Schmitt's and Lenin's Political Realism*. Westport, CT: Greenwood Press.

Buchanan, James M. 1949. "The Pure Theory of Government Finance: A Suggested Approach." *Journal of Political Economy* 57 (6): 496–505.

———. 1958. *Public Principles of Public Debt*. Homewood, IL: Richard D. Irwin.

———. 1960. "The Italian Tradition in Fiscal Theory." In *Fiscal Theory and Political Economy*, 27–74. Chapel Hill: University of North Carolina Press.

———. 1969. *Cost and Choice*. Chicago: Markham.

———. (1975) 2000. *The Limits of Liberty: Between Anarchy and Leviathan*. Vol. 7 of *The Collected Works of James M. Buchanan*. Indianapolis, IN: Liberty Fund.

———. 1982. "Order Defined in the Process of Its Emergence." *Literature of Liberty* 5 (4): 5.

———. 2005. "Afraid to Be Free: Dependency as Desideratum." *Public Choice* 124 (1–2): 19–31.

Buchanan, James M., and Gordon Tullock. (1962) 1999. *The Calculus of Consent: The Logical Foundations of Constitutional Democracy*. Vol. 3 of *The Collected Works of James M. Buchanan*. Indianapolis, IN: Liberty Fund.

Buchanan, James M., and Richard E. Wagner. 1977. *Democracy in Deficit*. New York: Academic Press.

Burnham, James. 1943. *The Machiavellians*. New York: John Day.

Candela, Rosolino, and Richard E. Wagner. 2016. "Vilfredo Pareto's Theory of Action: An Alternative to Behavioral Economics." *Il pensiero economico italiano* 24: 15–29.

Chaitin, Gregory, Newton da Costa, and Francisco A. Doria. 2012. *Gödel's Way: Exploits into an Undecidable World*. London: Taylor & Francis.

Cristi, Renato. 1998. *Carl Schmitt and Authoritarian Liberalism*. Cardiff: University of Wales Press.

Currie, Martin, and Ian Steedman. 1990. *Wrestling with Time: Problems in Economic Theory*. Ann Arbor: University of Michigan Press.

De Viti de Marco, Antonio. 1930. *Un Trentennio di Lotte Politiche: 1894–1922*. Naples: Giannini.

———. 1936. *First Principles of Public Finance*. London: Jonathan Cape.

Emmett, Ross B. 2006. "'Die gustibus est disputandum': Frank H. Knight's Response to George Stigler and Gary Becker's 'die gustibus non est disputandum.'" *Journal of Economic* Methodology 13 (1): 97–111.

Eucken, Walter. (1952) 1990. *Grundsätze der Wirtschaftspolitik.* Tübingen, Germany: Mohr.

Eusepi, Giuseppe, and Richard E. Wagner. 2013. "Tax Prices in a Democratic Polity: The Continuing Relevance of Antonio de Viti de Marco." *History of Political Economy* 45 (1): 99–121.

———. 2017. *Public Debt: An Illusion of Democratic Political Economy*. Cheltenham, U.K.: Edward Elgar.

Gladwell, Malcolm. 2008. *Outliers: The Story of Success.* Boston: Little, Brown.

Johnson, Marianne. 2014. "James M. Buchanan, Chicago, and Post-War Public Finance." *Journal of the History of Economic Thought* 36 (4): 479–97.

Katzner, Donald. 1998. *Time, Ignorance, and Uncertainty in Economic Models*. Ann Arbor: University of Michigan Press.

Keynes, John Maynard. 1936. *The General Theory of Employment, Interest and Money.* London: Palgrave Macmillan.

Knight, Frank H. 1960. *Intelligence and Democratic Action*. Cambridge, MA: Harvard University Press.

Latour, Bruno. 2005. *Reassembling the Social: An Introduction to Actor-Network Theory*. Oxford, U.K.: Oxford University Press.

Lerner, Abba P. 1944. *The Economics of Control: Principles of Welfare Economics.* New York: Macmillan.

Levy, David M., and Sandra J. Peart, eds. 2008. *The Street Porter and the Philosopher*. Ann Arbor: University of Michigan Press.

Lovejoy, Arthur O. 1936. *The Great Chain of Being*. Cambridge, MA: Harvard University Press.

———. 1961. *Reflections on Human Nature*. Baltimore, MD: Johns Hopkins University Press.

Michels, Roberto. 1915. *Political Parties: A Sociological Study of the Oligarchical Tendencies of Modern Democracy*. New York: Hearst's International Library.

Mill, John Stuart. 1863. *On Liberty*. Boston: Ticknor and Fields.

Mosca, Gaetano. 1939. *The Ruling Class*. New York: McGraw-Hill.

Ostrom, Vincent. 1987. *The Political Theory of a Compound Republic*, 2nd ed. Lincoln: University of Nebraska Press.

———. 1997. *The Meaning of Democracy and the Vulnerability of Societies: A Response to Tocqueville's Challenge*. Ann Arbor: University of Michigan Press.

Pareto, Vilfredo. 1935. *The Mind and Society: A Treatise on General Sociology*. New York: Harcourt Brace.

Persson, Torsten, and Guido Tabellini. 2000. *Political Economics*. Cambridge, MA: MIT Press.

Potts, Jason. 2000. *The New Evolutionary Microeconomics*. Cheltenham, U.K.: Edward Elgar.

Rajagopalan, Shruti, and Richard E. Wagner. 2013. "Constitutional Craftsmanship and the Rule of Law." *Constitutional Political Economy* 24 (4): 295–309.

Rawls, John. 1971. *A Theory of Justice.* Cambridge, MA: Harvard University Press.

Resnick, Mitchel. 1994. *Turtles, Termites, and Traffic Jams*. Cambridge, MA: MIT Press.

Robbins, Lionel R. B. 1952. *The Theory of Economic Policy in English Classical Economy.* New York: Macmillan.

Samuels, Warren J. 1966. *The Classical Theory of Economic Policy.* Cleveland, OH: World Publishing Co.

Scheiner, Samuel M., and Michael R. Willig, eds. 2011. *The Theory of Ecology*. Chicago: University of Chicago Press.

Schelling, Thomas C. 1978. *Micromotives and Macrobehavior*. New York: Norton.

Schmitt, Carl. (1932) 1996. *The Concept of the Political.* Chicago: University of Chicago Press.

Schoeck, Helmut. 1969. *Envy: A Theory of Social Behavior*. New York: Harcourt Brace.

Schumpeter, Joseph A. (1918) 1954. "The Crisis of the Tax State." *International Economic Papers* 4: 5–38.

———. 1934. *The Theory of Economic Development*, 2nd ed. Cambridge, MA: Harvard University Press.

Shackle, George L. S. 1961. *Decision, Order, and Time in Human Affairs*. Cambridge, U.K.: Cambridge University Press.

———. 1972. *Epistemics and Economics*. Cambridge, U.K.: Cambridge University Press.

Stephen, James Fitzjames. (1873) 1993. *Liberty, Equality, Fraternity*. Indianapolis, IN: Liberty Fund.

Sterpan, Ion, and Richard E. Wagner. 2017. "The Autonomy of the Political in Political Economy." *Advances in Austrian Economics* 22: 133–57.

Stoker, Thomas M. 1993. "Empirical Approaches to the Problem of Aggregation over Individuals." *Journal of Economic Literature* 31 (4): 1827–74.

Vickers, Douglas. 1994. *Economics and the Antagonism of Time: Time, Uncertainty, and Choice in Economic Theory*. Ann Arbor: University of Michigan Press.

Wagner, Richard E. 2012. "A Macro Economy as an Ecology of Plans." *Journal of Economic Behavior and Organization* 82 (2): 433–44.

———. 2013. "Choice vs. Interaction in Public Choice: Discerning the Legacy of *The Calculus of Consent*." In *Public Choice, Past and Present: The Legacy of James M. Buchanan and Gordon Tullock*, edited by Dwight R. Lee, 65–79. New York: Springer.

———. 2014. "James Buchanan's Public Debt Theory: A Rational Reconstruction." *Constitutional Political Economy* 25 (3): 253–64.

———. 2015. "Virginia Political Economy: A Rational Reconstruction." *Public Choice* 163 (1–2): 15–29.

———. 2017. *James M. Buchanan and Liberal Political Economy: A Rational Reconstruction*. Lanham, MD: Lexington Books.

Wieser, Friedrich. 1926. *Das Gesetz der Macht*. Vienna: Julius Springer.

CHAPTER TWO

BUCHANAN ON ETHICS AND SELF-INTEREST IN POLITICS

A CONTRADICTION OR RECONCILIATION?

ROGER D. CONGLETON

James M. Buchanan is well known for his pioneering contributions to public finance and constitutional political economy.[1] A third, less studied strand of his research attempts to determine how human nature and action should be characterized. Buchanan often wrote about the weaknesses of the mathematical models of rational choice that emerged in the first half of the 20th century, noting problems with both the utility-maximizing representation of decision-making and the utilitarian norms grounded in that model. Both were (and continue to be) routinely used by economists to model human decision-making and assess the relative merits of public policies and institutions. His perspective on ethics and moral choice are parts of his broader conception of human action that conceives each person as rule following, but partly self-created and evolving through time.

That extended model of human action and its implications for moral constraints appear to conflict with much of Buchanan's own research, which relies on—or is at least very consistent with—mainstream *homo economicus*–based analysis. For example, his claim that public choice takes the romance out of politics is largely based on results that are derived from narrow opportunistic representations of human interests and choices (Buchanan 1984). If conclusions from such models are realistic, then how important are Buchanan's critiques of the models of man used in economics?

If human interactions in society are bound by internalized norms (ethics), then one might expect politics to be partly grounded in ethics rather than entirely pragmatic or opportunistic.[2] There is a good deal of evidence that supports the contention that persons are interested in ethical issues and at least partly motivated by them. For example, most economists use ideas from utilitarian philosophy to demonstrate the possibility of government failure. Of course, such tools and conclusions are of interest only if they provide evidence of normative problems associated with public policy or democratic rule. Economists and public choice researchers who are concerned about what they refer to as "the welfare properties" of policies and institutions and are comfortable using utilitarian ideas in their analysis must have internalized norms that make such analyses salient for them.

This chapter argues that Buchanan's theory of the internalization and application of internal rules of conduct ultimately resolves this tension, but in a manner that is not entirely obvious. To appreciate his resolution requires understanding Buchanan's characterization of decision-making, especially with regard to moral constraints and constitutional rules. Most readers will be more familiar with the latter than the former; thus, this chapter begins with an overview of Buchanan's theories of choice and morality. The overview is followed by an analysis of the extent to which his theory of civic ethics overcomes the tensions between his richer model of man and his contributions to public choice. To the best of my knowledge, there is no single place where the entire argument can be found, although it seems to provide the organizing principle behind much of his work on morality and politics.

Buchanan's work on ethics began in the 1960s with a series of papers published in the philosophical journal of the same name. Another piece written at roughly the midpoint of his career provides the most complete overview of his perspective on man and internalized rules, and that piece is used extensively throughout this chapter (Buchanan [1979] 1999). These papers together with his work on constitutional political economy provide the basis for his analysis of the role of morality in politics. Quotes from throughout his career are used to demonstrate his sustained interest in decisions regarding personal and society-wide rules.

Buchanan argues (a) that there are moral dimensions to human decision-making and (b) that the same models of man should be used to analyze all human action, yet he concludes that (c) politics is largely amoral and opportunistic but (d) nonetheless potentially able to produce laws and decision-making procedures that are both moral and legitimate.

CREATING ONESELF

Buchanan often reminds his readers and students that the utility-maximizing model of neoclassical economics and game theory is useful, but flawed. The usual rational-choice model assumes that a person can be characterized by his or her preferences, which are transitive, complete, and durable. Preferences and their associated utility functions are assumed to be completely stable for the period of analysis. In such models, all people know their best course of action for every possible circumstance.

As a model, the *homo economicus* characterization of man neglects many aspects of human decision-making that we know to be important, but few have suggested a useful alternative that could replace it as an engine of analysis.

Buchanan argues that relatively few preferences are truly innate. Some are absorbed from one's local culture without much thought or action. Others emerge as one considers the alternatives in given circumstances or learns from experience. Decision-making is an active process, not simply a preprogrammed response to the circumstances at hand. Consequently, one's rankings of alternatives may be neither stable nor durable.

> Individual values are, of course, constantly changing; so a post-decision ordering may be different from a pre-decision ordering. (Buchanan 1954, 120)

> I am trying to develop this argument for a purpose, which is one of demonstrating that modern economic theory forces upon us patterns of thought that make elementary recognition of the whole "becoming" part of our behavior very difficult to analyze, and easy to neglect. (Buchanan [1979] 1999, 246)

> Each person is, of course, a product of his own history, the cultural environment, the conventions and traditions that exist and the public literature that explains these, all of which combine to describe the inclusive status quo that cannot be literally superseded. . . . This statement does not, however, imply dramatic shift to the other extreme of the spectrum; there should be no inference that a person, any person, is locked permanently into a predisposition as determined by personal history, experience and social environment. (Buchanan 2005, 102)

It bears noting that many of Buchanan's criticisms of the mainstream economic view of human nature would be uncontroversial to noneconomists, who often have a difficult time believing that people are routinely rational in their day-to-day lives instead of being occasionally rational at moments of reflection or major decisions. They are also skeptical of narrowly self-interested characterizations of human motives that ignore social pressures or broader ethical concerns. Buchanan, however, criticizes, not to chastise economists for their use of the *homo economicus* model, but to remind them that this model of man is incomplete and in some cases may mislead rather than enlighten. By neglecting broader interests, many choices that we routinely observe in our dealings with others remain unexplained and, in some cases, unexplainable.

In Buchanan's more encompassing characterization of decision-making, the implications of rational choice—even self-interested rational choice—are less restrictive and often less obvious and definite than they appear to be in the standard model.

Natural and Artifactual Man: Choices That Create Oneself

Buchanan begins his analysis of humans' capacity to create themselves with a discussion of human nature and imagination (Buchanan [1979] 1999). Imagination creates a very broad domain of choice, although one's imagined possibilities are constrained in various ways.

> It is useful to think of man as an imagining being, which in itself sets him apart from other species. A person sees himself or herself in many roles, capacities, and nature, in many settings, in many times, in many places. As one contemplates moving from imagination to potential behavior, however, constraints emerge to bound or limit the set of prospects severely.
>
> Once all the possible constraints are accounted for (historical, geographic, cultural, physical, genetic, sexual), there still remains a large set of possible persons that one might imagine himself to be, or might imagine himself capable of becoming. There is room for "improvement," for the construction of what might be. Further in thinking about realizable prospects, a person is able to rank these in some fashion.
>
> We move through time, constructing ourselves as artifactual persons. We are not, and cannot be, the "same person" in any utility maximizing sense. (Buchanan [1979] 1999, 250–51)

It is largely the ability to choose and internalize our own rules that make us artifactual beings.

> The same analysis [the decision to quit smoking] can be applied to any aspect of human behavior that represents "civility" in the larger meaning of this term. I refer here inclusively to manners, etiquette, codes of conduct, standards of deco-

> rum, and, most important, morals. A person conducts himself within the natural limits available to him, and the artifactual person he becomes does, at any moment, maximize utility subject to constraints. (Buchanan [1979] 1999, 252–53)

It is the freedom to choose, however limited, that ultimately makes us responsible individuals, according to Buchanan and other ethical theorists.[3] The ability to create oneself also provides a rationale for liberty itself and a demand for such.

> Man wants liberty to become the man he wants to become. He does so precisely because he does not know what man he will want to become in time. (Buchanan [1979] 1999, 259)

> By implicitly refusing to consider man as artifactual, we neglect the "constitution of private man," which translates into the necessary underpinning of a free society, the "character" of society, if you will. (Buchanan [1979] 1999, 252)

One's character or predispositions emerge gradually from choices over rules (maxims) to internalize, which are informed by the anticipated consequences of choices made under them. As a consequence, each individual's character evolves through time.

> Heraclitus noted that man does not step into the same river twice, first, because the stream has passed, and second because man too has moved forward in time. Choice is, and must be, irrevocable, and a person is constructed by the choices he has made sequentially through time, within the natural and artifactual constraints that have limited his possibilities. (Buchanan [1979] 1999, 257)

In the artifactual man essay, Buchanan mainly focuses on the domain of choice and how our choices ultimately determine our future selves. Choices over ethical rules of conduct are clearly a subset of those choices, but ones that he regards to be among the most important. According to Buchanan, the ability to develop one's own character is central to the demand for a classical liberal system of democratic governments and open markets.

Choices among Rules to Internalize

The rules of conduct that a person might adopt can be loosely grouped into three categories. People may adopt rules to improve their own character. Such rules would be adopted regardless of social setting and may be regarded as virtue or private ethics. Other rules are adopted and internalized because they make life in communities more attractive. Such rules may be regarded as civic ethics. In addition, there are principles and procedures that can be used for assessing the qualities of institutions and public policies, what might be regarded as constitutional or social ethics. One's choices over all three sets of normative principles have long-term consequences because they have significant effects on both one's choices and one's future selves, what philosophers refer to as character or will.[4]

Although Buchanan does occasionally discuss internal rules that improve one's character (Buchanan [1979] 1999; Brennan and Buchanan 1985, chap. 5), for the most part, he focuses on civic ethics, but from the perspective of individual interests rather than some overarching principle. With respect to social ethics, he has repeatedly argued in favor of the contractarian approach.

With respect to civic ethics, rather than appealing to altruistic impulses, rule-utilitarianism, or the Kantian categorical imperative, Buchanan argues that civic norms emerge from reciprocity. A person adopts many rules of conduct because he or she anticipates that others will reciprocate and adopt similar rules.

> Since we may assume that each [person] prefers to live in a setting of mutual self-respect, as shown by our ordering, the most likely outcome will surely be one where each and every person adopts and follows something that is akin to the Kantian categorical imperative. His standard for behavior will be some version of the generalization principle. (Buchanan 1965, 6–7)

Note that he does not say that such rules should satisfy the categorical imperative but rather that they will tend to satisfy it. Rules of conduct are adopted because behavior in accordance with those rules is expected to affect behavior of others (or not). In small communities in which repeat dealings are commonplace, treating potential trading partners honestly and with respect is likely to elicit the same behavior from those partners.

In Buchanan's analysis, it is reciprocity—mutual self-restraint—that generates universality, rather than Immanuel Kant's categorical imperative. Although this conclusion is not fully explained, Buchanan seems to have in mind a civic ethics based on common interests, shared moral intuitions, or both.[5] Buchanan assumes that people in the relevant community can imagine the responses that others will make. Each person's own interest may be quite narrow and self-centered, but the same people are inclined to adopt rules of civility not for their own sake, but because if the actions are reciprocated, all achieve more highly valued outcomes for themselves. In contrast with Jeremy Bentham and Immanuel Kant, ethics emerge from shared advantage, rather than from philosophical insight.[6]

> I am much more sympathetic to a quite different sort of moral constructivism, one that seeks to ground moral precepts for behavior within the rational self-interest of individuals, in the cognition and preferences that exist, rather than in some extra-individualistic sources.
>
> The rational morality of an individual does require constraints on the open-ended choice options that seem to describe particularized circumstances. But these constraints are themselves a product of, and are chosen by, a rationally based choice calculus at the higher level of dispositional alternatives. (Buchanan 1991, 232–33)

The rules of civic ethics are adopted for quasi-constitutional reasons, rather than Kantian ones, although they tend to satisfy Kantian norms of generality and also tend to elicit treatment of others as ends rather than means, because mutual respect and reciprocity facilitate market and other social interactions.[7]

Ethics and Markets

As an economist by training, Buchanan naturally applies his ideas about internalized rules of conduct to market-relevant decisions. He argues that morality plays a critical role in both exchange and production.

> Why does the individual trade at all? By stealing, cheating, or defrauding potential trading partners, the individual may secure a preferred bundle of goods by giving up a smaller share of the endowments initially possessed than that required in the trading process. The elementary exclusion of all such opportunistic behavior from analysis relies on the presumption that the effective price of any good obtained opportunistically is as high or higher than that which confronts the person in the straightforward exchange relationship. . . . Many persons do not behave opportunistically, even when the possibilities of apparent advantage are present, because they adhere to certain moral precepts or norms. . . . We should recognize that the efficacy of any market order depends critically on the endogenous behavioral constraints that are in existence. (Buchanan 1994, 124–25)

> One reason for the relatively enhanced productivity of the economy whose participants adhere to ethical constraints against opportunistic behavior lies in the implied efficacy of impersonal dealings. In an economy where widespread fraud is absent, persons can enter exchanges without the personalized relationships that may be necessary for the insurance of trust in the economy where fraud is preva-

> lent. The advantages of specialization can be more fully exploited as the scope for trading prospects is extended. (Buchanan 2005, 34)

Without a supportive internalized moral code, markets would be less productive; indeed, in many cases, exchange would be impossible.

Ethics and Politics

Perhaps surprisingly, Buchanan rarely mentions morality in his analyses of politics. Instead, he more or less routinely applies and defends the *homo economicus* model in that context.[8] Nonetheless, he occasionally acknowledges that internalized norms can have effects on policy choices. Laws may, for example, simply codify preexisting norms.

> The historically determined constraints may be descriptively summarized in the laws, institutions, customs, and traditions of the community, including the rules or institutions that define the means of making collective "choices." Again, as in the earlier analysis, the "choices" made by the collective unit as such in t_0 will modify the options that will emerge in t_1 and beyond, through influences on the constraints or preferences or both. (Brennan and Buchanan 1985, 87)

There is always some risk that other people will not follow the norms of one's own moral community. Informal sanctions may need to be "topped up" by formal sanctions against those violating community norms.

Moreover, civic morality may itself be a subject of public policy.

> With these considerations, the individual may, on quite rational grounds, invest current-period resources in the indoctrination, dissemination, and transmission of a set of general principles or rules that will, generally, influence behavior toward patterns of situational response that are predictably bounded. (Brennan and Buchanan 1985, 92)

> At the margin, the positive benefit–cost ratios from investment in ethics may be much larger than those from investment in politicization, which may indeed be negative. (Buchanan 2005, 97)

Because civic ethics are not uniquely determined by human nature, natural law, evolution, or holy scripture, members of a community will not usually internalize exactly the same rules or to the same degree. Public support for common civic norms can reduce transaction costs and broadly increase gains from social intercourse.

INTERNAL TENSIONS IN BUCHANAN'S APPROACH TO ETHICS, MARKETS, AND POLITICS

All the preceding demonstrates that Buchanan's model of man and approach to political economy include roles for personal decisions about ethics and ethical dispositions. We now turn to tensions and ambiguities generated by his interest-based approach to ethics and politics. There are at least three tensions associated with interest-based theories of ethical dispositions within his political economy: (a) If ethics emerge because they make people in a community better off, then why are people not uniformly ethical? (b) If ethics can substitute for law, why do we need laws or the organization that enforces laws? Herbert Spencer ([1851] 2011), for example, once argued that the state would wither away as social evolution produced the best possible set of internalized rules of conduct.[9] Buchanan is not as optimistic about ethics replacing law and politics as Spencer was in the mid–19th century, although this possibility is acknowledged in Buchanan's work (Buchanan 2005, 100). In addition, (c) there is a methodological tension between Buchanan's claim that there is a moral dimension to human choice and his claim that public choice removes the romance from politics.

Buchanan was aware of these tensions and largely resolved them through two hypotheses: what might be called the large-number hypothesis of civic ethics and the veil of uncertainty hypotheses of constitutional choice. Reciprocity constrains both sorts of decisions, but the personal choice calculus differs in small and large number choice settings. Individuals more completely adhere to the rules of civic ethics in small-number settings than in large-number decisions, because the anticipated reciprocity is greater in small-number settings than in large ones.

Individuals who are members of larger societies may nonetheless recognize that it would be useful to adopt durable rules that are fair and collectively advantageous. Moreover, Buchanan argues that such rules might be universally supported. The people attending a real or imagined constitutional or normative convention would try to account for every imaginable consequence associated with the rule that they might choose to adopt. By their doing so, a reflective form of encompassing interest emerges because of each person's uncertainties about the future.

Formal agreements are more likely to be necessary in large-number settings than small-number settings, because of the attenuation of reciprocity.

The Attenuation of Ethics in Large Communities

Recall that Buchanan's theory of civic ethics is grounded in reciprocity. People follow rules of civic ethics when they believe that their behavior will be reciprocated. Buchanan argues that this effect diminishes as the size of the group one interacts with increases. As group size increases, moral behavior tends to be replaced by opportunistic or narrowly self-interested behavior. There is less moral reciprocity and so informal civic norms are less binding.

> In a group of critically large size, the individual will tend to adopt the rule of following the expediency criterion even if he thinks that all of his fellow citizens are saints. (Buchanan 1965, 7)

> The extent that a person expects his own behavior to influence the behavior of those with whom he interacts will depend upon the size of the group. (Buchanan 1978, 365)

An implication of this large-number effect is that civic morality tends to become less common as polities become relatively large. Politics in the small tends to be constrained by the norms of civic morality, but those constraints become less binding and behavior becomes more opportunistic as the scale of politics increases.

> What can a person be predicted to do when the external institutions force upon him a role in a community that extends beyond his moral limits? The tension shifts toward the self-interest pole of behavior: moral ethical principles are necessarily sublimated. . . . Should we be at all surprised when we observe the increasing usage of the arms and agencies of the national government for the securing of private personal gain? (Buchanan 1978, 367)

From Buchanan's perspective, Spencer's prediction has some merit for small-scale local politics but not for larger-scale national politics. For example, small groups of lifetime friends will behave ethically toward each other without formal agreements, formal rules, or standing procedures for rule enforcement. Formal agreements and rules become more necessary as the group expands, and uninhibited self-interest replaces the morally constrained self-interest that characterizes behavior in small-number settings.

Buchanan argues that one's internal justification for adhering to civic norms rests on the likely effects that following such rules has on the behavior of others.

This reciprocity effect diminishes as repeat transactions become less frequent and relationships become more impersonal.

Constitutional Moments Do Not Require Moral Men and Women

If civic morality declines as large groups emerge, how is it possible that large groups can adopt morally appealing rules for conducting their affairs? Buchanan's answer to this is based on the nature of the choices and commitments made at constitutional moments.

> The veil of ignorance and/or uncertainty offers a means of bridging the apparent gap between furtherance of separately identified interests and agreement on the rules that conceptually define the "social contract." Potential contractors must recognize that the basic rules for social order—the ultimate constitutional structure—are explicitly chosen as permanent or quasi-permanent parameters within which social interaction is to take place over a whole sequence of periods. This temporal feature, in itself, shifts discussion away from that which might take place among fully identified bargainers toward discussion among participants who are unable to predict either their own position or how differing rules will affect whatever positions they come to occupy. . . . Criteria of fairness may replace those of advantage; agreement may emerge as the predicted working properties of alternative sets of rules are examined. . . .
>
> Each participant will also recognize that others will agree to impose constraints on their own behavior only as part of a reciprocal "exchange." In this preliminary sense, reciprocation implies generality. . . . Rules that apply to others must also apply to one's own behavior. (Buchanan and Congleton 1998, 6)

Again, reciprocity produces rules that satisfy the Kantian categorical imperative, but here the reciprocity is produced by discussion and agreement in a setting of extreme uncertainty, rather than by private assessments of how one's own behavior affects that of others.

This is not to say that common private moral perspectives do not facilitate agreement, but simply to say that a common ethos is not a prerequisite for the adoption of rules that are fair and uniformly applied. In large groups, the behavior induced by social contract–based law tends to be more appealing than the anticipated behavior of those agreeing to adopt and implement the contract agreed to! Neither altruism nor moral dispositions are required, although internalized norms or dispositions would tend to affect the kinds of agreement reached.[10]

CONCLUSION: ON THE TENSIONS BETWEEN MORAL DIMENSIONS OF CHOICE AND CONSTITUTIONAL POLITICAL ECONOMY

Buchanan's model of man is distinguished from the mainstream neoclassical one in many respects. Utility functions do not exist. Rankings of alternatives are not found in the minds of the choosers prior to choice but emerge through the process of deliberation and evaluation. Individuals are not static beings but ones that change through time, in part because they are able to imagine alternative future selves and take actions to realize those possibilities, including the adoption of moral principles. That which emerges is largely a consequence of biological and social evolution, but at the margin, it is self-created and artifactual. At the margin, we are responsible for who we are.

Buchanan does not carefully model the selection and internalization of rules of conduct, nor does he discuss it in much detail. He does not do so in part because his more complete model of man does not allow the superficial precision of the standard neoclassical models and, in part because to the extent possible, he resists the temptation to moralize and place one subset of rules of conduct above others. This approach nonetheless allowed him to analyze the extent to which internalized rules can advance individual interests and the extent to which social evolution and deliberate choices tend to generate support for morally attractive rules and government policies.

With respect to civic ethics, Buchanan accepts Kantian ideas about the nature of morality, although not Kant's motivation for them. He believes that self-interest and consensus favor rules of conduct that are consistent with Kant's categorical imperative. In small-number settings where one's behavior is likely to elicit similar responses from others, informal general rules emerge that reduce or eliminate opportunistic behavior. However, as the number of people dealt with increases, such reciprocity diminishes, and the normative rules of thumb (maxims) that best advance a person's interests become less and less universal and more opportunistic. Reciprocity is insufficient to motivate moral conduct in large-number settings. Private ethics and predispositions may still have effects on behavior, but these tend to be small and thus are little analyzed in Buchanan's political economy.

It is the large-number effect on ethical behavior that allows Buchanan to simultaneously argue that (a) there is an important moral dimension to human decision-making, (b) the same model of man should be used to analyze economic and political actions, and (c) morality plays little role in politics. Politics in today's world tends to be a large-number setting. The limits of morality in such settings, as in John Locke and Thomas Paine, provide rationales for government and law enforcement. In a large-number setting, reciprocity is insufficiently strong to generate behavior in accord with widely held norms and moral maxims.[11]

If pragmatism dominates day-to-day politics, why would the law or law enforcement be more than a system of rent-extracting rules? Buchanan's answer to that relies on the contract foundations of legitimate government and the veil of uncertainty associated with long-term commitments to rules. The people negotiating a social contract in a large-number setting are not inhibited by moral norms but nonetheless are induced to select fair and general rules because unanimous agreement is likely to require that everyone abide by the same rules. Here generality emerges from the necessity of agreement rather than from reciprocity.

There is a role for private and civic morality in such negotiations, but it is not an essential one. Such internalized rules and predispositions would tend to affect the particular constitutional rules agreed to, rather than the generality of the rules adopted.

Overall, this is a neat resolution of a fundamental tension between Buchanan's characterization of individuals as moral beings, his unromantic view of politics, and insistence that individuals do not change when they make politically relevant choices. Whether this is the last word or not, it is clearly one of the most sophisticated analyses of relationships between political and ethical issues.

Nonetheless, as Buchanan (2005) acknowledges, there may well be ethical foundations for a liberal constitutional order. Without ethical support and equality at a constitutional convention, social contracts may not produce liberal governance. The Hobbesian contract, for example, is not necessarily a liberal one (Buchanan [1999] 2000). Moreover, without a preexisting moral base in support of markets and democratic politics, the idea of a hypothetical constitutional convention with its associated veil of uncertainty is itself less than plausible. This final tension was left unresolved, but without the multilevel choice over rules framework developed by Buchanan, it could hardly be raised or addressed.

NOTES

1. For an overview of Buchanan's public finance work, see Congleton (1988), and for an overview of his constitutional political economy research, see Congleton (2014).

2. For the purposes of this piece, I use the terms norms and ethics as if they were equivalent terms, because both tend to have implications about personal conduct and both may be consciously adopted and revised. There are numerous distinctions, although these are not important for the purposes of this chapter. For the purposes of this chapter, it is sufficient to note that ethical rules are a proper subset of the norms that may be chosen and internalized. Rules for spelling are norms, but decisions to place "i" before "e" (or not) are not moral choices.

3. This rationale for individual responsibility is an ancient one with an intellectual history that includes most theologies and, in secular philosophers, back to Aristotle and beyond. Buchanan regards the interest in self-improvement and ability to do so to be a uniquely human characteristic (Buchanan [1979] 1999, 247).

4. Person-altering choices are related to, but are not the same as, what economists refer to as investments in human capital. They have different effects on preferences. The fundamental nature or preferences of a particular human are normally assumed to be unaffected choices to invest in this or that form of training, although some preferences over goods and services may be affected (Stigler and Becker 1977). A carpenter may have a stronger demand for hammers than a lab technician. In contrast, the decision to give up carpentry for the lab (or vice versa) may involve many changes in one's preferences over goods and services, interest in accuracy, rules and routines for engaging with fellow workers, and one's approach to life in general.

5. Buchanan's Kantian predictions about civic norms might also be regarded as similar to those developed by Rawls (2009) concerning rights and principles of distributive justice. That is to say, there are some conclusions about ethics that are natural or instinctive, because of human nature, evolution, or the "natural" meaning of morality.

6. In the *Critique of Practical Reason*, Kant repeatedly distinguishes between moral behavior and self-interested behavior. For example, "The direct opposite of the principle of morality is when the principle of private happiness is made the determining principle of the will" (Kant [1788] 2013, KL 10528–29). Kant goes on to argue that "All the morality of actions may be placed in the necessity of acting from duty and from respect for the [universal] law, not from love and inclination for that which the actions are to produce" (Kant [1788] 2013, KL 11273–74). [These excerpts are taken from *The Immanuel Kant Collection*; KL refers to Kindle locations in that collection.]

7. That characterization of moral principles, rules, and actions distinguishes his theory from that of Kant, who stresses that moral choice and self-interest are completely separate spheres of choice and conduct.

8. See, for example, Kirchgässner 2014.

9. "It is a mistake to assume that government must necessarily last forever. The institution marks a certain stage of civilization—is natural to a particular phase of human development. It is not essential but incidental. As amongst the Bushmen we find a state antecedent to government; so may there be one in which it shall have become extinct. Already has it lost something of its importance. . . . Government, however, is an institution originating in man's imperfection; an institution confessedly begotten by necessity out of evil; one which might be dispensed with were the world peopled with the unselfish, the conscientious, the philanthropic; one, in short, inconsistent with this same "highest conceivable perfection" (Spencer [1851] 2011, KL 39713–63).

10. Buchanan spends much of his book on liberalism (*Why I, Too, Am Not a Conservative: The Normative Vision of Classical Liberalism* [2005]) explaining why particular ethical predispositions tend to make a liberal political economic order more likely to emerge from constitutional negotiations.

11. Locke, for example, states that "And were it not for the corruption and virtuousness of degenerate men, there would be no need of any other; no necessity that men should separate from this great and natural community, and by positive agreements combine into smaller and divided associations" ([1690] 2011, KL 145). A century later, Paine sets out a similar idea: "Here then is the origin and rise of government; namely, a mode rendered necessary by the inability of moral virtue to govern the world; here too is the design and end of government, viz. freedom and security" ([1776] 2015, KL 97–99).

REFERENCES

Brennan, Geoffrey, and James M. Buchanan. 1985. *The Reason of Rules: Constitutional Political Economy.* Cambridge, U.K.: Cambridge University Press.

Buchanan, James M. 1954. "Social Choice, Democracy, and Free Markets." *Journal of Political Economy* 62 (2): 114–23.

———. 1965. "Ethical Rules, Expected Values, and Large Numbers." *Ethics* 76 (1): 1–13.

———. (1975) 2000. *The Limits of Liberty: Between Anarchy and Leviathan*. Vol. 7 of *The Collected Works of James M. Buchanan*. Indianapolis, IN: Liberty Fund.

———. 1978. "Markets, States, and the Extent of Morals." *American Economic Review* 68 (2): 364–68.

———. (1979) 1999. "Natural and Artifactual Man." In *What Should Economists Do?* Reprinted in *The Logical Foundations of Constitutional Liberty*. Vol. 1 of *The Collected Works of James M. Buchanan*. Indianapolis, IN: Liberty Fund.

———. 1984. "Politics without Romance: A Sketch of Positive Public Choice Theory and Its Normative Implications." In *The Theory of Public Choice II*, edited by J. M. Buchanan and R. D. Tollison, 11–22. Ann Arbor: University of Michigan Press.

———. 1991. *The Economics and the Ethics of Constitutional Order.* Ann Arbor: University of Michigan Press.

———. 1994. "Choosing What to Choose." *Journal of Institutional and Theoretical Economics* 150 (1): 123–35.

———. 2005. *Why I, Too, Am Not a Conservative: The Normative Vision of Classical Liberalism.* Cheltenham, U.K.: Edward Elgar.

Buchanan, James M., and Roger D. Congleton. 1998. *Politics by Principle Not Choice*. Cambridge, U.K.: Cambridge University Press.

Congleton, Roger D. 1988. "An Overview of the Contractarian Public Finance of James Buchanan." *Public Finance Quarterly* 16 (2): 131–57.

———. 2014. "The Contractarian Constitutional Political Economy of James Buchanan." *Constitutional Political Economy* 25 (1): 39–67.

Kant, Immanuel. (1788) 2013. *Critique of Practical Reason*. Reprinted in *The Immanuel Kant Collection: 8 Classic Works*. Waxkeep Publishing. Kindle.

Kirchgässner, Gebhard. 2014. "The Role of Homo Economicus in the Political Economy of James Buchanan." *Constitutional Political Economy* 25 (1): 2–17.

Locke, John. (1690) 2011. *Second Treatise of Government.* A Public Domain Book. Kindle.

Paine, Thomas. (1776) 2015. *Common Sense*. Best Illustrated edition. Kindle.

Rawls, John. 2009. *A Theory of Justice,* rev. ed. Cambridge, MA: Harvard University Press.

Spencer, Herbert. (1851) 2011. *Social Statics*. Reprinted in *The Complete Works of Herbert Spencer.* Kindle.

Stigler, George J., and Gary S. Becker. 1977. "De Gustibus Non Est Disputandum." *American Economic Review* 67 (2): 76–90.

CHAPTER THREE

CONSTITUTIONAL HOPES AND POST-CONSTITUTIONAL FEARS

THE ROLE OF RATIONAL CONSTRUCTION IN SKEPTICAL PUBLIC CHOICE

PETER J. BOETTKE AND JAYME S. LEMKE

Leviathan may maintain itself by force; the Hobbesian sovereign may be the only future. But alternative futures may be described and dreamed, and government may not yet be wholly out of hand. From current disillusionment can come constructive consensus on a new structure of checks and balances. (Buchanan [1975] 2000, 208)

Alexander Hamilton famously begins Federalist No. 1 (Hamilton, Jay, and Madison [1818] 2001, 1) with the following: "It has been frequently remarked, that it seems to have been reserved to the people of this country to decide, by their conduct and example, the important question, whether societies of men are really capable or not, of establishing good government from reflection and choice, or whether they are forever destined to depend, for their political constitutions, on accident and force." The entire field of constitutional political economy is based on an intellectual commitment to viewing the rules by which good government is defined as the product of reflection and choice rather than accident and force. Yet constitutional political economy also begins with an insistence that all analysis of rule changes must begin from a recognition of "here and now." The analysis must not assume some imaginary starting point from which it would be easy to generate agreement. History does indeed matter, every bit as much as the fundamental claim that institutions matter. Right from the start of the analysis, the constitutional political economy project is defined by a fundamental tension between evolution and design.

There are two ways in which the possibility of design generates tensions in the constitutional project. First, there is a tension between evolution and design within the constitutional process itself. To the extent that rules are a product of human design, they are open to reimagination and revision. To the extent that rules are an unintended byproduct of human action, they cannot be deliberately constructed. The attempt to engage in constitutional design presumes that individuals have the ability to improve their circumstances by crafting enforceable rules.[1] However, it is unlikely that those rules will effectively serve their intended purposes if the individuals participating in their construction do not account for the possibility that the rules may have consequences beyond what was originally intended. Constitutional design thus requires participants to take a position—either explicitly or implicitly—on how much of the social world they are capable of bringing under their control. So what exactly is the relationship between design and emergence in constitutional political economy? As we elaborate in the next section, few—if any—would argue that either intentional design or unintended evolutions are irrelevant. The question is instead one of the nature and relative explanatory significance of the two processes.

The fact that deliberate efforts to create rules play a causal but not deterministic role in shaping the constitutional order brings us to the second tension addressed in this chapter: the apparent tension within James Buchanan's thought over the extent to which individuals are capable of exercising reason to bring about mutually beneficial changes in rules. This particular question within the constitutional project involves presumptions of pessimism and optimism. As James Madison puts it in Federalist No. 51 (Hamilton, Jay, and Madison [1818] 2001, 269):

> But what is government itself, but the greatest of all reflections on human nature? If men were angels, no government would be necessary. If angels were to govern men, neither external nor internal controls on government would be necessary. In framing a government which is to be administered by men over men, the great difficulty lies in this: you must first enable the government to control the governed; and in the next place oblige it to control itself.

Constitutional theorists are by definition pessimistic about the self-governing capacity of mankind to discipline private predation and optimistic about the ability of constitutional constraints to curb public predation. The tensions and the presumptions are evident throughout Buchanan's work in his development of the field of constitutional political economy. At times—particularly when considering the constitutional level of analysis—Buchanan appears optimistic about the possibility that individuals can come up with systems of rules and enforcement mechanisms that adequately account for the possibility of unintended consequences. At other times—particularly when considering the post-constitutional stage—he seems more pessimistic about the capacity of individuals to control their environments.

Both of these tensions—the tension between emergence and design within constitutional theorizing and the tension between constitutional optimism and political pessimism within Buchanan's constitutional political economy—are fundamentally questions about the extent to which humans are capable of controlling their environments through the exercise of choice. Framing the issue in this way raises a set of questions that are critical for understanding the process of institutional development and change. If individuals' choices play a part in determining institutional rules, what part do they play? And what must be true about the nature of interaction and exchange in political contexts in order for the choices of individuals to be significant in bringing about institutional change?

In this chapter, we explore the above tensions and attempt a reconciliation of Buchanan's perspective on this issue. We suggest a twofold resolution. First, Buchanan's position on rational constitutional design is not as undetermined as it may appear. Rather, he is consistent on the fact that the design of an effective constitution is extraordinarily difficult but that it remains mankind's only real alternative to arbitrary state dominion. This is a consistent position, even if it is not always fully satisfying. It is vital, we argue, to continually remember that Buchanan's aspiration is to construct a government that exhibits neither discrimination nor dominion. Second, the constitutional process that Buchanan advocates becomes more fully realizable when combined with the idea of constructivism-on-the-margins, most thoroughly developed in the work of F. A. Hayek, Elinor Ostrom, and Vincent Ostrom. We postulate that, although Buchanan often saw himself in intellectual opposition to Hayek's evolutionary theory, this need not be the case in our reconstruction of constitutional political economy. In this sense, we argue that Buchanan is not as distant from spontaneous order theory as even he sometimes seems to think (Runst and Wagner 2011).

This chapter is structured as follows. The next section describes the tension between evolution and design in the constitutional project itself. Then we discuss the tension in Buchanan's thought over the extent to which individuals are capable of employing reason in the design of institutions—a prospect toward which his attitude can best be described as cautious optimism. The section following attempts to resolve these tensions by drawing on Hayek's idea that constitutional agents may make rational changes in rules—so long as those agents limit themselves to cultivating what is already grown, or constructing-on-the-margins—and Elinor and Vincent Ostrom's approach to operationalizing this idea. We then conclude.

THE TENSION BETWEEN EVOLUTION AND DESIGN IN THE CONSTITUTIONAL PROJECT

Constitutional political economy is a relatively modern term for a branch of inquiry that is deeply rooted within the Enlightenment tradition. Broadly speaking, *constitutional political economy* is that domain of economics that deals with "choice among constraints" (Buchanan 1990, 3). Its particular focus is on the way the members of a group choose the rules that they will use to constrain each other. As such, although the term constitutional political economy was not proposed until the 1980s, *The Calculus of Consent* (Buchanan and Tullock [1962] 1999) offers a critical modern contribution to a much older strand of inquiry. The theory dates back at least to Adam Smith, Thomas Hobbes, and John Locke; and the explicit practice on the national stage dates back at least to the American founding era, if not earlier.

The origins of the constitutional project lie in the belief that mankind is capable of both reason and cooperation. Reason is necessary in order for individuals to be able to identify ways to make themselves better off by using rules to constrain their own future behavior. This is true whether or not the rule has a social component. Consider Buchanan's example of Robinson Crusoe fashioning an alarm clock. When Crusoe sets an alarm, he is establishing a rule through which he limits his own options as to how long to sleep in the morning in order to be able to produce more with his day. For Buchanan, this is an act of self-governance. Crusoe's alarm is a contract with himself—a contract he agrees to knowing both that he will find the rule frustrating at times and that it is ultimately in his own best interest (Buchanan [1975] 2000, 118–20).

The basic logic of improving one's life through constraint is the impetus that propels any given person to participate in the creation of social rules, with one crucial distinction: in a social context, it is usually the behavior of *others* that the individual desires to constrain (Buchanan [1975] 2000, 136). Otherwise, no social contract would be required—the process would be entirely internal to the individual. The limitations on an individual's own actions are a price he or she pays in exchange for the promise that others will agree to constrain their actions. Still, the root motivation for supporting and participating in the rule-making process is that individuals perceive that their lives will be better with the behavior-constraining rule than without.

The possibility of social cooperation is also necessary for the success of the constitutional project. The recognition that rules would be beneficial if followed by a sufficiently large group are of little use if the group can't agree on the content and enforcement of those rules. The members of a society must be willing to come together to negotiate over the rules and how they will be enforced. And herein enters Buchanan's explanation for the creation of an official government apparatus. Any group of two or more people will prefer the rules they agree on to be enforced by a third party rather than having to rely on the people playing the game to enforce the rules. Essentially, they outsource the task to an entity that will have less of an incentive to cheat the enforcement process (Buchanan [1975] 2000, 121). Thus, states emerge when the members of a group come to believe three things: (a) life would be better with rules, (b) rules can govern social interactions only when others consent or are forced to obey them, and (c) a third party will provide superior enforcement to what could be arranged within the group.[2]

Buchanan was a faithful believer in the idea that individuals are capable of the reason and cooperation required to meaningfully participate in the process of governance. This is summarized succinctly in a 1977 letter to Vincent Ostrom, in which Buchanan (1977, 2) writes, "There are two basic articles of faith in our position: (1) Institutions matter. (2) Institutions can be constructed." The formulation of these two articles demonstrates the strength of Buchanan's commitment to the idea that groups of people are capable of making themselves better off through deliberate institutional design. They have both the knowledge and capability to engage in cooperative efforts to design constitutional rules.

However, there is here "a fork in the theoretical road," where reasoned constitutional design seems at odds with the appreciation of the traditional and emergent character of many constitutional rules (Runst and Wagner 2011, 133). In the same letter just mentioned, Buchanan (1977, 2) acknowledges the tension between the constitutional project and theories that emphasize the emergent character of rule formation: "George Stigler and the modern Chicago crowd . . . explicitly and implicitly deny the former of these two articles . . . [and] We have opposition from the 'evolutionists' (Hayek, Oakeshott, Popper, etc.) on the second article of faith [that institutions can be constructed]." Buchanan ([1987] 2001, 460) later describes himself as "modifying and going beyond emphasis on cultural evolution associated with the work of Professor F. A. Hayek."

Hayek began to theorize about spontaneous and unintended forms of organization during the socialist calculation debate. Even before Buchanan began teasing out the possible achievements of rational constitutional design, Hayek was already warning that the belief that social order is a consequence of deliberate design was one of the main reasons why intellectuals found socialist planning so attractive. He dubbed this position *rational constructivism*, and to Hayek it constituted one of the gravest errors in social theory. The key theoretical task, to Hayek, was to explain the emergence of institutions that are socially beneficial even when that was not the intention of the individuals whose actions resulted in their establishment. As Hayek (1952, 39) puts it in *The Counter-Revolution of Science*:

> The problems which they try to answer arise only in so far as the conscious action of many men produce undesigned results, in so far as regularities are observed which are not the result of anybody's design. If social phenomena showed no order except in so far as they were consciously designed, there would indeed be no room for theoretical sciences of society and there would be, as is often argued, only problems of psychology. It is only in so far as some sort of order arises as a result of individual action but without being designed by any individual that a problem is raised which demands a theoretical explanation.

Hayek went on in works such as *The Constitution of Liberty* (1960) and *Law, Legislation and Liberty* (1973) to argue forcefully that we do not have rules because of our reason but instead have reason because our ancestors followed rules. The errors of constructivism entail attributing conscious design to phenomena that, although the result of human action, are not the deliberate result of human design. He argued, in fact, that such institutions include money and markets as well as law and social mores. Hayek argued that his approach, following David Hume's, was to use reason to whittle down the claims of reason.

Given that Hayek was directly addressing the arguments for socialist reconstruction of modern society, as well as the progressive agenda to bypass the constitutional restrictions on governmental power, it made perfect sense that he stressed the wisdom of traditional rules and the evolution of constitutional practice from English and US history. As we will discuss, Hayek (1973, 45) denied neither the necessity of criticism nor the importance of rational design of organizations:

> At the moment our concern must be made clear that while the rules on which spontaneous order rests, may also be of spontaneous origin, this need not always be the case. Although undoubtedly an order originally formed itself spontaneously because the individuals followed rules which had not been deliberately made but had arisen spontaneously, people gradually learned to improve those rules; and it is at least conceivable that the formation of a spontaneous order relies entirely on rules that were deliberately made.

What he was clear about, however, was that one cannot remake society anew as if from scratch, or on the basis of a root and branch reconstruction.

Hayek's criticism of rational constructivism and his emphasis on the long evolutionary process of trial and error of rules that came to define western civilization seemed to Buchanan to suggest acquiescence to accident and force in our constitutional constructions. Buchanan's criticism of the evolutionists therefore suggests that he found the limits on the possibility of design argued for by the spontaneous order theorists to be too confining. However, he did not find the idea of rules as evolved phenomena to be irrelevant. Ten years after penning the previously quoted letter to Vincent Ostrom, he writes:

> the rules for social order are not *exclusively* the product of some process of cultural evolution, rules that we have inherited and that we abide by without understanding their purpose or function. At least within limits, the supposition here is that rules are deliberately "constructed" from the choices of those persons who are to be subject to the constraints that these rules embody. (Buchanan [1987] 2001, 460, emphasis added)

Buchanan's argument as such seems to be that choice plays a part in determining institutional rules rather than the more difficult to defend notion that institutions are purely determined products of choice.[3]

So, if choice plays a part in determining institutional rules, what part does it play? And what must be true about the nature of nonmarket exchange in order for the choices of individuals to be significant in bringing about institutional change?

Buchanan certainly did not think that institutional design could be masterminded. He was a staunch critic of experts' attempts to maximize social well-being, particularly when their attempts to do so involved social welfare functions (Buchanan 1949, 1959). The root of his critique lies in his understanding of subjective value. Since value is determined subjectively, the only information the economist can have about individuals' preferences is knowledge of which of the alternatives available to them was the most preferred. The economist is ignorant of everything except what is chosen. As such, it is not possible for the economist to independently gather the full preference scales of a group of people in order to aggregate those individual values and identify the alternative with the greatest social value (Buchanan 1959, 193–96).

In light of the economist's inability to identify the socially preferred alternative, Buchanan proposes that the economist "does not recommend policy A over policy B. He presents policy A as a hypothesis subject to testing" (Buchanan 1959, 195). Buchanan goes on to explain that whether or not policy A is judged to improve welfare can be determined only through observation of whether or not the group is able to come to a consensus that the policy will indeed be an improvement. The extent to which we can expect changes in the rules to be improvements will then depend on the decision rules in effect in a society, and the extent to which they require individuals to choose rather than permitting others to make decisions without the consent of the affected parties. This is outlined most completely in *The Calculus of Consent*, in which Buchanan and Gordon Tullock ([1962] 1999) establish unanimity as the only decision rule under which a collective decision can be ensured to be in the interest of all members of a social group.

The idea that any policy to which all members of a group consent will be an improvement rests on the implicit assumption that individuals understand enough about the consequences of the policy to be able to engage in subjective valuation. Knowledge about how a particular rule will work out is certainly not perfect. Individuals are limited in their "cognitive capacity to discern and anticipate reliably the general operating properties of alternative rules" (Vanberg and Buchanan [1991] 2001, 131). If individuals do not accurately anticipate the effects of a policy or rule change, they may initially support a policy that they will experience as a cost in the future. Individuals may also wind up supporting a policy or rule against their own interests if their interests change between the time they weigh in on the policy and the time the consequences of the policy are felt. Individuals may not be much better than the economists observing them at identifying the policies that will prove to be in their interest. (However, this does not imply that the economist or some other type of expert will be a better judge, as is sometimes implied when individuals' ability to engage in intelligent decision-making is criticized.)

These difficulties associated with even identifying beneficial rules—let alone securing the appropriate level of agreement and successfully devising and executing an enforcement scheme—suggest a kind of constitutional ignorance that calls the possibility of deliberate constitutional design into question. The ignorance of the individual participant in the political process has been well established with respect to voting (Aranson 1990; Caplan 2011; Downs 1957); the ignorance of the individual participant has been less fully explored in the constitutional process. Yet there does seem to be a knowledge requirement for individuals hoping to effectively participate in the constitutional process, particularly to the extent that individuals are expected to be able to extrapolate from themselves and from their own particular interests at the moment of choice. Buchanan and Tullock ([1962] 1999, 96) write: "At the constitutional level, *identifiable* self-interest is not present in terms of external characteristics. The self-interest of the individual participant at this level leads him to take a position as a 'representative' or 'randomly distributed' participant in the succession of collective choices anticipated." What kind of knowledge would be required for an individual to take such a representative position and, while in that position, be able to successfully identify policies and rule changes that will be beneficial for all the members of the group? The ability of the individual to gather and interpret such knowledge would seem to fall short, and for the same reasons that the expert observer would be unable to gather full preference scales for all members of a society.

The fact that interests are clearly defined only at the moment of choice—and that even then all that can be known is that what is chosen is the most valued—is an important part of why individuals must directly participate in the design of institutions if Buchanan's contractarian approach to the creation and enforcement of rules is to have any of its advertised benefits. Buchanan is clear on the fact that he does not believe individuals to be able to hold clearly defined objectives independent of choice, even internally:

> I am here advancing the more radical notion that *not even* individuals have well-defined and well-articulated objectives that exist independently of choices themselves. Introspectively, we must realize that we do not. My plea is that we begin to temper our analytical-explanatory thought patterns to allow for what we know to be real, regardless of the havoc wrought to our aesthetically appealing logical structures. (Buchanan [1979] 1999, 258, emphasis in original)

This does not mean that individuals do not understand their own interests or that some other party is capable of understanding them better (Buchanan [1977] 2000). If that were true, the only possible political order would be the arbitrary dominion of whatever individual or group happens to grab power over the rest. There is no conceptual path forward for political organization for the sake of mutual benefit.

What the significance of the moment of choice does mean, however, is that the participation and consent of all members of the society are perhaps more important to the constitutional project than has commonly been appreciated. Essentially, reason enters into the constitutional process exclusively through meaningful individual participation. The aspect of constitutional political economy that this problematizes is the idea that the constitutional process can meaningfully take place "as if" all members of the group are participating. This idea raises important questions about the feasible size and structure of political units. If constitutions can persist only when unanimously consented to by all members of the group, then how big can a polity possibly be? It may be possible for the community to outsource many functions to larger external organizations; however, the realistic political unit may wind up being capped at no more than a few hundred people, and even that size may be difficult to manage. Even in small organizations, the problem remains of ensuring that all members of the community participate in a way that reveals the best of that community's knowledge about the likely effects of a particular rule.

Constitutional discourse, meaning "everything that advances the acquisition, communication and processing of general constitutional information and knowledge," is one proposed solution to the knowledge problem inherent in attempts to identify the most preferable set of rules and enforcement mechanisms (Vanberg and Buchanan [1991] 2001, 131). However, individuals are limited both in their willingness to participate in constitutional discourse and in their ability to translate whatever information they do gather into accurate working knowledge of how a particular rule will function in practice. And here the Hayekian critique of rational construction returns. To the extent that we are unable to predict the future consequences of rules enacted today, no amount of discourse could enable us to identify a priori the optimal set of constitutional rules (Buchanan 1959, 140).

CONSTITUTIONAL HOPES AND POST-CONSTITUTIONAL FEARS

Buchanan's own thought on the question of whether or not individuals are capable of navigating the process of designing improvements in their complex environments seems to vacillate between optimism and despair. The hopefulness tends to be concentrated at the constitutional stage; the fear recognizes the great opportunity for predation and exploitation that enters at the post-constitutional stage.[4] The question of which of the two mental states *should* dominate is for Buchanan a question of the extent to which the paradigm of politics as exchange is capable of triumphing over the ever-present danger of state predation and violence. In his words: "The control of government scarcely emerges as an issue when we treat collective action in strictly contractarian terms. Such control becomes a central problem when political power over and beyond plausible contractarian limits is acknowledged to exist" (Buchanan [1975] 2000, 12).

Buchanan's views on the possibilities for peaceful social coordination seem to have been challenged by his observations of the United States in the 1960s and 1970s (Buchanan 1970a, 1970b). He describes the United States as in a state of "constitutional anarchy" within which "the range and extent of federal government influence over individual behavior depend largely on the accidental preferences of politicians in judicial, legislative, and executive positions of power" (Buchanan [1975] 2000, 19). To the extent this characterization is true, Buchanan is describing a world in which his own constitutional vision is robbed of predictive power.

The post-constitutional ideal of politics as exchange is also put at risk because of the discretionary influence that particular individuals have over the political process in modern democracies. If the resources of a society are managed to a significant degree by the public sector, "neglect of the influence of politicians and bureaucrats on budgetary results may severely weaken the relevance of any analysis," presumably including Buchanan's own preferred models (Buchanan [1975] 2000, 197). Once the influence of politicians and bureaucrats is considered, it quickly becomes clear that these individuals are almost certain to use their influence to expand both the size and scope of government (Higgs 1987; Tullock 2005).

This less optimistic side of Buchanan's thought—and its relationship to his constitutional vision—is perhaps articulated most clearly in *The Limits of Liberty: Between Anarchy and Leviathan* ([1975] 2000). In the first chapter of this volume, Buchanan describes *The Calculus of Consent*—his joint project with Tullock in which they show that many features of public systems can be understood as outcomes of a process of rational choice and exchange—as an exercise in "indulg[ing] our fancies" despite the fact that "[z]ero-sum and negative-sum analogues yield better explanatory results in many areas of modern politics" (Buchanan [1975] 2000, 10). To the extent this is true, the implication is that thinking about politics as a positive-sum process of exchange, arguably the very foundation of Virginia public choice (Buchanan 1987), yields inferior explanatory results relative to theories that focus on individuals' capacities for predation and violence.

One possible explanation for the different perspectives at the constitutional and post-constitutional levels of organization is that the productive state and the protective state have different knowledge requirements. Although the protective and productive functions of the state are difficult to separate when considering an actual government, they are at least conceptually separable. The productive functions of the state clearly require knowledge of individuals' relative valuations of different goods and services. This knowledge is an important prerequisite to being able to make decisions about whether provision of the goods through public means will be worthwhile (Buchanan [1975] 2000, 125–58). Because this knowledge is so important to making decisions about what will be provided publicly, there must be some way to aggregate and act on this information. The unanimity principle has been proposed as a solution to this problem: if all members of the group voluntarily consent to a particular rule and method of enforcement, an observer can be confident that the rule serves the interest of all members of the group, even if getting to that agreement requires the use of logrolling or other types of side payments (Buchanan and Tullock [1962] 1999, 131–46).

If the state does not require local knowledge of individuals' interests in order to execute its protective functions, there is possibly more hope for the constitutional project when it is limited to a basic set of protective functions. For example, if all know and agree to some natural or universal set of rights to be protected, perhaps there would be no problem obtaining the information needed to come to consensus, or an approximation thereof.

However, even a limited constitution may not be able to last, especially once its formation is no longer in living memory. The binds of any agreement designed to constrain behavior will always chafe at the moment of constraint. For most citizens in a modern state, this chafing is their only experience with the constitutional order. The understanding of the state as an entity created out of a self-governing impulse is gone. All that remains for individuals is their experience with the coercion exercised by the state; they no longer have any sense that this coercion was voluntarily submitted to or serves some valuable grand purpose (Buchanan [1975] 2000, 123). This is further exacerbated by the fact that, once a state is established, the agents left in charge will often be tempted to expand the state's authority beyond what was originally agreed to by the contracting group (Buchanan [1975] 2000, 133–34).

The fragility of the constitutional agreement and the contempt that many may come to feel for it are not sufficient justification to abandon the constitutional project, certainly not in Buchanan's mind. A number of unanswered questions remain. How long can a community maintain the sense that it created its own government? Are there ways, such as the cultivation of particular habits or attitudes, to prolong the sense of self-governance? (Buchanan [1979] 1999; Ostrom 1997, 2008) To the extent that constitutional negotiations resulting in outsourcing of enforcement to a third-party government are flawed, is there any better alternative? (Boettke and Leeson 2015; Leeson 2007) Depending on one's expectations about the possibilities for internal group enforcement of rules—in other words, how bad you think anarchy is likely to get—even a short-lived, imperfect constitutional order may seem significantly preferable.

This could be why Buchanan viewed respect for law as particularly significant to the maintenance of constitutional order. Strong commitment to being rule-abiding can substitute for the need for an enforcement mechanism and, as an empirical matter, may explain much observed rule-following behavior even when there are punishments in place for those who violate the law. Conversely, the attitude that obeying the law is not valuable for its own sake can make the problem of enforcement significantly more difficult. The fact that the "principle of respect for law, as such, may be subject to rapid erosion once a critical minority is observed to violate the principle" makes the matter of this underlying ethic a significant issue of concern for Buchanan ([1975] 2000, 151). He sees how much could be accomplished through the constitutional process but at the same time recognizes how dependent the efficacy of that process is on the attitudes and character of the individuals involved.

This is why the "flaunting of traditional codes of conduct" and the way in which the culture of the 1960s challenged commonly accepted ideals about acceptable behavior was such a matter of concern for Buchanan ([1975] 2000, 26). At some points, he expresses general concern over the erosion of traditional institutions within families, schools, and churches because of the corrosive effect that loss may have on constitutional order during a time at which significant reform seems a real possibility (Buchanan 1970b). At other points, his concern seems to be less about the specific changes taking place and more about the fact that the agreed-upon standards of behavior were changing in the minds of only part of the population. If people cannot come to agreement about the basic rules for social interaction, it becomes harder to imagine those interactions resulting in the creation of agreed-upon constitutional rules: "How could two men, meeting for the first time, carry out the simplest form of interchange without implicit acceptance of some behavioral limits?" (Buchanan [1975] 2000, 28)

Buchanan's answer to the problem of needing to come to some degree of initial shared expectations before the constitutional process can begin in earnest is the cultivation of the constitutional habit, or *constitutional attitude*. The use of rules and constraints to cultivate a better life is part of man's nature. It is an important feature of human life to be able to "within limits, shape the form of being that we shall be between now and the time of death" (Buchanan [1979] 1999, 247). However, our creative, artifactual impulses are a part of our character that could potentially be ignored, to our detriment: "By implicitly refusing to consider man as artifactual, we neglect the 'constitution of private man,' which roughly translates as 'character,' as well as the 'constitution of public men,' which translates into the necessary underpinning of a free society, the 'character' of society, if you will" (Buchanan [1979] 1999, 252). If we ignore our artifactual character, it may not be possible for us to reform either ourselves or our communities.

There is a sense in which Buchanan emphasizes the constitutional attitude not because of any of its actual merits but because it is the only alternative between anarchy and Leviathan. As a philosophical ideal, Buchanan considers his own constitutional/contractarian position to be second best relative to a world in which individuals cooperate to effectively protect individual rights without need for the external enforcement provided by a government. However, he also views humankind as not up to the challenge of statelessness. His criticism seems to be primarily pragmatic—that is, anarchism is empirically less likely to succeed—and strategic: "Where the contractarian paradigm comes on at its strongest [relative to anarchism], is at the bridge between negative criticism and constructive proposals for change"

(Buchanan [1977] 2001, 23). The concept of unanimity gives the social scientists a platform from which to develop proposals for advantageous social reforms and a method for evaluating whether or not they prove to be desirable in practice (Buchanan 1959).

Given his concerns about both the pragmatism and strategic value of anarchy, Buchanan understandably considers the cultivation of a constitutional attitude as a task that is both extraordinarily challenging and more likely to succeed than an available alternative. For him, a constitutional attitude is the only realistic way to preserve some degree of self-governance (Buchanan [1977] 2001, 16). As such, Buchanan's view is that the available choices are either to adopt a constitutional attitude or to turn ourselves over to Leviathan.

Buchanan's ([1975] 2000, chap. 7) conceptualization of law as a stock of public capital suggests two reasons he views the constitutional attitude as such a critical component of the constitutional project. First, like other capital investments, constitutional negotiation can be extraordinarily costly, and its benefits have the potential to accrue over quite a long period of time. Whether or not the process of negotiation is considered worthwhile will depend in part on how far into the future the participants are willing to consider when calculating the present value of a potential investment in the public capital stock. An ideology or attitude that prioritizes the value of mutually restraining rules may promote this kind of long-term vision. Much like individuals in their 30s will likely anticipate greater net present benefit from a long-term investment than peers in their 80s, individuals abstracting away from their own position and interests to devise a set of generally beneficial rules will likely perceive higher net present benefits from an investment in public capital than those who don't see the long-term value of constitutional constraints. Second, like other forms of capital, public capital is subject to erosion over time and often requires maintenance to procure the most efficient return. A belief that recognizes good rules as an asset will allow future owners of the legal capital stock to recognize its productive capacity and to take actions that will ensure a continued flow of returns. When there is no constitutional attitude and the importance of rules is not recognized, the legal capital stock that has been built may lie fallow, an underappreciated profit opportunity.

In "Natural and Artifactual Man," Buchanan ([1979] 1999) makes the provocative claim that "Man wants Liberty to be the man he wants to become," but two decades later (Buchanan 2005), his concern turns to the situation when men are "afraid to be free." As Buchanan argues, the contemporary threat to the liberal order no longer comes from managerial socialism, or even paternalistic government, but from the desire of the population to demand the government take on the role of parent—to provide protection, to provide security. A similar theme is voiced in Buchanan's (2000) essay "The Soul of Classical Liberalism," where he states that classical liberals have relied too much on economic efficiency arguments rather than on more philosophical arguments that address questions of justice and aspirational ideals for human societies. Liberalism must be reconstituted in Buchanan's mind for this new generation in a way that excites the imagination. Just as Hayek did before him, Buchanan stresses social mores, law, and markets. Ideas, as well as interests, rule the world.

The tensions in Buchanan's constitutional political economy project are not evidence of fatal contradictions but are instead reflections of the very "crooked timber of humanity" out of which nothing straight can ever be made. Throughout all Buchanan's writings the phrase "relatively absolute absolutes" is invoked at various times to reflect this recognition of the tensions (see, for example, Brennan and Buchanan [1985] 2000, 85).

EXPERIMENTATION AND ADAPTATION IN THE CONSTITUTIONAL PROCESS

The liberal order must be continually reconstituted. The constitutional order of a free people is plagued by a variety of tensions, including the durability of the constitutional contract. Buchanan has introduced the useful terminology of the *protective state* (law and order), the *productive state* (public goods), and the *redistributive or predatory state* (rent-seeking society) (Buchanan [1975] 2000). The first fundamental tension that Buchanan argues must be recognized is whether the protective and productive state can be empowered without unleashing the predatory state. For most of his career, Buchanan wrestled with this tension in an analytical manner. Institutional problems demanded institutional solutions, and we can analyze institutional designs using the tools of economic reasoning. Throughout his career, however, Buchanan also stressed the importance of ideas; and, toward the end of his career, he continually stressed this element in the constitutional reconstruction of the liberal society. This willingness to wrestle with tensions enabled Buchanan to offer an answer to the paradox of governance laid out in Federalist No. 51 in a way that answered the question in Federalist No. 1 about reflection and choice as opposed to accident and force (Hamilton, Jay, and Madison [1818] 2001).

Although he often contrasted his social contract perspective with Hayek's evolutionist perspective, the analytical and social philosophical differences between Hayek's *The Constitution of Liberty* (1960) and Buchanan's *Freedom in Constitutional Contract* ([1977] 2000) are minuscule compared with the differences between their philosophies and those of their scientific and scholarly peers in post–

World War II economics. A classic demonstration of just how far apart Hayek and Buchanan were from their peers is Buchanan's exchange with Richard Musgrave. Buchanan simply asked Musgrave whether, if he had a pet tiger, he would put a muzzle on it. Musgrave took the bait and actually argued that he would not want to muzzle the tiger in case it wanted to eat (Buchanan and Musgrave 1999, 88–89). But Buchanan's question puts the stress on the analytical puzzle of finding that set of constitutional restrictions that will do the job.

Buchanan's insistence that all constitutional bargains must begin from the "here and now" is a concession to the imprint of history, and his focus on the constitutional attitude and the maintenance of public capital is a concession to ideology. Once Buchanan's social contractarianism is infused with history and ideology, the gap between Hayek and Buchanan fades. There is an inevitability in arriving at this conclusion. Humans are creatures who live in groups, and those groups would not have survived without some rules of conduct, even if only simple prohibitions on murder and theft (Runst and Wagner 2011, 134). Certainly no civilization could have developed to the point of being able to create something like a formally articulated constitution without first having some rules of just conduct that made coexistence tolerably productive. The initial emergence of rules is clearly not an intentional process, yet people clearly do engage in the intentional design of rules as well. When design and emergent elements are both taken seriously, we arrive at a situation in which critical theorists must be free to question all of society's arrangements—values, laws, fundamental institutions of governance—but they cannot question all of society's arrangements at once. Change is always on the margin.

Our final conjecture in this chapter is that the most direct path to the resolution of the apparent tension between constitutional hope and post-constitutional fear in Buchanan's work is to study the conditions under which mankind, with all its flaws and limitations, can make marginal changes to the rules in a way that maximizes the opportunity for constitutional improvements while minimizing the damage from potentially harmful changes. If we take both Buchanan's and Hayek's fears about human cognitive limitations seriously, the extent to which the system in question can survive poorly made decisions must be a particularly important evaluative criterion. Effective constitutional rules will minimize the possibility that a bad or uninformed actor within them can do too much harm—hence, the importance of balanced powers, procedural checks, and other constitutional limits on powers. Similarly, the institutional background for effective constitution-making minimizes the impact of bad decisions at the constitutional level.

The idea that different institutional backgrounds will result in different rule-making processes originates in the work of Hayek and is perhaps most developed by two of Buchanan's constitutional fellow travelers, Elinor and Vincent Ostrom.[5] The Ostroms' lifetime of research speaks to two simple questions: (a) How do imperfect people with diverse interests come together to govern themselves? and (b) How do the rules of the game affect this process of self-governance? (Boettke, Lemke, and Palagashvili 2015) Buchanan shared these concerns. As demonstrated earlier in this chapter, he was very aware of both the limits of human understanding and the possibility of predatory outcomes if the political game is played by the wrong rules. Given how committed Buchanan remained to the constitutional project despite his acute awareness of these limitations, the Ostroms' questions must be answered in order to reconcile Buchanan's project.

Elinor and Vincent Ostrom viewed the competitive, polycentric framework as the context within which institutional design could avoid the pitfalls of radical constructivism. In brief, a polycentric framework is a system within which many different groups have genuine autonomy to make their own decisions about the rules they will follow and enforce (Aligica and Boettke 2009; Ostrom 1972; Ostrom, Tiebout, and Warren 1961). Usually the polycentric framework is discussed as occurring within some type of general rule of law, similar to Buchanan's view that general agreement on what constitutes acceptable social behavior must come before any type of further negotiation. The various relationships between the different autonomous political units will be constituted according to what type and scale of organization will help the people involved most effectively solve whatever communal problem it is that they are trying to address. The nature of the political organization is expected to emerge from a process in which the people involved participate in both the creation and enforcement of the rules. In these fundamentals, there is a strong similarity between Buchanan's political economy and the Ostroms' polycentric framework. Both require a particular type of foundation before they can be expected to operate effectively; both view the design of rules as an attempt at mutual problem-solving; and both view the involvement of the affected individuals as critical to the identification and implementation of good rules.

The significant contribution the Ostroms bring to the Buchananite framework is the way their apparatus enables the study of rule formation at the local level and the process through which good rules rise to the top. This is true both in their theoretical emphasis and in their choice of method. On the level of method, fieldwork had been an important part of the Ostroms' research program since its inception (Boettke, Palagashvili, and Lemke 2013). It was important to them to directly study and participate in the process of rule formation because of the difference between rules in form and rules in use and because of their interest in understanding details about the participants that would be difficult to observe from a distance. This concern is seen in both Elinor Ostrom's (1990) design principles, which emphasize the importance of direct buy-in and participation in the enforcement process, and in Vincent Ostrom's (1997, 14) emphasis on the "habits of the heart" and "character of the mind" that individuals bring to the constitutional process.

The local constitutional process takes on additional significance when it occurs in a system in which there is meaningful contestation. Contestation can take place both horizontally and vertically. Horizontally, different groups offering different solutions to the same common problem—say, maintaining law and order or preventing overuse of a common resource—will face competition and draw ideas from each other. This is a common feature of theories of decentralized political structures (Frey 2001; Ostrom, Tiebout, and Warren 1961; Tiebout 1956). Contestation can also take place vertically, between a political organization and a related counterpart with more or less overarching political authority. This kind of contestation has potential to serve as a meaningful constraint also depending on the rules that govern the relationships between vertical political units. As with horizontal competition, if lower-level units can meaningfully check political organizations that have a more comprehensive type of authority, there is potential for organizations that solve problems well to gain authority and for organizations that solve problems poorly to lose authority. It is the combination of the bottom-up nature of the rule-making process and the fact that the rule-making process is occurring within a system with contestation between different systems of rules that lends continuing hope to the constitutional project. Without these elements, the constitutional vision is devastated by the critiques of epistemic overreach and predatory capture that it was designed to overcome. The element of choice prevents predation and provides a mechanism through which learning can take place; the fact that the project of designing rules is undertaken by many different groups independently of each other is the sole, albeit imperfect, way around the problem that people usually simply do not know in advance what the best rules will be (Ostrom 1980).

Buchanan, however, was not unequivocally in favor of competition and contestation within political systems. (Of course, the question always remains, "in favor" relative to what alternative?) Particularly notable is the work of Buchanan and Charles Goetz (1972), which draws attention to the limits of the efficiency processes of Tiebout competition. Buchanan and Goetz note that differences in the value of private goods across localities mean that sorting along private good margins will muddle the proposed efficiency properties of Tiebout sorting. Specifically, the wealthy will tend to self-segregate, increasing the tax base in already-wealthy areas and further decreasing the tax base in already-poor areas. Further, the interpersonal and interjurisdictional transfers required to internalize the problem of income-based segregation are politically infeasible because of the discrimination in tax burden and service benefits that resolution would require. Poorer localities *could* charge wealthy business owners a lower tax rate or offer them superior public services in order to prevent flight to wealthier urban centers with greater private profit opportunities, but it would be almost impossible to do so in a way that would be both constitutional and acceptable to the voting public. Consequently, even the idealized Tiebout model is a significant departure from market-like efficiency in the provision of local public goods.

Unlike Charles Tiebout's (1956) conclusion that competition between localities would lead to a public goods law of one price in which tax rates and public services would equalize across jurisdictions, Buchanan saw Tiebout competition as likely to exacerbate the problem of urbanization and self-segregation by the wealthy. This concern was the motivating insight behind Buchanan's argument in favor of equalizing interstate transfers, a proposal he advanced multiple times in the 1940s and 1950s. Boettke and Alain Marciano (2016) walk through the process by which Buchanan moderated this view in the 1960s. Essentially, Buchanan came to recognize that *not even* interstate transfers could prevent flight to wealthier areas with greater opportunities. The proposed interstate transfers would equalize only marginal benefit, so the fact that the total surplus was greater in some localities would still drive migration. What was necessary instead was a mechanism that would allow attractive localities to exclude newcomers who would erode the value of their local public goods by overdrawing on services or insufficiently contributing. Shortly after, the theory of clubs was born (Boettke and Marciano 2016; Buchanan 1965).

What do Buchanan's criticisms of competition imply for our argument in favor of bottom-up, consensus-based local public goods provision within a polycentric system? Most obviously, they raise the question of whether or not heterogeneity across communities is as troublesome as Buchanan seems to fear in his responses to the idea of Tiebout competition. The alternative perspective is that, given heterogeneity across people, heterogeneity of institutional solutions has value (see, for example, Aligica 2014; Aligica and Tarko 2013; Ostrom 1990). Increasing diversity of the interests of a population increases the cost of negotiation over what optimal rules will be, and also increases the externalities that will be imposed on individuals who have nonstandard preferences.

Further, heterogeneous communities enable a kind of institutional discovery process. Hayek (1960, 23–24) emphasized throughout his work, "We are as little able to conceive what civilization will be, or can be, five hundred or even fifty years hence as our medieval forefathers or even our grandparents were able to foresee our manner of life today." If we cannot conceive what civilization will be like, it follows that we will not be able to predict in advance exactly which rules we will need to follow in order to be able to continue to engage in mutual cooperation. This suggests a benefit to enabling a wide degree of institutional experimentation. Further, once the limits of human reason are taken into consideration, the value of institutional experimentation seems to close the gap between the visions of the contractarian constitutionalists and those who instead prefer, either ideologically or analytically, the idea of cooperation within anarchy. At the end of the day, both are systems in which the only hope for finding a good form of cooperation comes from experimenting and seeing what happens.

CONCLUSION

Systemic competition and contestation are important features of the constitutional process. Once this fact is recognized, Buchanan's contractarian vision seems obviously consistent with his skeptical view of much of the operation of actual governments. Much as someone who understands the beneficial properties of exchange can critique a particular market or firm without experiencing any cognitive dissonance, Buchanan successfully abstracts away from specific existing political systems in order to understand the underlying properties of political exchange. It is true that no perfect manifestation of the constitutional vision exists in the world, past or present. However, this is no more valid as a critique of the constitutional vision than a criticism of the market exchange process that is based on empirical observations of imperfect markets. Yes, failure and error occur. Bad actors, or good actors facing perverse incentives, engage in abuse and exploitation. Yet, underneath the human imperfections, the process of individuals seeking to create rules persists. Constitutional political economy is the theory through which this process can be understood.

Although Buchanan was perfectly comfortable with the normative implications of his theorizing, these statements can also be considered in a purely positive sense. Denying the law of demand will do nothing to interfere with its operation. Similarly, the program of constitutional political economy is aimed at teasing out the truth of the abstract relationships that exist between people, rules, and power. Our understanding of these relationships can continue to evolve, and we can disagree over the specifics of particular cases; but there's no getting away from the basic fact that people can and do benefit themselves by engaging in mutual constraint. This action will produce different outcomes depending on the institutional environment. This is a matter for study and institutional analysis, but, again, it does not change the fact that there is a constitutional impulse—similar to Adam Smith's "propensity to truck, barter, and exchange"—that is there to be described and understood.

The critical question Buchanan begins and ends with is how to marshal this constitutional impulse in a way that muzzles rather than releases the predatory Leviathan he fears. This chapter's suggested approach to answering this question is to advance Buchanan's constitutional project in a way that is rooted in a Hayekian understanding of human limitations and embraces a practical Ostromian emphasis on the importance of individuals and small-scale, local activity. If this approach is adopted, perhaps the constitutional project can be rescued from the misconception that it is an unattainable dream.

NOTES

The authors thank Rosolino Candela and the participants at the symposium on "Tensions in the Political Economy Project of James M. Buchanan," in Fairfax, Virginia, on December 14–15, 2016, for valuable comments. They also thank the anonymous referees who provided many useful suggestions on how to improve the paper. Any remaining errors are the authors' own.

1. This presumes that individuals actually do attempt to create constitutional rules. The other possible explanation is that most attempts to craft constitutions are merely dressed-up versions of rent-seeking or other forms of negotiation between special interests.

2. One problem with this belief is that there is no true third party to be found. There is no agent outside the system. The only possible enforcement is that conducted by individuals who are a part of the system and subject to the rules themselves—in this sense the departure from anarchy may not be possible.

3. This quote suggests that Buchanan seems to have a better appreciation for spontaneous order than is sometimes recognized. And, on the basis of the quote from Hayek (1973) in the previous paragraph, Hayek seems to have a better appreciation for the role of intentional design than is sometimes recognized. So Buchanan and Hayek's views seem in actuality to be quite similar. Thank you to Rosolino Candela for bringing the Hayek quote to our attention and noting the value of the juxtaposition.

4. An open question is whether Buchanan's hopefulness is better described as being attached to theoretical inquiry and his optimism as a function of observing the actual exercise of politics.

5. Runst and Wagner (2011, 135) offer the relationship between grammar and language as an example of the interplay between the rules and the process of change. Grammar comes to exist only after language; however, once the grammatical rules are codified, they shape the way that language is used and so influence its further development.

REFERENCES

Aligica, Paul Dragos. 2014. *Institutional Diversity and Political Economy: The Ostroms and Beyond.* New York: Oxford University Press.

Aligica, Paul Dragos, and Peter J. Boettke. 2009. *Challenging Institutional Analysis and Development: The Bloomington School.* New York: Routledge.

Aligica, Paul Dragos, and Vlad Tarko. 2013. "Co-Production, Polycentricity, and Value Heterogeneity: The Ostroms' Public Choice Institutionalism Revisited." *American Political Science Review* 107 (4): 726–41.

Aranson, Peter H. 1990. "Rational Ignorance in Politics, Economics and Law." *Journal Des Économistes et Des Études Humaines* 1 (1): 25–42.

Boettke, Peter J., and Peter T. Leeson. 2015. "Introduction: 'The Economic Role of the State.'" In *The Economic Role of the State*, edited by Peter J. Boettke and Peter T. Leeson, xi–xxv. Northhampton, U.K.: Edward Elgar Publishing.

Boettke, Peter J., and Alain Marciano. 2016. "The Distance between Buchanan's 'An Economic Theory of Clubs' and Tiebout's 'A Pure Theory of Local Public Expenditures.' New Insights Based on an Unpublished Manuscript." *European Journal of the History of Economic Thought* 24 (2): 205–37.

Boettke, Peter J., Jayme S. Lemke, and Liya Palagashvili. 2015. "Polycentricity, Self-Governance, and the Art and Science of Association." *Review of Austrian Economics* 28 (3): 311–35.

Boettke, Peter J., Liya Palagashvili, and Jayme S. Lemke. 2013. "Riding in Cars with Boys: Elinor Ostrom's Adventures with the Police." *Journal of Institutional Economics* 9 (4): 407–25.

Brennan, Geoffrey, and James M. Buchanan. (1985) 2000. *The Reason of Rules: Constitutional Political Economy*. Vol. 10 of *The Collected Works of James M. Buchanan*. Indianapolis, IN: Liberty Fund, Inc.

Buchanan, James M. 1949. "The Pure Theory of Government Finance: A Suggested Approach." *Journal of Political Economy* 5 (6): 496–505.

———. 1959. "Positive Economics, Welfare Economics, and Political Economy." In *The Logical Foundations of Constitutional Liberty*, 191–209. Indianapolis, IN: Liberty Fund, Inc.

———. 1965. "An Economic Theory of Clubs." *Economica* 32 (125): 1–14.

———. 1970a. "Political Economy and National Priorities, A Review Essay of the Economic Report of the President and the Annual Report of the Council of Economic Advisers." *Journal of Money, Credit and Banking* 2 (4): 486–92.

———. 1970b. "The 'Social' Efficiency of Education." *Il Politico* 35 (4): 653–62.

———. 1977. "Letter to Vincent Ostrom, March 18, 1977." James M. Buchanan papers, C0247, Special Collections Research Center, George Mason University Libraries.

———. 1987. "The Constitution of Economic Policy." *American Economic Review* 77 (3): 243–50.

———. 1990. "The Domain of Constitutional Economics." *Constitutional Political Economy* 1 (1): 1–18.

———. (1979) 1999. "Natural and Artifactual Man." In *The Logical Foundations of Constitutional Liberty*. Vol. 1 of *The Collected Works of James M. Buchanan*, 246–59. Indianapolis, IN: Liberty Fund, Inc.

———. 2000. "The Soul of Classical Liberalism." *Independent Review: A Journal of Political Economy* 5 (1): 111–19.

———. (1975) 2000. *The Limits of Liberty: Between Anarchy and Leviathan*. Vol. 7 of *The Collected Works of James M. Buchanan*. Indianapolis, IN: Liberty Fund, Inc.

———. (1977) 2000. *Freedom in Constitutional Contract: Perspectives of a Political Economist*. College Station: Texas A&M University Press.

———. (1977) 2001. "A Contractarian Perspective on Anarchy." In *Choice, Contract, and Constitutions*. Vol. 16 of *The Collected Works of James M. Buchanan*, 15–27. Indianapolis, IN: Liberty Fund, Inc.

———. (1987) 2001. "Constructivism, Cognition, and Value." In *Moral Science and Moral Order*. Vol. 17 of *The Collected Works of James M. Buchanan*, 459–68. Indianapolis, IN: Liberty Fund, Inc.

———. 2005. "Afraid to Be Free: Dependency as Desideratum." *Public Choice* 124 (1–2): 19–31.

Buchanan, James M., and Charles J. Goetz. 1972. "Efficiency Limits of Fiscal Mobility: An Assessment of the Tiebout Model." *Journal of Public Economics* 1 (1): 25–43.

Buchanan, James M., and Richard A. Musgrave. 1999. *Public Finance and Public Choice: Two Contrasting Visions of the State*. Cambridge, MA: MIT Press.

Buchanan, James M., and Gordon Tullock. (1962) 1999. *The Calculus of Consent: Logical Foundations of Constitutional Democracy*. Vol. 3 of *The Collected Works of James M. Buchanan*. Indianapolis, IN: Liberty Fund, Inc.

Caplan, Bryan. 2011. *The Myth of the Rational Voter: Why Democracies Choose Bad Policies*. Princeton, NJ: Princeton University Press.

Downs, Anthony. 1957. "An Economic Theory of Political Action in a Democracy." *Journal of Political Economy* 65 (2): 135–50.

Frey, Bruno S. 2001. "A Utopia? Government without Territorial Monopoly." *Journal of Institutional and Theoretical Economics* 157 (1): 162–75.

Hamilton, Alexander, John Jay, and James Madison. (1818) 2001. *The Federalist: The Gideon Edition*, edited by George W. Carey and James McClellan. Indianapolis, IN: Liberty Fund, Inc.

Hayek, F. A. 1952. *The Counter-Revolution of Science: Studies on the Abuse of Reason*. Glencoe, IL: Free Press of Glencoe, Collier-Macmillan.

———. 1960. *The Constitution of Liberty*. Chicago: University of Chicago Press.

———. 1973. *Law, Legislation and Liberty, Volume 1: Rules and Order*. Chicago: University of Chicago Press.

Higgs, Robert. 1987. *Crisis and Leviathan: Critical Episodes in the Growth of American Government.* New York: Oxford University Press.

Leeson, Peter T. 2007. "Better Off Stateless: Somalia before and after Government Collapse." *Journal of Comparative Economics* 35 (4): 689–710.

Ostrom, Elinor. 1990. *Governing the Commons: The Evolution of Institutions for the Study of Collective Action.* Cambridge, U.K.: Cambridge University Press.

Ostrom, Vincent. 1972. "Polycentricity." Workshop Archives, Workshop in Political Theory and Policy Analysis, Indiana University, Bloomington. Presented at the Workshop on Metropolitan Governance, American Political Science Association Meeting, Washington, DC, September 5–8.

———. 1980. "Artisanship and Artifact." *Public Administration Review* 40 (4): 309–17.

———. 1997. *The Meaning of Democracy and the Vulnerability of Democracies: A Response to Tocqueville's Challenge.* Ann Arbor: University of Michigan Press.

———. 2008. *The Political Theory of a Compound Republic: Designing the American Experiment.* 3rd ed. Lanham, MD: Lexington Books.

Ostrom, Vincent, Charles Tiebout, and Robert Warren. 1961. "The Organization of Government in Metropolitan Areas." *American Political Science Review* 55 (4): 831–42.

Runst, Petrik, and Richard E. Wagner. 2011. "Choice, Emergence, and Constitutional Process: A Framework for Positive Analysis." *Journal of Institutional Economics* 7 (1): 131–45.

Tiebout, Charles M. 1956. "A Pure Theory of Local Expenditures." *Journal of Political Economy* 64 (5): 416–24.

Tullock, Gordon. 2005. *The Collected Works of Gordon Tullock, Volume 6: Bureaucracy.* Edited by C. K. Rowley. Indianapolis, IN: Liberty Fund, Inc.

Vanberg, Viktor J., and James M. Buchanan. (1991) 2001. "Constitutional Choice, Rational Ignorance and the Limits of Reason." In *Choice, Contract, and Constitutions.* Vol. 16 of *The Collected Works of James M. Buchanan*, 127–47. Indianapolis, IN: Liberty Fund, Inc.

CHAPTER FOUR

CAN CONSENT LIMIT LIBERTY?

AN ANALYSIS OF BUCHANAN'S CLASSICAL LIBERAL CONTRACTARIANISM

RANDALL G. HOLCOMBE

The title of James M. Buchanan's 1975 book, *The Limits of Liberty: Between Anarchy and Leviathan* ([1975] 2000), nicely summarizes the challenge he sees to maintaining a classical liberal society. The title states his normative goal—liberty—and the threats he sees to liberty from both sides. Those threats are too little government—anarchy—and too much government—Leviathan. Here Buchanan is concerned about the lack of constraints on people coercing each other under anarchy on one side of classical liberalism and the lack of constraints on a Leviathan government that can coerce and oppress people on the other side. The book's title also reveals Buchanan's classical liberal orientation, which he discusses in many other works. Buchanan (2000, 117) says, "A motivating element [underlying classical liberalism] is, of course, the individual's desire for liberty from the coercive power of others—an element that may be almost universally shared." He goes on to say, "Classical liberalism sketches out a world as I should like to bring into being were I granted omnipotence" (Buchanan 2005a, 98).

Buchanan's (1975) title reflects the challenges he sees to achieving his normative goal of a classical liberal society, and the book describes a contractarian framework for achieving that goal. People agree to a set of constitutional rules that both give government the power to protect its citizens from having their rights violated by others and constrain government from using its power to violate people's rights. People would agree to such constitutional constraints on government because, Buchanan (2000, 117) notes, the desire to be free from the coercion of others "may be almost universally shared." But a more pessimistic Buchanan (2005b, 19) suggests that people might prefer a state that "stands in loco parentis." People might prefer to give the state power over their lives "because ceding control over their actions to others allows individuals to escape, evade, and even deny personal responsibilities." Buchanan himself explains why there is a tension between his contractarian framework and his classical liberal goals. Not only could people agree to an illiberal state but many also prefer it because they prefer a state that allows them to "evade and even deny their personal responsibilities" to one that protects their freedom.

Both Buchanan's classical liberalism and his contractarianism have normative foundations. Buchanan's classical liberalism is not based just on a utilitarian argument that it works better,[1] but on an ideological soul that values freedom for its own sake (2000). Meanwhile, his contractarianism is based on the normative principle of agreement. Desirable rules are those that command consensus. Buchanan's classical liberalism rests on a different normative principle from his contractarianism, and the two may find themselves in conflict if people agree to illiberal rules.

ANARCHY AND LEVIATHAN

Although Buchanan looks at the limits of liberty as anarchy at one end and Leviathan at the other, he spends relatively little time discussing the anarchy end. He primarily evaluates potential institutional constraints that can limit the power of government (see Holcombe 2013). Buchanan's vision of anarchy follows Thomas Hobbes ([1651] 2012), in which life is a war of all against all and is "nasty, brutish, and short." Then, referring to the individual who wants to preserve classical liberal values, Buchanan (1975, 6) says,

> When he recognizes that there are limits to the other-regardingness of men, and that personal conflict would be ubiquitous in anarchy, the extreme individualist is forced to acknowledge the necessity of some enforcing agent, some institutionalized means of resolving interpersonal disputes.

Buchanan cites Murray Rothbard (1973) to recognize that not everyone holds this Hobbesian view of anarchy but dismisses libertarian anarchism as unrealistic, saying, "To the individualist, utopia is anarchist, but as a realist he recognizes the necessity of an enforcing agent, a collectivity, a state" (Buchanan 1975, 12). Government is necessary to avoid a Hobbesian anarchy, Buchanan concludes.

One can debate the viability of a libertarian anarchy (see Holcombe 2004), but Buchanan dismisses the idea as unrealistic. He continues to hold this position in his later work. Geoffrey Brennan and Buchanan (1985, 5) reference Hobbes to say that we benefit from a set of rules that govern people's interactions with each other because

> without them we would surely fight. We would fight because the object of desire for one individual would be claimed by another. Rules define the private spaces within which each of us can carry out our own activities.

Buchanan begins with the idea that to preserve his normative value of liberty requires a government to prevent violence and protect individual rights.

To avoid Hobbesian anarchy, Buchanan argues for the existence of some third-party enforcer for those rules, which is government. That is what Buchanan labels the *protective state*. People might want more than this from government, however. Some production can be undertaken more efficiently when it is a collective undertaking rather than being left to bilateral transactions, so Buchanan also sees a role for the productive state to produce these goods and services. The *productive state*, Buchanan (1975, 97) says:

> enables the community of persons to increase their overall levels of economic well-being, to shift toward the efficiency frontier. Only through governmental-collective processes can individuals secure the net benefits of goods and services that are characterized by extreme jointness efficiencies and by extreme nonexcludability, goods and services that would tend to be produced suboptimally or not at all in the absence of collective-governmental action.

In *The Limits of Liberty* ([1975] 2000), Buchanan envisions people agreeing to government not only to preserve their liberty but also to produce public goods.

At the other end of the spectrum, Buchanan recognizes the potential for Leviathan government to compromise liberty. In *The Calculus of Consent*, Buchanan and Gordon Tullock (1962) adopt a framework that depicts politics as exchange: people use government to collectively attain ends that would be difficult or impossible to attain individually. Buchanan (1975, 6–7) later questions this politics as exchange approach, saying:

> The framework for analysis was necessarily contractarian, in that we tried to explain the emergence of observed institutions and to provide norms for changes in existing rules by conceptually placing persons in idealized positions from which

> mutual agreement might be expected. . . . I have come to be increasingly disturbed by this basically optimistic ontology. . . . Zero-sum and negative-sum analogues yield better explanatory results in many areas of modern politics.

So, at the Leviathan end of the spectrum, the issue becomes devising a method of designing constraints on government to prevent—or at least minimize—those zero-sum and negative-sum outcomes.

Buchanan recognizes the tension between classical liberalism and his contractarian approach to designing a social contract in the preceding quotation. As *The Limits of Liberty* ([1975] 2000) was being written, the rent-seeking literature based on Tullock (1967, 1975) and Anne Krueger (1974) was gaining prominence, which was perhaps a factor causing Buchanan to question—but not abandon—his basically optimistic contractarian ontology. Brennan and Buchanan (1980) use that framework to recommend a fiscal constitution, and Brennan and Buchanan (1985) further defend the normative foundations of constitutional economics.

Even while using it, Buchanan (1975, 8) questions the applicability of the politics as exchange approach to analyzing government, saying:

> So long as collective action is interpreted largely as the embodiment of individual behavior aimed at securing the efficiency attainable from cooperative effort, there was a natural tendency to neglect the problems that arise in controlling the self-perpetuating and self-enhancing arms of the collectivity itself. The control of government scarcely emerges as an issue when we treat collective action in strictly contractarian terms. Such control becomes a central problem when political power over and beyond plausible contractarian limits is acknowledged to exist.

That is, the Leviathan government threatens liberty, which explains why Buchanan's framework places liberty between anarchy and Leviathan. Buchanan (1990) describes constitutional economics as analyzing the choice among constraints, reinforcing his contractarian approach to constitutional economics and, in the context of his normative goals, looking for those constraints that can design a society that fits between anarchy and Leviathan.

POLITICS AS EXCHANGE

Buchanan viewed public choice as analyzing politics as exchange. Early in *The Calculus of Consent,* Buchanan and Tullock (1962) draw the parallel between market exchange and political exchange:

> Men co-operate through exchange of goods and services in organized markets, and such co-operation implies mutual gain. . . . At base, political or collective action under the individualistic view of the State is much the same. Two or more individuals find it mutually advantageous to join forces to accomplish certain common purposes.

Buchanan (2000, 115) expands on this idea of politics as exchange and relates it to classical liberalism:

> The encompassing vision that informs classical liberalism is described by an interaction of persons and groups within a rule-bound set of behavioral norms that allow each person or agent to achieve internally defined goals that are mutually achievable by all participants. . . . There is, and can be, no social or collective purpose to be expected from the process of interaction; only private purposes are realized, even under the idealized operation of the structure and even if collectivized institutions may be instruments toward such achievements.

Buchanan has consistently been inclined to look at political activity within the framework of collective agreement, as opposed to viewing that some use the force of government to coerce others. Buchanan (1990, 1) states that his constitutional political economy research program emphasizes "cooperative rather than conflictual" interaction among individuals. This idea appears in Buchanan's earliest work. Buchanan (1949, 498) says: "The state has no ends other than those of its individual members and is not a separate decision-making unit. State decisions are, in the final analysis, the collective decisions of individuals." This vision of politics as exchange depicts government as a mechanism that allows individuals to work together collectively to accomplish their individual ends that would be difficult or impossible to accomplish without collective action.

From a classical liberal perspective, the virtue of market exchange is that it occurs only if all parties to the exchange agree. Buchanan's classical liberal ideal of a society in which nobody coerces anyone else fits market exchange well. People transact with each other because they receive mutual benefits from doing so. For the politics as exchange framework to conform to Buchanan's classical liberal ideal, everyone must agree to the collective actions taken by the group. Buchanan and Tullock (1962, 72) state, "The only means whereby the individual can insure that the actions of others will never impose costs on him is through the strict application of the rule of unanimity for all decisions, public and private." They go on to note "that the rule of unanimity does possess certain special attributes, since it is only through the adoption of this rule that the individual can insure himself against the external damage that may be caused by the actions of other individuals, privately or collectively" (Buchanan and Tullock 1962, 81).

Buchanan and Tullock (1962, 88) reemphasize this point:

> This single decision-making rule acquires a unique position in the whole analysis which suggests that if costs of decision-making could be reduced to negligible proportions, the rational individual should always support the requirement of unanimous consent before political decisions are finally made.

They go on to say, "Only the unanimity rule will insure that all external effects will be eliminated by collectivization" (Buchanan and Tullock 1962, 89). The external costs, also discussed by Buchanan (1962a), are the costs that individuals bear because a political exchange leaves them worse off. It would be as if, in a market exchange, one party could force the other party into a trade the other party did not want to make.

Ultimately Buchanan and Tullock (1962, 96) conclude that their politics as exchange framework rests on the conceptual foundation of unanimous agreement to collective activity: "The individualistic theory of the constitution that we have been able to develop assigns a central role to a single decision-making rule—that of general consensus or unanimity." This is entirely consistent with Buchanan's classical liberal norm that individuals are free from the coercive powers of others. To preserve this norm, in markets and in politics, exchange occurs only when everyone agrees.

A tension arises from the fact that in politics it is rare to require unanimous agreement for collective action (Holcombe 2015).[2] Buchanan (1954, 334) himself notes many problems with "the prosaic 'one-dollar-one-vote' analogy, which is, at best, only partially appropriate and which tends to conceal extremely important differences." Despite these differences that Buchanan notes well before the publication of *The Calculus of Consent*, Buchanan's constitutional framework leans heavily on the analogy of politics as exchange.

THE CONCEPT OF AGREEMENT

Buchanan's classical liberal norm depicts a society in which individuals are free of coercion from others. His contractarian norm of unanimous agreement over the rules that govern collective action depicts individuals cooperating to achieve collectively goals they would be unable to attain through individual action. Buchanan recognizes, as shown in the many quotations in the previous section, the potential tension between these two norms. Buchanan extends the politics as exchange framework by developing a distinction between constitutional and post-constitutional decisions, initially with Tullock in *The Calculus of Consent* and extended himself in *The Limits of Liberty*. For the politics as exchange concept to hold, agreement must take place at the constitutional level but might not take place at the post-constitutional level.

In perhaps the most-cited chapter of *The Calculus of Consent* (chap. 6), Buchanan and Tullock (1962) develop a generalized economic theory of constitutions. They distinguish external costs, which are the costs individuals bear when collective action imposes costs on them, from decision-making costs, which are the costs individuals bear in the collective decision-making process. There is a trade-off, and individuals find that the value they get from collective action can rise if they move away from unanimous agreement, in which there are no external costs, toward less-inclusive decision rules, which will impose expected external costs on individuals in exchange for lower decision-making costs. Thus, members of a group could unanimously agree to a less than unanimous collective decision-making rule for certain decisions, which could make everyone in the group better off. Unanimity remains at the constitutional level. Everyone agrees on the rules, even though at the post-constitutional level some collective actions make individuals worse off. They are better off with the constitutional rules that create some external costs that will be imposed on them through post-constitutional decisions than if they did not have the rules.

A good example from Buchanan (1962b) that helps illustrate the point is the use of traffic signals to regulate traffic. The constitutional framework consists of rules that give the right-of-way to automobiles facing a green light and require automobiles coming to a red light to stop. On occasion a driver will come to a red light and have to stop even when there is no conflicting traffic. Clearly in this case it is suboptimal for the driver to have to stop when there is no other traffic, so the rule imposes costs on the driver with no offsetting gain to anyone. Yet overall, drivers are surely better off following the traffic rules than disregarding them, despite individual cases in which the rules impose costs greater than their benefits. Everyone is better off following the constitutional rules, despite the fact that some post-constitutional decisions (stopping at traffic lights when no other traffic is in the vicinity) make them worse off. We unanimously agree to the rules because overall, we are better off with the rules than without them, even though following them imposes costs in excess of benefits on us in certain situations.

CONSTITUTIONAL AND POST-CONSTITUTIONAL AGREEMENT

Buchanan's constitutional framework in which people unanimously agree to rules that sometimes produce outcomes with which they disagree offers an elegant explanation for why people can generally agree to an institutional framework that sometimes imposes costs on them. They agree with the rules at the constitutional level even though sometimes they bear external costs at the post-constitutional level. The idea was introduced by Buchanan and Tullock (1962) in their generalized theory of constitutions. Considering more deeply the broad idea of external costs at the post-constitutional level within the Buchanan and Tullock framework, it appears that there are ambiguities not answered by the broader framework.

Consider again the traffic light example. The driver stopped at the red light with no other traffic nearby can recognize that the rule is imposing an external cost on her, but can still be happy to bear that momentary cost in exchange for a more orderly flow of traffic. Now consider the case of the Affordable Care Act of 2009, which has been interpreted to require that health plans provide certain types of coverage to enrollees that the enrollees say they do not want, and sometimes say violate their ethical beliefs. Some people who supported the Affordable Care Act but oppose insurance plans with these provisions might say that, if they had known their plans would require coverage of these things they object to, they would not have supported the act. In the first situation, people bear post-constitutional external costs willingly because they believe they are better off with the constitutional rule. In the second situation, people believe that the unforeseen post-constitutional external costs outweigh the benefits, making them regret agreeing to the constitutional rule.

Of course, not everybody agreed to the Affordable Care Act; even if they had, the point is that, had those individuals been able to foresee the external costs of the constitutional rule, they would not have favored it. This aspect of external costs appears ambiguous in Buchanan's constitutional framework. In the Buchanan and Tullock (1962) framework, people weigh the expected external costs against the decision-making costs and favor the constitution if it provides net benefits. But Brennan and Buchanan (1985) say that constitutional rules must be sufficiently general and must apply to future decisions in which there is sufficient uncertainty that people cannot foresee their potential burden of external costs, an idea echoed in Buchanan and Roger Congleton (1998).

This might be illustrated with the traffic light example. Drivers will not know ahead of time whether they will drive up to a green light and be given the right of way or have to stop at a red light, even when there is no opposing traffic. Given the uncertain future, another possibility is that they find themselves at an intersection where the light always stays red, also marked with a "No Turn on Red" sign. If that intersection is the only route by which some residents can leave their homes, the light prevents them from ever being able to drive. This is an unlikely real-world outcome with the traffic light, but the analogy to real-world post-constitutional decisions seems plausible. People might agree to a constitutional rule ahead of time that, in hindsight, has made them worse off. The traffic light example is supposed to illustrate the case in which, even though people bear post-constitutional external costs, they still find themselves in agreement with the constitutional rules. The bizarre always-red traffic light example, however, suggests the possibility that, if people had been able to foresee the post-constitutional effects of the constitutional rules, they would no longer agree with those rules.

The problem is easier to resolve if all individuals find themselves worse off under the constitutional rules. They can agree to change the rules. But what if one of the unanticipated effects of the constitutional rules was to systematically benefit some at the expense of others? Those who benefit from the rules would not agree to change them. Even if somehow everyone originally agreed to the constitutional rules, does this mean that an oppressed minority is stuck with those rules, or can people agitate for change, even by secession or revolution?

In *The Limits of Liberty*, Buchanan (1975, 74) says:

> Contractual obligation, expressed by the willingness of individuals to behave in accordance with specified terms, depends critically on explicit or imagined participation. Individuals, having "given their word" are "honor bound" to live up to the terms. This remains true even if, subsequent to the agreement, these terms come to be viewed as "unfair" or "unjust."

If individuals agree to a process—on the basis of "explicit or imagined participation"—they are bound to the outcome of the process, even if the outcome was something they did not anticipate. Following the logic of Buchanan and Tullock (1962, chap. 6), one might agree to abide by majority rule for certain decisions, and the majority might decide on something substantially illiberal that the classical liberal minority did not foresee. Nevertheless, everyone is still bound by the outcome produced by the procedure to which they agreed.

Buchanan (1975, 75) goes on to say, "Individuals must ask themselves how their own positions compare with those they might have expected to secure in a renegotiated contractual settlement." This suggests that, if their positions leave them worse off because of an unforeseen post-constitutional decision, they are justified in backing out of an unfair or unjust agreement. And because, as the previous quotation notes, the agreement could be "imagined participation," this opens up additional ambiguities. How can someone be honor bound to live up to an imaginary agreement?

Buchanan (1975, 38–39) asks:

> Does a "social contract" in which all members of the community agree to make all collective choices relating to the provision and cost-sharing of a purely public good embody coercion as meaningfully defined? Ex ante, each participant knows that he will secure gains under such a contract, gains over and beyond those secured when none of the pure public good is provided. . . . Hence, it would seem that an agreement to join a collectivity that would make its decisions only under a rule of unanimity could be reached noncoercively.

He then notes:

> It is important to recognize both the purpose and the limits of the constitutional constraints that may be imposed on the operation of nonunanimity rules for collective decision-making at the postconstitutional stage of social interaction. To remain within what we may call broad contractual bounds, individuals must be assured that, in the net, operational politics will produce for them benefits rather than damages. (Buchanan 1975, 47)

This means that individuals must believe they are at least as well off as they would be if the contract were renegotiated from anarchy.

On the one hand, Buchanan argues that, once the constitutional contract is agreed to, one is bound to it "even if, subsequent to the agreement, these terms come to be viewed as 'unfair' or 'unjust.'" On the other hand, Buchanan says, "To remain within what we may call broad contractual bounds, individuals must be assured that, in the net, operational politics will produce for them benefits rather than damages." There is more than an apparent tension—there is an apparent contradiction—between these two passages from the same book.

AGREEMENT WITH THE CONSTITUTION

The problem of agreement is complicated by the fact that one set of constitutional rules applies to everyone. Because people have different preferences, there can be little doubt that most people do not agree with every individual provision of the social contract. However, the contractarian framework requires only agreement with the social contract itself. Consider Buchanan's (1975) contractarian model in which people begin from a Hobbesian anarchy and agree to constitutional rules that make everyone better off. People would rather live under the social contract and find themselves better off than if they remained in the state of Hobbesian anarchy. Because one set of rules applies to everyone, surely most people would find some constitutional rules with which they do not agree. Taken together, they prefer the whole set of rules to no rules, which would appear to indicate agreement under Buchanan's framework. If the requirement was that everyone had to agree with every single rule, there can be little doubt that, in any group larger than just a handful of people, there would be very few rules that would command unanimous agreement.

Consider an example. Some, such as Buchanan and Richard Wagner (1977), would argue that not only would people agree to a balanced budget constraint for government but also such a constraint actually was a part of the fiscal constitution at one point, even if not explicitly articulated. Buchanan and Wagner are not in agreement with a constitutional framework that allows governments to run deficits in normal times and have used the contractarian argument to support a balanced budget amendment to the Constitution. However, one can be fairly certain that Buchanan and Wagner are better off under the full set of current constitutional rules than they would be in Hobbesian anarchy. If they agree that all the constitutional rules taken together make them better off than having none, and if the current rule is that governments can run deficits at their discretion, are they then in agreement with the deficit rule?

Their opposition to deficit finance is far from unanimously shared. Among economists, many argue the merits of the discretionary fiscal policy that has led to budget deficits. If everyone agreed, the answer would be easy: establish a constitutional rule prohibiting deficit finance during normal times. But everyone does not agree, so when some people get the fiscal rule they prefer, others are left with a fiscal rule they oppose.

In contrast, Buchanan and Nicos Devletoglou (1970) argue that students who cause campus unrest because of their objections to the Vietnam War and racial inequities should be prevented from renegotiating the social contract. In a separate work, Buchanan (1970, 659) says:

> We see students now being allowed to act out what we previously allowed only as academic fantasies. Unrestrained and with little or no sense of mutual respect and tolerance, they flaunt ordinary rules of conduct; they disrupt others in the pursuit of their affairs; they have almost destroyed the basic order that once prevailed on campuses everywhere.

Keeping in mind that the military draft meant that those students could be involuntarily conscripted to go to war, it should be no surprise that some students believed the draft was not a legitimate part of the social contract and that they would not agree to any social contract that had involuntary conscription as a component. Buchanan (1970, 670) says, "the simple solution is one of cutting off the external sources of support." Students who are attempting to renegotiate the social contract should be prevented from doing so.

When Buchanan and Wagner object to contemporary policies, they perceive their attempt to renegotiate the social contract as legitimate; however, when college students object to contemporary policies and attempt to renegotiate the social contract, Buchanan sees their objections as illegitimate. If one starts with the presumption that in the United States everyone is better off living under the government's rules and policies than in Hobbesian anarchy, everyone is in agreement with the social contract as Buchanan (1975) sees it. A tension appears between Buchanan and Wagner's (1977) argument that the social contract should be modified and Buchanan and Devletoglou's (1970) argument that it should not.

The fact that one set of rules applies to everyone complicates the question of what constitutes agreeing with the social contract. Because all the rules apply to everyone, nobody will find every constitutional rule to be the one most preferred. Agreement, in Buchanan's terms, would seem to mean agreement that the set of rules—the social contract—taken in its entirety is preferred by everybody over Hobbesian anarchy. If Buchanan prefers the current set of constitutional rules to Hobbesian anarchy but opposes a fiscal constitution that allows continual deficit finance, one could argue that, by agreeing to the status quo, he also conceptually agrees with the fiscal constitution that is part of that status quo—according to his own criterion of hypothetical renegotiation of the social contract from anarchy.

Following this line of reasoning makes it very easy to argue that everyone is in agreement with the social contract and makes it difficult to argue that any current constitutional rule is not a part of the social contract. Comparing the status quo with Hobbesian anarchy sets a low bar, in the sense that in most places around the world the order provided by government makes people better off than the situation in which life is a war of all against all. Recognizing that we must agree to a set of rules that applies to everyone, it is then easy to argue, using Buchanan's criterion, that the compromise necessary to reach agreement means that individuals would agree with the whole set of rules even if they disagree with some specific rules.

THE TERMS OF THE CONTRACT

The two big challenges facing any social contract theory of the state are, first, determining what provisions are in the social contract and, second, establishing what it means to be in agreement with the social contract when in fact people did not agree to it. The preceding sections dealt with some ambiguities in determining what is in the social contract. What specific constitutional rules did people agree to follow? The second challenge any social contractarian faces is explaining how people can be said to be in agreement with constitutional rules when in fact they did not agree. Two 20th century contractarians, John Rawls (1971) and Buchanan (1975), offer similar but different mechanisms to answer both questions.

Rawls (1971) uses the device of a hypothetical veil of ignorance. People would step behind a veil of ignorance where they would know nothing about their individual characteristics. They would not know their race or gender, their height or physical strength, their level of intelligence, or any other personal characteristics. Behind the veil, they would have an equal probability of being anyone once the veil was lifted. Behind the veil of ignorance they would agree to a social contract; after that agreement, the veil would be lifted and people would be bound by the social contract to which they agreed before they knew their own personal characteristics.

Rawls's device of the veil of ignorance answers both of the two big challenges facing social contractarians. People would be said to be in agreement with the social contract if they agreed from behind a veil of ignorance. The provisions of the social contract are those provisions that people would agree to from behind a veil of ignorance. This is a procedural theory. The theory does not specify the outcome—the specific provisions of the social contract. Rather, the outcome—the social contract—is what is produced by the procedure of agreement from behind the veil of ignorance.

Buchanan (1975) uses a similar but different device of a hypothetical renegotiation of the social contract from Hobbesian anarchy. People do not actually have to go back to Hobbesian anarchy but rather to imagine a renegotiation of the social contract in that situation in which life is "nasty, brutish, and short," and a war of all against all. There are no social institutions in Hobbesian anarchy, so people have no social status, no political connections or privileges, and no socially ascribed characteristics of any kind. Douglass North, John Wallace, and Barry Weingast (2009) make the distinction between people's personal characteristics and their socially ascribed characteristics. *Personal characteristics* are those such as race, gender, height, intelligence, and the like. *Socially ascribed characteristics* come from one's job, political connections, educational affiliation, and, more generally, people's interactions with other people. One potentially significant difference between Rawls's device of the veil of ignorance and Buchanan's device of renegotiation from anarchy is that, behind the veil of ignorance, people have no personal characteristics or socially ascribed characteristics, whereas in a renegotiation from anarchy people lose their socially ascribed characteristics but retain their personal characteristics.

Buchanan (1975) defines a *natural distribution* that would exist among individuals in Hobbesian anarchy and imagines a bargaining process that begins from that natural distribution. He says:

> The specific distribution of rights that comes in the initial leap from anarchy is linked to the relative commands over goods and the relative freedom of behavior enjoyed by the separate persons in the previously existing natural state. This is a necessary consequence of contractual agreement. (Buchanan 1975, 25)

People agree to constitutional rules only when they are better off with them than without them. People are aware of their personal characteristics because those characteristics are a major component of how well off people would be in the natural state.

The contract includes a government to enforce the rules of the contract, designed to prevent opportunistic behavior that can lead to a devolution back to anarchy. Buchanan (1975, 32) says:

> The final or ultimate constitutional contract will define the rights assigned to each person in the inclusive community. And each person will find his own position improved over that which he might have enjoyed in any one of the natural distributions noted above, because he will not have to exert or contribute effort to defense and predation, either as an individual on his own account or as a contributing member of a subset of the total community.[3]

The social contractarian frameworks of both Rawls and Buchanan are procedural, meaning that the social contract that emerges is determined by the procedure that produces agreement. The social contract, following Rawls, is agreed to from behind a veil of ignorance; and the social contract, following Buchanan, is agreed to if people renegotiated from Hobbesian anarchy. A potentially significant difference between those procedures is that, behind a veil of ignorance, people do not know their personal characteristics whereas, when renegotiating from anarchy, they do.

Rawls conjectures that, from behind a veil of ignorance, people would design a social contract that would maximize the well-being of the least well off. His logic is that, behind the veil, everyone has an equal probability of being the least well off. They would therefore be willing to give up a little if they happened to be well off as insurance against the possibility they would be less fortunate. Setting aside whether people would actually agree to this "maximin" principle behind the veil, people renegotiating from anarchy would have a better idea about their post-constitutional prospects because, unlike those behind the veil, they know their personal characteristics.

Consider a simple two-person example of a weak person and a strong person devising a social contract that would allow them to coexist peacefully together. Behind a veil of ignorance, neither would know who would be the strong one or the weak one until after the veil was lifted. They might agree to a social contract that treated them both equally, perhaps incorporating some variant of Rawls' maximin principle. Renegotiating from anarchy, they would know which one of them was the weak and which the strong, giving a bargaining advantage to the strong (see Holcombe 2014). For example, the strong person could offer not to harm the weak person in exchange for the weak's paying 20 percent of his income as tribute to the strong person.

This simple example, which is similar to the way governments actually operate (Holcombe 2008), shows that the terms of the social contract are likely to be different if they are negotiated from behind a veil of ignorance than if they are negotiated from a hypothetical Hobbesian anarchy. This example raises the question about what happens to the social contract once the negotiating is complete. A social contract negotiated behind a veil of ignorance and incorporating the maximin principle might be disregarded by the strong once the veil was lifted and they saw the opportunity to take from the weak. A social contract negotiated from behind a veil of ignorance would certainly be more fragile than one renegotiated from anarchy. In this sense, Buchanan's renegotiation from anarchy, where people know their personal characteristics, would seem to be a better guide to understanding the real-world social contract than Rawls's negotiation from behind a veil of ignorance.

Both Rawls and Buchanan specify a process by which a social contract is (hypothetically) negotiated, but neither offers a clear specification of what provisions would be in the final contract. The simple example above shows that the terms of the social contract can depend on the details under which those terms are negotiated. There is a good chance that, despite the similarities in their theories, the actual provisions of the contract would not be the same if determined following Rawls's procedure than if determined following Buchanan's. Modern contractarianism leaves one of the main questions the theory must answer—What are the terms of the social contract?—without a clear answer.

In *The Limits of Liberty*, Buchanan (1975, 75) says:

> That set of rights which might be widely accepted as being within the limits of what we may call here the "renegotiation expectations" of individuals will not be uniform over communities and over time. . . . This suggests that there can be no resort to idealized general standards through which a legal or constitutional struc-

> ture in a particular community at a particular stage of historical development might be judged.

Buchanan himself notes that his contractarian framework does not specify the exact terms of the social contract.

Buchanan's admission that his social contract theory does not specify the terms of the social contract suggests that the hypothetical procedure he offers would not necessarily guarantee freedom of speech, protection of private property, freedom of trade, or the freedom to participate in one's government. What if citizens of a society became particularly enamored with a charismatic leader and unanimously agreed to make that person the dictator? What if that dictator then took away the rights to freedom of speech, property ownership, and so forth? Even if people later came to view the outcome as unfair or unjust, would they still would be bound by the agreement? Some passages in Buchanan (1975) appear to say yes and others no. If people looked at the outcome and determined that their own positions were worse than they thought would exist under a renegotiation, perhaps this outcome would not meet the test of this framework and the contract could be renegotiated. There is some ambiguity on this question in Buchanan's work.

This puts Buchanan in a different camp from many libertarian thinkers, who see clear limits to the legitimate role of government. Libertarian anarchists like Rothbard (1982) argue that all government activity is unethical. Ayn Rand (1961) and Robert Nozick (1974), however, see a legitimate role for government, but one with clear, defined limits beyond which government action is illegitimate. Rather than specify limits beyond which government action is illegitimate, both Rawls and Buchanan say it is whatever people would agree to under their hypothetical conditions. This position presents an obvious tension between Buchanan's contractarianism and his classical liberalism because one could envision a group agreeing to an illiberal social contract.

HYPOTHETICAL UNANIMOUS AGREEMENT

One feature of the agreement in both Rawls' and Buchanan's social contract theories is that they do not rest on an actual agreement with the contract; instead, they devise mechanisms to argue that hypothetically, people would agree. As Leland Yeager (1985, 2001) has emphasized, saying that people could hypothetically agree means that they did not actually agree. This idea highlights another major source of tension between Buchanan's classical liberalism and his contractarianism.

A major point in Yeager's critique is that all government activity is backed by force and that the only reason to have a government is to force people to do things they otherwise would choose not to do, or prohibit them from doing things they otherwise would choose to do. If people voluntarily paid for the public goods, redistribution programs, and other activities the government undertakes, there would be no reason to force them to pay taxes. If people voluntarily agreed to do the things government regulations required, and not do those things government regulations prohibited, there would be no reason for government to force them to abide by those regulations. This argument holds no matter how much citizens approve of what their governments do. Even for those who completely approve of everything government does, the threat of force still stands behind all government activity. Ultimately, all government activity is based on force; even in the contractarian framework, the purpose of government is to force people to do things they would not voluntarily choose to do.

Yeager's criticism—very relevant to Buchanan's classical liberalism—is that the contractarian framework depicts government activity as the result of agreement, when in fact it is always based on coercion. Some contractarians might be able to justify this by saying that people conceptually agree to their coercive state, but a classical liberal contractarian faces the criticism that he is trying to pass off the product of coercion as the result of agreement. In fact, there was no agreement, and government is forcing people to comply with its demands.

PEOPLE CAN AGREE TO BE COERCED

When weighing Buchanan's contractarian framework against the metric of his classical liberal values, a common argument is that people can agree to be coerced. This idea is apparent in the theory of constitutions in *The Calculus of Consent* (Buchanan and Tullock 1962, chap. 6), which makes the argument that people could unanimously agree to less-than-unanimous post-constitutional decision rules. It is even more clearly depicted in Harold Hochman and James Rodgers (1969), who offer a theory of Pareto optimal redistribution. Hochman and Rodgers hypothesize that the welfare of poor people enters as an argument in rich people's utility functions, so an increase in the welfare of poor people increases the utility of rich people. But redistribution, depicted this way, is a public good and induces a free rider problem. Each rich individual would be happy to give to the poor if all rich people did, but each individual's contribution alone would have little impact Everyone has an incentive, therefore, to free ride off the contributions of others, and charitable redistribution is less than optimal from the standpoint of the rich as well as the poor. In this model, everyone's utility would be higher if the rich could make a contract with each other that all would contribute to help the poor, and such an agreement is effectively put into effect through compulsory government redistribution plans. All people, including the rich, would be better off, so conceptually they would all agree to be coerced. The argument applies to all prisoners' dilemma situations in which participants are better off if they are forced to accept the cooperative solution rather than left with the individual utility-maximizing option to not cooperate.

One difference between the Hochman and Rodgers framework and the Buchanan and Tullock theory of constitutions is that the former has no external costs. Everyone is always better off because the coercion eliminates a welfare-reducing free rider problem. More generally, however, the "agree to be coerced" argument fits with Buchanan and Tullock's (1962) theory of constitutions, Hochman and Rodgers' (1969) theory of Pareto optimal redistribution, and Buchanan's (1975) contractarianism. Hypothetically, everyone would agree to government coercion at the constitutional level, which makes everyone better off in the post-constitutional world.

Although the argument is not entirely implausible, it fits uncomfortably with classical liberalism for several reasons. First, as Yeager (1985) emphasizes, the argument depicts government coercion as the product of agreement, when in fact there was no such agreement. In the Hochman and Rodgers framework, despite the plausibility of the argument, people did not agree to pay their taxes: they were forced to pay. A classical liberal should have a serious problem with an argument claiming that coercive acts of government are the product of agreement because in some hypothetical circumstance people might have agreed to them. The argument applies to Buchanan's agreement with constitutional rules just as much as Hochman and Rodgers' redistribution. One might say that under some circumstances people could have agreed to bear the external costs imposed on them by government action; in fact they did not agree, and the coercion was not the product of agreement. Depicting coercion as agreement is at odds with classical liberalism.

The argument in the previous paragraph applies to Buchanan and Tullock (1962), Rawls (1971), and Buchanan (1975); but a further argument applies to both Rawls and Buchanan. Buchanan and Tullock stop with the argument that people might agree to constitutional rules that permit post-constitutional actions that impose external costs on them. Buchanan and Tullock do not, however, specify what would constitute agreement to those constitutional rules. Rawls (1971) and Buchanan (1975) go further with their criteria of hypothetical agreement from behind a veil of ignorance and hypothetical agreement in a renegotiation from anarchy. These criteria do not represent real-world agreement among real-world people. They create a situation in which the theorist could argue that people who are not in agreement actually agree.

The idea of agreement lies at the center of *The Limits of Liberty* because Buchanan argues that everyone would benefit by escaping Hobbesian anarchy for a more orderly society. Buchanan (1975, 94) says, "Two or more persons may rationally choose to be governed by prior selection and implementation of enforcement institutions." Government follows a set of rules predetermined and agreed on by those who are governed, and Buchanan (1975, 95) says this "resort to third-party adjudication produces 'government' of the ideal type in practicality." Essentially, all individuals find it in their own self-interests to agree to be coerced.

Consider an individual who, when asked, says, "I do not agree with government spending programs that provide housing subsidies to low-income individuals." One response might be, "If you did not know your socially ascribed characteristics and might have been one of those low-income individuals, you would have agreed from behind a veil of ignorance, or in a renegotiation from anarchy; therefore, you are in agreement." The individual responds, "No, I am not in agreement," but the contractarian answer is "Even if you say you disagree, under hypothetical circumstances you would agree, so you are conceptually in agreement." In this dispute, it would seem that the classical liberal would have to side with the individual who says she is not in agreement rather than the theorist who makes the argument that the person who disagrees is hypothetically in agreement. There is an apparent tension between Buchanan's classical liberalism and his contractarianism.

In this dispute between the individual and the theorist, the individual might say, "You're wrong; I would not agree in a renegotiation from anarchy." Alternatively, the individual might say, "I'm not behind a veil of ignorance or renegotiating from anarchy, and in my current situation I don't agree." From a classical liberal perspective, would it matter which response the individual gave? In either case, the individual is being coerced by government into paying for a government program with which she disagrees. The classical liberal would have to conclude that the individual is being coerced—an outcome that the classical liberal Buchanan would find objectionable.

This argument is not passing judgment on the normative conclusions of social contractarians. Perhaps desirable constitutional rules are those rules with which people would agree from behind a veil of ignorance, or in a renegotiation from anarchy. However, if real-world people conclude that they are being coerced by their real-world governments, this is at odds with Buchanan's own vision of a classical liberal society in which people are free from the coercion of others. The argument that, hypothetically, people could agree to be coerced when in fact they have not agreed, and instead object to the coercion, is at odds with classical liberalism. The reality is that the individual is being coerced (Holcombe 2011).

CONCLUSION

The tensions between Buchanan's classical liberalism and his contractarianism grow deeper the further one digs into his contractarian framework. They offer different normative criteria for determining desirable social rules—the social contract. Consistent with the ideas of John Locke ([1690] 1960), F. A. Hayek (1944), Rothbard (1982), and other classical liberal or libertarian writers, Buchanan (2000, 117) says, "A motivating element [underlying classical liberalism] is, of course, the individual's desire for liberty from the coercive power of others—an element that may be almost universally shared." Buchanan's vision of a classical liberal society in which people are free from the coercive power of others is the norm shared by classical liberals. Meanwhile, the normative criterion for determining desirable social rules in Buchanan's contractarianism is consensus of agreement. Desirable social rules are those that command unanimous agreement.

The tension arises immediately because of the possibility that people would agree to rules that would create an illiberal society. Buchanan (2005b, 19) recognizes the possibility, saying that people might choose to live in a state that has coercive power over their lives "because ceding control over their actions to others allows individuals to escape, evade, and even deny personal responsibilities." However, Buchanan does not acknowledge that tension between his classical liberal views and his contractarian constitutional economics.

Acknowledging that people did not actually agree to a social contract, Buchanan (1975) describes a contractarian framework in which, hypothetically, people could agree to constitutional rules in an imagined renegotiation of the social contract from anarchy. This creates an additional tension because saying people could hypothetically agree under imagined circumstances is not the same thing as people actually agreeing. Coercion underlies all government activity, and this fiction that people agree to government coercion seems at odds with the classical liberal ideal of people being free from coercion. Buchanan's contractarian framework opens the possibility that government coercion can be justified with the argument that under hypothetical circumstances people could agree to be coerced. People who legitimately argue that they do not agree with government coercion could be met with Buchanan's contractarian argument that under hypothetical circumstances they might have agreed.

Buchanan's social contract theory is a procedural theory: it offers a procedure for agreeing to a social contract but does not identify the provisions of the social contract that would emerge from that procedure. Therefore, not only is there no assurance that the social contract produced by the imagined procedure will be consistent with classical liberalism, but there is also a more general ambiguity about the specific provisions that would constitute a social contract within Buchanan's framework. Joseph Schumpeter (1950, 198) observed, "The theory which construes taxes on the analogy of club dues or of the purchase of the services of, say, a doctor only proves how far removed this part of the social sciences is from scientific habits of mind."

My observations on the tensions between Buchanan's classical liberalism and his contractarianism are not meant as an attack on either. Buchanan's constitutional project is ongoing, even after his passing, with unresolved issues and research opportunities as in any area of academic inquiry. From a classical liberal perspective, one major issue is whether the constitutional rules with which people agree are also rules that preserve people's liberty.

NOTES

The paper has benefited from comments from an anonymous reviewer and from discussion at a workshop at the Mercatus Center at George Mason University in December 2016. Any remaining shortcomings are the responsibility of the author.

1. The utilitarian justification for classical liberalism (for example, Friedman [1962]) also is based on a normative foundation—although one that is widely supported—which is that it is desirable to use economic resources more efficiently. The utilitarian justification for free markets emphasizes economic efficiency over equity as a value, suggesting a possible tension that is outside the scope of this chapter on Buchanan's work.

2. As noted elsewhere, it is the requirement of unanimous agreement that makes this decision rule analogous to market exchange and that without the requirement a unanimous agreement (under majority rule, for example) might leave some people worse off (Holcombe 1986). This is because an individual's one vote will often not be decisive but will always determine whether the individual is in the minority or the majority, and it is often advantageous to vote with the majority. Thus, under less-inclusive decision rules, voters who see which way a vote is going might vote against the outcome that would best serve their own interests so that they can show solidarity with the majority rather than cast a losing vote that identifies them as members of the minority.

3. This quotation raises another question, peripheral to the arguments discussed in this section, which is that it would appear that individuals would have to contribute efforts to their own protection, at least in the form of payment of taxes. Buchanan makes it appear (in this quotation) that protection is free; in fact it has an opportunity cost, and individuals would weigh the cost of collective protection efforts against going it alone. For example, people install burglar alarms in their homes because, collectively, government protection is not sufficient to prevent all the burglaries that individuals would want to prevent.

REFERENCES

Brennan, Geoffrey, and James M. Buchanan. 1980. *The Power to Tax: Analytical Foundations of a Fiscal Constitution*. Cambridge, U.K.: Cambridge University Press.

———. 1985. *The Reason of Rules: Constitutional Political Economy*. Cambridge, U.K.: Cambridge University Press.

Buchanan, James M. 1949. "The Pure Theory of Government Finance: A Suggested Approach." *Journal of Political Economy* 57 (6): 496–505.

———. 1954. "Individual Choice in Voting and the Market." *Journal of Political Economy* 62 (4): 334–43.

———. 1962a. "Politics, Policy, and the Pigouvian Margins." *Economica* n.s. 29 (113): 17–28.

———. 1962b. "The Relevance of Pareto Optimality." *Journal of Conflict Resolution* 6 (4): 341–54.

———. 1970. "The 'Social' Efficiency of Education." *Il Politico* 35 (4): 653–62.

———. 1975. *The Limits of Liberty: Between Anarchy and Leviathan*. Chicago: University of Chicago Press.

———. 1990. "The Domain of Constitutional Economics." *Constitutional Political Economy* 1 (1): 1–18.

———. 2000. "The Soul of Classical Liberalism." *Independent Review* 5 (1): 111–19.

———. 2005a. *Why I, Too, Am Not a Conservative: The Normative Vision of Classical Liberalism*. Cheltenham, U.K.: Edward Elgar.

———. 2005b. "Afraid to Be Free: Dependency as Desideratum." *Public Choice* 124 (1/2): 19–31.

Buchanan, James M., and Roger D. Congleton. 1998. *Politics by Principle, Not Interest: Towards Nondiscriminatory Democracy*. Cambridge, U.K.: Cambridge University Press.

Buchanan, James M., and Nicos E. Devletoglou. 1970. *Academia in Anarchy: An Economic Diagnosis*. New York: Basic Books.

Buchanan, James M., and Gordon Tullock. 1962. *The Calculus of Consent: Logical Foundations of Constitutional Democracy*. Ann Arbor: University of Michigan Press.

Buchanan, James M., and Richard E. Wagner. 1977. *Democracy in Deficit: The Political Legacy of Lord Keynes*. New York: Academic Press.

Friedman, Milton. 1962. *Capitalism and Freedom*. Chicago: University of Chicago Press.

Hayek, F. A. 1944. *The Road to Serfdom*. Chicago: University of Chicago Press.

Hobbes, Thomas. (1651) 2012. *Leviathan*. Oxford, U.K.: Oxford University Press.

Hochman, Harold M., and James D. Rodgers. 1969. "Pareto Optimal Redistribution." *American Economic Review* 59 (September): 542–57.

Holcombe, Randall G. 1986. "Non-optimal Unanimous Agreement." *Public Choice* 48 (3): 229–44.

———. 2004. "Government: Unnecessary but Inevitable." *Independent Review* 8 (3): 325–42.

———. 2008. "Why Does Government Produce National Defense?" *Public Choice* 137 (1/2): 11–19.

———. 2011. "Consent or Coercion? A Critical Analysis of the Constitutional Contract." In *Constitutional Mythologies: New Perspectives on Controlling the State,* edited by Alain Marciano, 9–23. New York: Springer.

———. 2013. "Institutions and Constitutions: The Economic World of James M. Buchanan." Chap. 2 in *Public Choice: Past and Present,* edited by Dwight R. Lee. New York: Springer.

———. 2014. "Consenting to Collective Action: The Classical Liberal Constitutional Calculus of James M. Buchanan." *Independent Review* 18 (3): 359–72.

———. 2015. "Unanimous Consent and Constitutional Economics." In *The Elgar Handbook of Social Choice and Voting,* edited by Jac Heckelman and Nicholas Miller, 35–53. Cheltenham, U.K.: Edward Elgar.

Krueger, Anne O. 1974. "The Political Economy of the Rent-Seeking Society." *American Economic Review* 64 (3): 291–303.

Locke, John. (1690) 1960. *Two Treatises of Government*. Cambridge, U.K.: Cambridge University Press.

Nozick, Robert. 1974. *Anarchy, State, and Utopia*. New York: Basic Books.

North, Douglass C., John Joseph Wallace, and Barry R. Weingast. 2009. *Violence and Social Orders: A Conceptual Framework for Interpreting Recorded Human History*. Cambridge, U.K.: Cambridge University Press.

Rand, Ayn. 1961. "The Nature of Government." Chap. 14 in *The Virtue of Selfishness*. New York: Signet.

Rawls, John. 1971. *A Theory of Justice.* Cambridge, MA: Belknap Press.

Rothbard, Murray N. 1973. *For a New Liberty*. New York: Macmillan.

———. 1982. *The Ethics of Liberty*. Atlantic Highlands, NJ: Humanities Press.

Schumpeter, Joseph A. 1950. *Capitalism, Socialism and Democracy*, 3rd ed. New York: Harper & Row.

Tullock, Gordon. 1967. "The Welfare Costs of Tariffs, Monopolies, and Theft." *Western Economic Journal* 5 (3): 224–32.

———. 1975. "The Transitional Gains Trap." *Bell Journal of Economics* 6 (2): 671–78.

Yeager, Leland B. 1985. "Rights, Contract, and Utility in Policy Espousal." *Cato Journal* 5 (1): 259–94.

———. 2001. *Ethics as a Social Science.* Cheltenham, U.K.: Edward Elgar.

CHAPTER FIVE

UNREASONABLENESS AND HETEROGENEITY IN BUCHANAN'S CONSTITUTIONAL PROJECT

STEFANIE HAEFFELE AND VIRGIL HENRY STORR

James M. Buchanan's research program is expansive, including areas such as the economic analysis of political action (public choice), the analysis of the rules that form and constrain institutions (constitutional political economy), and the creation, legitimacy, and ethical considerations of social orders (contractual constitutionalism). While these topics are wide-ranging, they are all concerned with the ability of individuals to live peacefully together through contractual social orders. In other words, Buchanan is committed to exploring the capabilities and limitations of political arrangements that are likely to facilitate collective action in a free and liberal society.

Ultimately, Buchanan believes that a society of free individuals is possible and advances both positive and normative analysis that provide the foundation for the establishment and sustainability of a free and liberal society. Such a society, he argues, allows for individuals to grow and improve themselves, their prospects, and their society (Buchanan [1979] 1999, [1975] 2000). Furthermore, Buchanan (2006) argues for classical liberalism, which views individuals as equals in their capacity to make decisions, be accountable for their actions, and participate in self-governance.

Yet Buchanan also worries that such a society is not possible if individuals are too unreasonable and too different from one another to agree to constitutional rules (Buchanan and Tullock [1962] 1999; Buchanan [1975] 1999; Brennan and Buchanan [1985] 2000). In this scenario, Buchanan often argues that it is acceptable to curtail the range of political decisions that can and should be made via unanimous consent. Stated another way, for Buchanan, it appears to be acceptable to relax or abandon the strictures of his own contractual constitutional project whenever they become too inconvenient. As such, unreasonableness and heterogeneity become acceptable exceptions to his typical insistence on an inclusive and democratic constitutional order, characterized by voluntary collective action based on consensus.

These exceptions, however, are not without their issues. First, in suggesting that his analysis is applicable only to reasonable people within homogeneous societies, Buchanan limits his constitutional analysis to only the most straightforward cases (i.e., the cases that least require formal rules to ensure peaceful social interactions). Second, he offers no systematic treatment of what would constitute intolerable levels of unreasonableness and heterogeneity. Third, opening the door for political actors to legitimately disregard or exclude certain individuals on the basis of their unreasonableness creates an incentive to define as unreasonable and then exclude those individuals who make social choice complicated or costly. Finally, Buchanan's theoretical constitutional political economy would seem to be inapplicable to real-world societies that are populated with individuals from diverse backgrounds and with diverse capabilities and goals.

This tension in Buchanan's project, we argue, limits the applicability and tractability of his contractual framework. Either current societies are incapable of being truly liberal in a contractual sense or these exceptions are not as damaging as Buchanan may believe. In this chapter, we (a) explore this tension, (b) discuss the implications for defining or categorizing certain individuals as unreasonable and certain populations as too heterogeneous, and (c) hint at some alternative ways of constructing the political arrangements of a free and liberal society. Specifically, we argue that a radical inclusiveness is necessary for establishing a truly liberal society.

The chapter proceeds as follows. In the next two sections, we outline the ability of a free and liberal society to improve the prospects and capabilities of individuals and examine Buchanan's framework for creating and sustaining political arrangements for a free society. Then, we explore the exceptions of limiting unreasonableness and heterogeneity within Buchanan's research program and their implications for real-world social order. In the final section, we suggest three alternative approaches to social order that avoid excluding difficult or different members of society.

A FREE SOCIETY AS PRIMARILY A SPACE FOR GROWTH AND IMPROVEMENT

The freer the society, the more diverse the population that can peacefully live, work, and exchange together and the greater the space for growth and improvement. Buchanan endorsed this view for several reasons: a free and liberal society (a) facilitates exchange between diverse individuals, (b) makes individuals responsible for their actions, and (c) allows for self-improvement.

First, mutual gains from trade exist only because people are different—they have different preferences and backgrounds that translate into different goals and desires. These differences allow for exchange that makes both participants better off. By promoting mutually beneficial voluntary exchange between diverse individuals, free societies are also more prosperous than less free societies.[1] Indeed, to truly understand why free societies are more prosperous, it is important to understand and appreciate the differences that make society worthwhile. Buchanan ([1975] 2000, 15) states: "In a world of equals, most of the motivation for trade disappears. Exchange of rights takes place because persons are different, whether these differences are due to physical capacities, to some assignment of endowments, or to differences in tastes or preferences."

Second, a free and liberal society ensures that individuals are held accountable for their actions. Buchanan ([1991] 1999, 291) argues that

> The normative individualist whose ontology is subjectivist [rather than epistemic] operates on the presumption that, by their very being as individuals, members of humankind are and must be treated as responsible for their own choices. Individuals are not to be "protected from their own folly," even if this basic stance is tempered with ordinary compassion.

Likewise, "If individual man is to be free, he is to be held accountable, he is to be deemed responsible for his actions. . . . A determined and programmed existence is replaced by the uncertain and exciting quest that life must be" (Buchanan [1979] 1999, 257–58). A free and liberal society necessitates that people be responsible for their actions and consistently aim to pursue their interests while respecting others. By making individuals responsible for their actions, a free society ensures that they learn from their successes and, perhaps more important, their failures.

Third, individuals who take responsibility for their actions and recognize and appreciate the differences in the other members of their society are individuals who can aim to become better citizens. Individual freedom is a prerequisite. Buchanan argues that this desire improves not only individuals but also society. He states:

> If man can envisage himself as a product of his own making, as embodying prospects for changing himself into one of the imagined possibilities that he might be, it becomes relatively easy for him to envisage changing the basic rules of social order in the direction of imagined good societies. . . . Individually, man invests in becoming that which he is not. Collectively, men agree to modify the artifactual rules within which they interact one with another so as to allow individualized pursuit of whatever men may choose. (Buchanan [1979] 1999, 258)

Furthermore, he concludes that

> *Man wants liberty to become the man he wants to become.* He does so precisely because he does not know what man he will want to become in time. Let us remove once and for all the instrumental defense of liberty, the only one that can possibly be derived directly from orthodox economic analysis. Man does not want liberty in order to maximize his utility, or that of the society of which he is part. *He wants liberty to become the man he wants to become.* (Buchanan [1979] 1999, 259)

According to Buchanan, this act of striving and becoming better people is the ultimate desire for a free and liberal society.

THE POLITICAL ARRANGEMENTS NECESSARY FOR A FREE SOCIETY

Buchanan, in his expansive research program, is ultimately concerned with how people find ways to live peacefully together. People who wish to pursue their own interests have long realized that they can prosper by finding ways to cooperate with one another. In *The Limits of Liberty,* Buchanan ([1975] 2000, 3) states this sentiment concisely: "We live together," he explains, "because social organization provides the efficient means of achieving our individual objectives and not because society offers us a means of arriving at some transcendental common bliss." Human beings are, of course, social creatures. But it is not our sociability alone that makes society desirable and possible. Society is also desirable and possible because we are better off individually when we can discover ways to live and work together.

For social organization to work, however, it needs rules that proscribe the extent to which members of the society can harm one another. Additionally, it requires mechanisms not only for enforcing these rules but also for facilitating collective action. For this reason, when informal rules and norms are inadequate, people will seek to constrain behavior through constitutional rules. As

Buchanan ([1975] 2000, 28) notes, "a necessary starting position for a society of free individuals, related one to another in a network of interdependence, is some agreement on a structure of rights which, in effect, defines the entities who enter negotiations." Similarly, as Buchanan and Gordon Tullock ([1962] 1999, 301) note in *The Calculus of Consent*, "the acceptance of the right of the individual to do as he desires so long as his action does not infringe on the freedom of other individuals to do likewise must be a characteristic trait in any 'good' society." The equality of individuals in a society and their expectation that they will not be interfered with within certain domains are critical to the maintenance of a free society.

Indeed, the rules and structure of rights in society define the limits of social interaction. Geoffrey Brennan and Buchanan, in *The Reason of Rules*, make this point explicitly. As they explain, "We require rules for living together for the simple reason that without them we would surely fight. We would fight because the object of desire for one individual would be claimed by another. Rules define the private spaces within which each of us can carry on our own activities" ([1985] 2000, 5). This sphere of freedom could be relatively large as it is in, say, the West, where someone's religious activities tend to be viewed as private. Or, this sphere of freedom could be relatively restrictive as it is in states governed by sharia law, where religious observance is a public matter rather than just a private one. Regardless of the size of the sphere of freedom, the mere existence of rules that delineate between public and private (assuming they are enforced and viewed as legitimate) facilitates social organization.

Furthermore, the rules also set the expectations for social interaction. As Brennan and Buchanan ([1985] 2000, 10) write, "Rules provide to each actor predictability about the behavior of others. This predictability takes the form of information or informational boundaries about the actions of those involved in the interaction." Think, for example, of rules that define and enforce private property rights. These rules mean that the parties to an exchange can form reasonable expectations around the nature of their likely interactions. Where there are private property rights, members of a community cannot be legitimately alienated from their possessions without their prior agreement. Moreover, the parties involved in any exchange would have to more or less agree on the terms of trade before that trade could take place. Parties involved in an exchange can reasonably assume that they would retain possession of the goods they had prior to the trade unless they agreed to part with them. They would also expect to have to give up something of value in order to obtain something that does not belong to them. Thus, the rules around private property generate certain expectations that allow for and even encourage voluntary exchange.

While the presence of rules that delineate the public from the private sphere is critical to social organization, the content of those rules that are in place in any particular society shapes the interactions of individuals within that context. So, although social organization is possible within both Western-style democracies and states governed by sharia law, the nature of social and religious life in both systems is likely to differ substantially. As Brennan and Buchanan ([1985] 2000, 3–4) explain:

> In the limiting case, or in more general settings where at least some part of behavior is explicitly "social," the rules that coordinate the actions of individuals are important and are crucial to any understanding of the interdependence process. The same individuals, with the same motivations and capacities, will interact to generate quite different aggregate outcomes under differing sets of rules, with quite different implications for the well-being of every participant.

Therefore, *what* the rules are matters a great deal.

Buchanan also believes that *how* the rules come about matters. Although the informal rules of conduct might emerge spontaneously and evolve over time, the formal rules do not just appear but instead must be deliberated and agreed to by the members of a society. Moreover, the formal rules are legitimate only if this process of deliberation and agreement is inclusive and voluntary. As Brennan and Buchanan ([1985] 2000, 112) explain:

> A rule is legitimate, and violations of it constitute unjust behavior, when the rule is the object of voluntary consent among participants in the rule-governed order. Why is this so? Because the provision of consent on a voluntary basis amounts to offering a *promise* to abide by the rules. Just conduct is conduct in accord with promises given.

Leaving aside for the moment what exactly would constitute giving one's voluntary consent to a system of formal rules—whether consent can be assumed by one's continued presence within the rule regime's jurisdiction or must be explicitly voiced—voluntary consent is at the heart of any legitimate system of rules. Imposed rules and even inherited rules, in Buchanan's account, cannot and do not carry the same moral force as rules that come about through voluntarily agreement. If they are to be successful, the formal rules are also likely to be decided through rational deliberation. As Buchanan ([1975] 2000, xv) describes, "Precepts for living together are not going to be handed down from on high. Men must use their own intelligence in imposing order on chaos, intelligence not in scientific problem-solving but in the more difficult sense of finding and maintaining agreement among themselves." Ideally, this agreement will be reached through an inclusive deliberative process. As Buchanan ([1975] 2000, 4–5) insists:

> The approach must be *democratic,* which in this sense is merely a variant of the definitional norm for individualism. Each man counts for one, and that is that. Once this basic premise is fully acknowledged, an escape route from cynicism seems to be offered. A criterion for "betterness" is suggested. A situation is judged "good" to the extent that it allows individuals to get what they want to get, whatsoever this might be, limited only by the principle of mutual agreement. Individual freedom becomes the overriding objective for social policy, not as an instrumental element in attaining economic or cultural bliss, and not as some metaphysically superior value, but much more simply as a necessary consequence of an individualist-democratic methodology.

Because every individual has a say in the development of these rules and must consent to them, the rules agreed to through this process are likely to be rules that promote individual freedom.

In *The Calculus of Consent,* Buchanan and Tullock ([1962] 1999) describe the emergence and likely functioning of a social order that is based on constitutional rules arrived at through unanimous consent. For individuals to agree on a set of rules that constrain behavior in ways that will make all individuals better off regardless of their position in society, background, or ability, a certain level of uncertainty over the future is necessary. As Buchanan and Tullock ([1962] 1999, 78) state:

> Essential to the analysis is the presumption that the individual is *uncertain* as to what his own precise role will be in any one of the whole chain of later collective choices that will actually have to be made. For this reason he is considered not to have a particular and distinguishable interest separate and apart from his fellows. This is not to suggest that he will act contrary to his own interest; but the individual will not find it advantageous to vote for rules that may promote sectional, class, or group interests because, by presupposition, he is unable to predict the role that he will be playing in the actual collective decision-making process at any particular time in the future. He cannot predict with any degree of certainty whether he is more likely to be in a winning or a losing coalition on any specific issue. Therefore, he will assume that occasionally he will be in one group and occasionally in the other. His own self-interest will lead him to choose rules that will maximize the utility of an individual in a series of collec-

> tive decisions with his own preferences on the separate issues being more or less randomly distributed.

Similarly, Brennan and Buchanan ([1985] 2000, 35) point to uncertainty as increasing the potential for consensus by stating:

> The uncertainty introduced in any choice among rules or institutions serves the salutary function of making potential agreement more rather than less likely. Faced with genuine uncertainty about how his position will be affected by the operation of a particular rule, the individual is led by his self-interest calculus to concentrate on choice options that eliminate or minimize prospects for potentially disastrous results. . . . To the extent that a person faced with constitutional choice remains uncertain as to what his position will be under separate choice options, he will tend to agree on arrangements that might be called "fair" in the sense that patterns of outcomes generated under such arrangements will be broadly acceptable, regardless of where the participant might be located in such outcomes.

Under this arrangement, Buchanan argues, society can establish rules that improve social interaction and constrain harmful and exploitative behavior.

However, once political institutions are established through consensus-based constitutional rules, there is a new threat of oppression and exploitation through political action. Buchanan and Tullock ([1962] 1999, 301) state:

> It should be emphasized that no social organization in which men (some men or all men) are allowed freedom of choice can prevent the exploitation of man by man and group by group. Our construction is helpful in that it enables us to illustrate this point quite clearly. The relevant choice among alternative institutions reduces to that of selecting that set which effectively minimizes the costs (maximizes the benefits) of living in association.

This potential for government to do precisely what social rules attempt to constrain is what Buchanan calls the paradox of government. "Men want freedom from constraints," Buchanan ([1975] 2000, xv) writes, "while at the same time they recognize the necessity of order. This paradox of being governed becomes more intense as the politicized share in life increases, as the state takes on more power over personal affairs." This paradox becomes more palpable the more political institutions grow and expand outside of maintaining social order, delegating decisions to experts and bureaucracies.[2]

The solution to this issue, according to Buchanan, is to develop and adopt constitutional rules that constrain government action. Buchanan argues ([1975] 2000, 207–08):

> If our Leviathan is to be controlled, politicians and judges must come to have respect for limits. Their continued efforts to use assigned authority to impose naively formulated constructs of social order must produce a decline in their own standing. . . . Leviathan may maintain itself by force; the Hobbesian sovereign may be the only future. But alternative futures may be described and dreamed, and government may not yet be wholly out of hand. From current disillusionment can come constructive consensus on a new structure of checks and balances.

Despite this threat of government expansion, Buchanan argues that people can create beneficial and sustainable political institutions. Although a classical liberal vision of a free and liberal society may be utopian, Buchanan views it as not only desirable and worth striving for but also possible.

A FREE SOCIETY LIMITED TO REASONABLE INDIVIDUALS WITH HOMOGENEOUS BACKGROUNDS

A free and liberal society—based on a social contract that allows responsible individuals to interact in ways that allow them to live better together—may be harder to operationalize than may be expected given the discussion so far. Although Buchanan believed that a society of free and accountable individuals is possible, he worried about the issues that might arise when society includes individuals who are unreasonable and when the population is too diverse.[3] In this scenario, Buchanan argues that it is acceptable to curtail the range of political decisions that can and should be made via unanimous consent. As such, unreasonableness and heterogeneity become acceptable exceptions to his typical insistence on an inclusive constitutional order, characterized by voluntary collective action based on consensus.

The Unreasonableness of Individuals

Buchanan, in "Positive Economics, Welfare Economics, and Political Economy," acknowledges that his argument for a free society is based on the assumption of reasonable persons who are able to take responsibility for their actions and come together to discuss and agree on collective action. As Buchanan ([1959] 1999, 204) states:

> I have assumed that the social group is composed of reasonable men, capable of recognizing what they want, of acting on this recognition, and of being convinced of their own advantage after reasonable discussion. Governmental action, at the important margins of decision, is assumed to arise when such individuals agree that certain tasks should be collectively performed.

His constitutional project, it appears, assumes that it is possible to know which rules individuals ought to adopt and to assess the reasonableness of individuals on the basis of whether or not they are willing to go along with these rules assumed to be reasonable.

However, as Buchanan himself acknowledges, the real world is not populated only with reasonable people. In any deliberative process in the real world, there are likely to be holdouts. Unanimous agreement to even the most "reasonable" rules, in this scenario, will be difficult to attain. As Buchanan ([1959] 1999, 204) notes:

> I am aware of the limitations of this conception of society, and I can appreciate the force of the objection that may be raised on these grounds. Societies in the real world are not made up exclusively of reasonable men, and this fact introduces disturbing complications in any attempt to discuss the formation of social policy. . . . Insofar as "antisocial" or unreasonable individuals are members of the group, consensus, even where genuine "mutual gains" might be present, may be impossible. Here the absolute unanimity rule must be broken; the political economist must try, as best he can, to judge the extent of unanimity required to verify (not refute) his hypothesis.

In response to the recognition that unreasonable men exist in society, Buchanan suggests that unanimous consent is no longer a desirable feature of the political decision-making process, be it constitutional or post-constitutional decision-making.[4] In other words, unreasonable men can and should be excluded from participating in the political process.

This insistence on excluding certain dissenters because they are too unreasonable raises important questions for constitutional political economy: Who identifies which individuals are unreasonable? And who determines when an individual who is typically reasonable is being unreasonable? Interestingly, despite Buchanan's critique of the expert in other contexts, he suggests that it is up to the political economist to decide who is unreasonable or when someone is being unreasonable. Specifically, Buchanan ([1959] 1999, 205) argues:

> The necessary modification does not materially reduce the strength of the argument presented. But it does place an additional responsibility upon the political economist. *He is forced to discriminate between reasonable and unreasonable men in his search for consensus.* This choice need not reflect the introduction of personal evaluation. *Relatively objective standards may be adduced to aid in the discrimination process.* Reflection from everyday experience with groups which use unanimity as the customary, but not essential, means of reaching decisions should reveal that *the genuinely unreasonable individual can be readily identified.* This reduction of the unanimity requirement to some relative unanimity does not suggest that "unreasonable" as a characteristic behavior pattern can be determined on the basis of one issue alone. And it should be emphasized that in no way whatsoever does continuing disagreement with majority opinion suggest unreasonableness. (emphasis added)

Buchanan here assumes that the political economist can objectively distinguish between reasonable and unreasonable men; that the political economist can overcome the knowledge problems inherent in identifying the range of reasonable perspectives across a number of constitutional choices; that the political economist can overcome incentive problems in making this determination and so avoid being influenced by personal preferences; and that it is the political economist's opinion that will carry the day in the political process. Buchanan, of course, insists that describing someone as unreasonable is not to be done lightly. As he suggests, a disagreement with the dominant view on one or a range of issues is not sufficient grounds to classify someone as unreasonable. He does, however, also believe that identifying the unreasonable person is likely to be unproblematic.

This potential role for the political economist or policymaker (i.e., identifying and isolating the unreasonable person) directly contradicts Buchanan's stance that constitutional political economy must "involve the generalization of individualistic and rationality postulates to *all* persons in the political community" (Buchanan 1990, 15, emphasis in original). Further, he states:

> Who is to count as an autonomous individual? How are children to be treated, and at what age or stage of development does childhood cease and full membership in community granted? How are the mentally and emotionally incompetent to be handled, and who is to decide who is incompetent? Is the community

> considered to be open to potential entrants? These and related issues are relevant for inquiries in constitutional economics, but the program, by its nature, cannot address them readily. (Buchanan 1990, 15–16)

The Heterogeneity of the Community

Although differences among individuals are necessary for mutual gains from trade, these same differences may increase the cost and difficulty of achieving consensus for social rules. In *The Reason of Rules*, Brennan and Buchanan ([1985] 2000, 15) discuss this increased cost to political order, stating that it is possible to imagine a simple two-person game in which "the two players prefer different rules despite the fact that both prefer either rule to no rule." This disagreement over which rule to adopt will likely become more pronounced and more difficult to resolve the more players are added to the game and the greater the number of rules that are supported.

Indeed, the more the members of a group differ in terms of backgrounds, preferences, and values, the more likely there are to be disagreements of the rules. In *The Calculus of Consent*, Buchanan and Tullock ([1962] 1999, 115) state this explicitly:

> It seems reasonable to expect that more will be invested in bargaining in a group composed of members who have distinctly different external characteristics than in a group composed of roughly homogeneous members. Increased uncertainty about the tastes and the bargaining skills of his fellows will lead the individual to be more stubborn in his own efforts. When he knows his fellows better, the individual will surely be less stubborn in his bargaining, and for perfectly rational reasons. The overall costs of decision-making will be lower, given any collective-choice rule, in communities characterized by a reasonably homogeneous population than in those characterized by a heterogeneous population.

They go on to say:

> The community that includes sharp differences among individual citizens and groups cannot afford the decision-making costs involved in near-unanimity rules for collective choice, but the very real fears of destruction of life and property from collective action will prompt the individual to refuse anything other than such rules. . . . Regardless of the compromises on decision-making rules that may be adopted, the relative costs of collective organization of activity can be ex-

> pected to be much greater in a community lacking some basic consensus among its members on fundamental values. (Buchanan and Tullock [1962] 1999, 116)

When groups are diverse, collective decision-making will be costly. And, when groups are too diverse, unanimous consent can be too costly and movements away from unanimity may be required. Or, when groups are too diverse, the range of collective activity should be curtailed. Buchanan and Tullock ([1962] 1999, 116) explain:

> The implication of this is the obvious conclusion that the range of collective activity should be more sharply curtailed in such communities, assuming, of course, that the individualistic postulates are accepted. Many activities that may be quite rationally collectivized in Sweden, a country with a relatively homogeneous population, should be privately organized in India, Switzerland, or the United States.

Moreover, it is possible that the social cleavages are so entrenched and extreme that no social organization is possible. As Buchanan and Tullock ([1962] 1999, 81) explain:

> Our analysis of the constitution-making process has little relevance for a society that is characterized by a sharp cleavage of the population into distinguishable social classes or separate racial, religious, or ethnic groupings sufficient to encourage the formation of predictable political coalitions and in which one of these coalitions has a clearly advantageous position at the constitutional stage.

Although they note that sharp cleavages are detrimental to forming a consensus around political rules, Buchanan and Tullock also concede that this is a major problem only when people are so different that no real society can be said to exist. They suggest:

> This qualification should not be overemphasized, however. The requisite equality mentioned above can be secured in social groupings containing widely diverse groups and classes. So long as some mobility among groups is guaranteed, coalitions will tend to be impermanent. The individual calculus of constitutional choice presented here breaks down fully only in those groups where no real constitution is possible under democratic forms, that is to say, only for those groups which do not effectively form a "society." (Buchanan and Tullock [1962] 1999, 81)

When society does exist, deviating from unanimity or curtailing the range of collective activity should be sufficient to get agreement over the rules.

The Problems with Relaxing the Unanimity Assumption

Moving away from unanimity when group members are too unreasonable or too heterogeneous is not without its issues. First, in suggesting that his analysis is applicable only to reasonable people within homogeneous societies, Buchanan limits his constitutional analysis to only the most straightforward cases (i.e., the cases that least require formal rules to ensure peaceful social interactions). As such, Buchanan potentially reduces constitutional political economy to an analysis of how to develop formal, written constitutions when informal, unwritten constitutions are sufficient for fostering cooperation and collective action. In relatively homogeneous societies, social cooperation will have less to do with formal rules and more to do with the existence of informal rules and norms that regulate and restrict social interactions within tolerable bounds. In these environments, formal constitutions can negatively affect social cooperation—if, for example, they were to undermine these informal constraints. And, at best, they can play only a limited positive role, perhaps serving as a focal point in individual and collective decision-making.

Second, there is no systematic treatment of what would constitute intolerable levels of unreasonableness and heterogeneity. Indeed, Buchanan presents us with something of a tautology (i.e., someone is too unreasonable or society is too heterogeneous when unanimity at even the constitutional level is impossible). Buchanan, however, does not provide us with any real guidance as to when the costs are so high that we should formally relax our concern with consensus, when the costs are too high to expect consensus across a wide range of issues but we should still insist on consensus at the constitutional level, and when the costs of reaching agreement are high but we should redouble our efforts to find areas of agreement.

Third, opening the door for political actors to legitimately disregard or exclude certain individuals on the basis of their unreasonableness creates an incentive to define certain individuals as unreasonable because they may make social choice complicated or costly. There have been multiple instances in which members of certain groups (defined by race, ethnicity, religion, gender, etc.) were excluded from the constitutional decision-making process. This exception to universality that Buchanan adopts would seem to offer an easy way to legitimize efforts to exclude certain community members. It is unclear why we should expect constitutions to tend toward general, inclusive rules if there are defensible strategies to exclude certain individuals from the constitutional process.

Finally, Buchanan's theoretical constitutional political economy would seem to be inapplicable to real-world societies, which are populated with individuals from diverse backgrounds, capabilities, and goals. In fact, the trend seems to be toward countries becoming increasingly diverse. The need for constitutional frameworks that facilitate the peaceful coexistence of members of society is greater the more societies must confront and overcome demographic cleavages. Thus, Buchanan's project has the least to say in precisely the arena in which we would want it to speak the loudest. In other words, Buchanan's abstract theorizing does not seem to apply to concrete, real-world situations.

TWO STRATEGIES FOR SOCIETIES OF UNREASONABLE AND HETEROGENEOUS AGENTS

Buchanan is ultimately concerned with how to construct and sustain a free and liberal society. He, along with Tullock and Brennan, advances a social order based on deliberation and consensus of all members, not just the elite or powerful. However, they also make qualifications on such contractual societies, including the issues of unreasonable participants and heterogeneous populations.

Instead of advancing a social order that maintains a free and liberal society, we argue that these qualifications open the door for discrimination. To the extent that Buchanan and other political economists have refused to tackle the hard cases (how to get social cooperation when some members of society are disagreeable and difficult to deal with), they have advanced a notion of a free and liberal society that is weak and fragile. In other words, they have advanced the idea that a free society is suitable only for a population of angels (when, in reality, people are prone to err and create conflict). Such a society would be easy to govern (with or without formal constitutions), and would neglect the complexities of reality.

In contrast, real-world communities are populated by unreasonable and heterogeneous agents. Still, we must find alternative solutions to these challenges in order to advance a free and liberal society. Three alternatives may reconcile this tension. First, we might consider simultaneously insisting on unanimity and a radically inclusive constitutional decision-making process (see, for example, Gaus 2011). This would have the effect of privatizing a wide range of collective activities that we might assume need to happen via a public process. This might also mean that the constitutional rules that are ultimately agreed to will tend to be abstract and general.

Second, we might consider advocating increasingly polycentric systems (see, for example, Ostrom, Tiebout, and Warren 1961; Ostrom [1972] 1999, [1991] 2014). Buchanan and Tullock would seem to be in favor of decentralized political orders as a solution to the challenges created by unreasonableness and heterogeneity. As they write, "If the organization of collective activity can be effectively decentralized, this decentralization provides one means of introducing market-like alternatives into the political process" (Buchanan and Tullock [1962] 1999, 114–15).

Finally, a constitutional design of political turn-taking may reduce the potential of certain groups to form lasting political coalitions and enable all members of society to actively participate in governance (Durant 2011; Durant and Weintraub 2014a, 2014b). Under a turn-taking institution, the only way to obtain or maintain lasting political power is to form a coalition that is sufficiently inclusive to win a super majority. "The gist of the proposed turn-taking institution," Durant (2011, 143) describes, "is to allot the whole term only to a candidate who builds a sufficiently inclusive supermajority consensus; otherwise, major candidates take turns in office." Unlike in majority-rule, winner-take-all systems, under the turn-taking institution small groups of political elites will be unable to hold political power for long periods. As such, under a turn-taking institution, an inclusive and diverse society may be more likely to emerge and will be more sustainable as ethnic political conflicts become less necessary and so less likely.

Ultimately, these institutional proposals limit the scope or scale of political orders. Perhaps constitutional rules that allow for a radical inclusiveness and constrain coalition building can be devised and agreed on. Or perhaps the most suitable constitutional organizations are polycentric political orders. Either way, a truly free and liberal society depends on an ability to constrain conflict and induce cooperation across *all* populations of society.

NOTES

1. Buchanan follows in the comparative institutional tradition of Adam Smith (see Buchanan 1990).

2. Buchanan ([1975] 2000, 126) saw the post-1960 U.S. government as an exemplar of government overreach and examines what reforms and constraints are possible to restrict government and foster better social interaction.

3. It should be noted that Buchanan isn't alone in worrying about whether unreasonable individuals can or should participate in a free society. For example, John Stuart Mill ([1851] 1989, 13) identified children and barbarians as exceptions to a free society, noting, "Those who are still in a state to require being taken care of by others, must be protected against their own actions as well as against external injury" and "Despotism is a legitimate mode of government in dealing with barbarians, provided the end be their improvement, and the means justified by actually effecting that end." Likewise, F. A. Hayek ([1960] 1978, 77) presumed that some individuals were unable to be held accountable for their actions: "The complementary of liberty and responsibility means that the argument for liberty can apply only to those who can be held responsible. It cannot apply to infants, idiots, or the insane."

4. It should be noted that, in *The Calculus of Consent*, Buchanan and Tullock ([1962] 1999, 296) also note that the real world is not full of completely reasonable people, stating:

> We know, of course, that in the economic as well as the political relationship, individuals are not entirely rational, they are not well informed, and they do not follow self-interest in all circumstances. Yet we can observe that people purchase more goods at lower prices, that wage rates for similar occupations tend to equality, that the return on investment will tend to be equalized in different employments, and many other propositions of "positive" economics that can be subjected to empirical testing.

Although on first read this passage may seem more amenable to accepting the role of unreasonable people in society, the notion that we can generally see patterns of activity as if all people acted reasonably may allow for social rules to be determined as if they were based on unanimous consent.

> Buchanan and Tullock, however, do warn against disregarding unanimity too quickly. They say: The analysis has shown that the rule of unanimity does possess certain special attributes, since it is only through the adoption of this rule that the individual can insure himself against the external damage that may be caused by the actions of other individuals, privately or collectively. However, in our preliminary analysis, once the rule of unanimity is departed from, there seems to be nothing to distinguish sharply any one rule from any other. (Buchanan and Tullock [1962] 1999, 81)

REFERENCES

Brennan, Geoffrey, and James M. Buchanan. (1985) 2000. *The Reason of Rules: Constitutional Political Economy.* Vol. 10 of *The Collected Works of James M. Buchanan.* Indianapolis, IN: Liberty Fund.

Buchanan, James M. 1990. "The Domain of Constitutional Economics." *Constitutional Political Economy* 1 (1): 1–18.

———. (1959) 1999. "Positive Economics, Welfare Economics, and Political Economy." In *The Logical Foundations of Constitutional Liberty.* Vol. 1 of *The Collected Works of James M. Buchanan,* 191–209. Indianapolis, IN: Liberty Fund.

———. (1979) 1999. "Natural and Artifactual Man." In *The Logical Foundations of Constitutional Liberty.* Vol. 1 of *The Collected Works of James M. Buchanan,* 246–59. Indianapolis, IN: Liberty Fund.

———. (1991) 1999. "The Foundations for Normative Individualism." In *The Logical Foundations of Constitutional Liberty.* Vol. 1 of *The Collected Works of James M. Buchanan,* 281–91. Indianapolis, IN: Liberty Fund.

———. (1975) 2000. *The Limits of Liberty: Between Anarchy and Leviathan.* Vol. 7 of *The Collected Works of James M. Buchanan.* Indianapolis, IN: Liberty Fund.

———. 2006. *Why I, Too, Am Not a Conservative: The Normative Vision of Classical Liberalism.* Northampton, MA: Edward Elgar Publishing.

Buchanan, James M., and Gordon Tullock. (1962) 1999. *The Calculus of Consent: Logical Foundations of Constitutional Democracy.* Vol. 3 of *The Collected Works of James M. Buchanan.* Indianapolis, IN: Liberty Fund.

Durant, T. Clark. 2011. "Making Executive Politics Mutually Productive and Fair." *Constitutional Political Economy* 22 (2): 141–72.

Durant, T. Clark, and Michael Weintraub. 2014a. "An Institutional Remedy for Ethnic Patronage Politics." *Journal of Theoretical Politics* 26 (1): 59–78.

———. 2014b. "How to Make Democracy Self-Enforcing after Civil War: Enabling Credible Yet Adaptable Elite Pacts." *Conflict Management and Peace Science* 31 (5): 521–40.

Gaus, Gerald. 2011. *The Order of Public Reason: A Theory of Freedom and Morality in a Diverse and Bounded World.* Cambridge, U.K.: Cambridge University Press.

Hayek, F. A. (1960) 1978. *The Constitution of Liberty.* Chicago: University of Chicago Press.

Mill, John Stuart. (1851) 1989. *On Liberty and Other Writings.* New York: Cambridge University Press.

Ostrom, Vincent. (1972) 1999. "Polycentricity (Part 1)." In *Polycentricity and Local Public Economies: Readings from the Workshop in Political Theory and Policy Analysis*, edited by M. D. McGinnis, 52–74. Ann Arbor: University of Michigan Press.

———. (1991) 2014. "Polycentricity: The Structural Basis of Self-Governing Systems." In *Choice, Rules and Collective Action*, edited by P. Aligica and F. Sabetti, 45–60. Colchester, U.K.: ECPR Press.

Ostrom, Vincent, Charles M. Tiebout, and Robert Warren. 1961. "The Organization of Government in Metropolitan Areas: A Theoretical Inquiry." *American Political Science Review* 55 (4): 831–42.

CHAPTER SIX

IT CAN'T BE RATIONAL CHOICE ALL THE WAY DOWN

COMPREHENSIVE HOBBESIANISM AND THE ORIGINS OF THE MORAL ORDER

GERALD GAUS

OVERCOMING THE FATAL LACUNA IN "HOBBESIAN" POLITICAL THEORY

James M. Buchanan grounded his constitutional political economy project on what is commonly understood as Hobbesian contractarianism.[1] In this familiar view, the Hobbesian models individual agents as essentially self-interested, strategic, maximizers; the aim is to analyze the political order that emerges from the choices and actions of these Hobbesian agents. Because the aim is to demonstrate how certain legal and political orders can arise out of the interactions of self-interested agents, the assumed baseline condition is a normless interaction in a "state of nature." The model then shows that these agents would be caught in mixed motive games such as prisoner's dilemmas, in which noncooperation is the dominant strategy, or at best stag hunt/assurance games, with a strong tendency for players to play the risk-dominant equilibrium.[2] In either case, an agreement to end the war and accept a regime of rights benefits each agent, so a large set of possible "social contracts" is on the Paretian frontier. Buchanan ([1975] 2000, 2001a), of course, argues that agents will accept not the orthodox "Hobbesian" contract instituting a Leviathan with unlimited authority but, rather, a constitutional regime. Specifying the rules—especially the basic procedural rules—of that regime is critical to the constitutional political economy project.

This familiar Hobbesian project is of special interest to economists who turn their attention to political philosophy because it is common to equate Hobbesian self-interested agents with the basic model agents of rational choice theory (see Kliemt 2009, 46ff.; for a criticism, see Gaus 2008, 19ff.). Insofar as economists are interested in the application of rational choice models, "Hobbesian contractarianism" is thus tempting, as it certainly was for Buchanan's political economy project. It would be a satisfying and elegant analysis of a sophisticated rule-based political order that it can emerge from the choices of rational, self-interested individuals. And, insofar as one is, like Buchanan (see Buchanan and Tullock [1962] 1999, 307–22), committed to a normative individualism that accords foundational value to respect for individual choices, understanding what political institutions would emerge from these choices helps us gain insight into long-standing normative questions in political theory (Thrasher and Gaus, forthcoming).

Straightforward, basic, Hobbesian contractarianism, though, is undermined by what we might call its "fatal lacuna." It supposes simply two relevant social states: Hobbesian agents acting (a) in a (literally) "unruly" condition (b) in a rule-based political order, where (a) helps us see why we end up in a particular type of (b). This, however, supposes that no "ruly" social and moral order exists before the state. But it does: outside of, and in an important sense prior to, political and legal order are moral orders, including the general moral order of large-scale civil society. Overlooking the informal moral order underlying the legal-constitutional order, T. H. Green ([1889] 1986, 89) insisted, leads to the false conclusion that the state, not the preexisting moral order, is the fountainhead of individual rights. Moral orders are not simply the reflection or creation of the political, but are independent sources of moral rights and claims. Now, if individuals possess moral rights independently of the state, then the set of Paretian political institutions ("social contracts") cannot be defined by the unruly baseline of the state of nature but must refer to the more ruly baseline of the informal moral order. Moreover, the informal moral order does not simply constrain political and legal options; it creates them. As Montesquieu ([1748] 1949, 292–315) stressed, the effectiveness of any constitution depends on the habits, manners, and morals of the population. Some societies' informal morals, Montesquieu held, simply do not support free constitutions; others do. The fatal lacuna of the straightforward Hobbesian social contract is that it is blind to this critical role of the underlying moral order, depicting effective social order as simply the artifact of a politico-legal regime.

The next section of this chapter defends the core of the fatal lacuna thesis—Montesquieu's claim that an effective constitutional order depends on an informal social and moral order. Given this, a plausible Hobbesian political theory cannot jump from the unruly condition to a lawful ruly one: the success of the latter depends on informal moral rules, and on getting them right. However, in the following section we see that, despite what may be the popular reading, Buchanan's Hobbesian analysis does not manifest the fatal lacuna: he proposes what we might call "Comprehensive Hobbesianism." The legal, political, *and* moral orders all can be justified by Hobbesian analyses: as we go deeper and deeper into the basis of order, we encounter deeper and deeper Hobbesian arguments. It is, as it were, Hobbesian rational choice all the way down. The following section sketches Buchanan's Hobbesian model of the origins of the moral order. I argue that it pretty clearly fails as a rational reconstruction of the origin of the large-scale moral order needed to support a large-scale political and economic order, though it is an insightful model of stabilization of a preexisting informal order. As is so often the case with innovative thinkers, even they do not achieve their ultimate goals (in this case, reconstructing norm origins); they enlighten us about the overall phenomenon (norm stabilization). Again taking a cue from Buchanan, I generalize this problem to Comprehensive Hobbesian analyses of moral order in general. A serious tension in his political economy project is revealed: Buchanan's analysis justifies large-scale politico-legal orders but is unable to show how these large-scale moral orders can come about. I conclude by evaluating the upshot of my analysis for the overall project of constitutional political economy.

THE IMPORTANCE OF THE MORAL ORDER

Moral Norms

Normative guidance—motivation to comply with social rules despite the fact that cheating would be to our material advantage—goes far back in human evolutionary history and is probably one of the defining features of our species (Kitcher 2011; Boehm 2012; Gaus 2015). This is captured by Cristina Bicchieri's (2006, 52–55; 2016, chap. 1) formalization of a social norm, in which it is characterized as an individualized sensitivity to a shared social rule (one that is actually followed in one's group or culture) that leads one to forgo material gains.[3] Critical to her analysis is that norm followers are moved both by their empirical expectations as to what others will actually do (Will others follow the rule?) and their beliefs about what others in their network normatively expect of them (Will others hold me responsible for failing to conform?). She has measured these expectations in an impressive series of experiments and shown that they are good predictors of behavior in ultimatum and dictator games (see, for example, Bicchieri and Chavez 2010; Bicchieri and Xiao 2009).[4] She has subsequently shown that her model allows measurement of norms in field settings in both small- and large-scale societies (Bicchieri 2016).

It should be stressed that, by Bicchieri's account, compliance with social norms cannot be reduced to either (a) personal approval of the behavior required by the norm or (b) a person's desire to escape punishment. As regards (a), she has provided compelling evidence that attitude change often fails to translate into action change—partly because individuals are moved not simply by their own attitudes but, critically, by their beliefs about what others with whom they interact normatively expect from them. Bicchieri (2016, chap. 1) draws our attention to a United Nations Children's Fund study on violence toward children, which reported both high rates of caregiver disapproval of punishment and of caregiver punishment. Similar findings have been reported concerning prison guards (Bicchieri 2016, 180). And, as she reports, in some African countries there appears to be a similar pattern concerning female genital cutting—high disapproval rates combined with high participation rates (Bicchieri 2016, chap. 1). Concerning (b), informal social rules are of course typically enforced by punishment (Gaus 2011, 103–22); however, we also know that, when punishment fails to correspond to what people believe are legitimate normative expectations, punishment easily turns into "antisocial" counterpunishment. As Samuel Bowles and Herbert Gintis (2011, 26) stress, effective punishment depends on beliefs about its legitimacy: unless those to be punished and their friends and allies are convinced that the rule being enforced is legitimate, a punishing action taken as a means to protect social cooperation can lead to weakening it. Experimental evidence confirms that attempts to punish readily evoke counterpunishment when the offender does not experience guilt, which is associated with moral norm violation (see, for example, Hopfensitz and Reuben 2009). Thus the internalization of moral norms is critical: in most cases the acceptance of a moral norm motivates individual compliance (see Gaus 2011, chapter 4; for cognitive modeling of norm internalization processes, see Andrighetto, Villatoro, and Conte 2010).

Most economists recognize that the spontaneous order of the market presupposes legal institutions (Buchanan 2001a, 27). Far fewer follow F. A. Hayek (1988, 6):

> To understand our civilisation one must appreciate that the extended order resulted not from human design or intention but spontaneously: it arose from the unintentional conforming to certain traditional and largely *moral* practices, many

> of which men tend to dislike, whose significance they usually fail to understand, whose validity they cannot prove, and which have nonetheless fairly rapidly spread by means of an evolutionary selection. . . .

However, the last twenty years have seen a growing consensus that market orders rest on the evolved informal moral order, and in particular on moral norms and rules (Schwab and Ostrom 2008; Friedman 2008; Richerson and Boyd 2005; Rose 2011; Platteau 2000, 325ff.; Gaus 2015).

Law and Moral Norms

There is, I think, a tendency to suppose that, although informal social rules are important to small-scale societies, in large-scale societies they are supplanted by formal legal institutions. And this common view captures an important truth: in large-scale economic orders, formal law sometimes competes with, and supplants, smaller informal networks with overlapping competencies, say, about contractual performance. In Taiwan, for example, numerous small norm networks provide the basis for contractual enforcement in small- and medium-sized firms, thwarting the development of western formal legal contractual relationships (Platteau 2000, 285–87). As formal legal institutions expand their effective jurisdictions, they tend to supplant these informal competing networks. This should not be denied.

Nevertheless, this common view misses the fundamental role of moral norms in upholding legal systems and rendering them effective (Platteau 2000, 290ff.). We can distinguish two ways in which the informal morality is critical to the effectiveness of law: (a) at the level of a specific law, L, its effectiveness often depends on its relation to a specific informal moral norm, N; and (b) at the general level of legality as such, whether there is a norm upholding obedience to law (Tyler 1990).

Regarding (a), as William J. Stuntz (2000, 1871) points out:

> The mass of the population avoids seriously bad behavior not because they know it can be found in the codes, but because they know the behavior is thought to be seriously bad (and only secondarily because seriously bad behavior can often get you thrown in jail). For the most part, criminal law regulates actors in the legal system, while popular norms—morals—regulate the conduct of the citizenry.

Platteau (2000, 290) concludes, "Clearly, the fact that laws provide external validation of underlying social norms appears to be an important factor of effective implementation of the former." Although, as Montesquieu ([1748] 1949, 304–05) stressed, there are mutual influences between moral norms and legal regulation, it is generally more accurate to see the informal norms shaping the law than vice versa (Robinson 2000). Laws that run counter to the moral norms of the populace are apt to be not only ineffective but also, according to Stuntz (2000), self-defeating: laws against normatively approved behavior often strengthen, not weaken, the norm in the population. Thus, laws that depart from the basic moral norms of a society most likely will be ignored, often engendering contempt for the law. Gerry Mackie (forthcoming) has recently noted that, in hundreds of critical cases around the world, widely criminalized practices—among them female genital cutting, caste discrimination, and child marriage—continue to be practiced because they are supported by local informal norms. Mackie, following Iris Marion Young (2011), concludes:

> Criminalization is an appropriate response to a criminal injustice, a deviation from accepted norms, its harmful consequences intended, knowingly committed by identifiable individuals, whose wrongdoing should be punished. It is not an appropriate response to a structural injustice, in compliance with accepted norms, its harmful consequences unintended byproducts, and caused by everyone and no one. The proper remedy for a harmful social norm is organized social change, not fault, blame, punishment. (Mackie, forthcoming)

"[W]hen manners and customs are to be changed," Montesquieu ([1748] 1949, 289) observed, "it ought not to be done by laws; this would have too much the air of tyranny: it would be better to change them by introducing other manners and other customs."

Regarding (b), Tom Tyler's (1990, 59) panel study of compliance in Chicago showed that a people's moral convictions about fairness and justice are important determinants of whether they will comply with laws that conform or conflict with those convictions. But Tyler also found that whether citizens accepted the legitimacy of politico-legal procedures has a strong impact on whether people comply with the law. In this vein Mackie (forthcoming) argues that the data indicate that an effective legal system requires a generalized norm supporting legal obedience. Recent political philosophy has tended to be dismissive of a general obedience to the law, or a general recognition of its moral authority; however, without some such support in the informal moral order, legal regulation is apt to be ineffective (Gaus 2011, 449ff.).

The Fatal Lacuna

We are now in a position to appreciate the fatal lacuna in the standard Hobbesian social contract. The typical analysis begins with essentially self-interested individuals (call them "egoists") in a normless environment and then asks to what formal institutions they would agree in order to improve their deeply suboptimal relations. In its most plausible versions, the answer to this question should, first, help us evaluate our current institutions to see if they satisfy the test of mutual benefit and, second, point the way to reforming them. However, if the individuals already endorse and live by an informal moral order (call them norm-followers), then (a) their problems will not be the same problems as those of egoists, (b) the solutions viable for egoists and norm-followers will be different, and (c) norm-followers will evaluate proposals differently because the proposals must correspond to their already-endorsed moral norms. This is not to say the norm-followers will be entirely uninterested in the Hobbesian conclusions; in some cases, they may approve of institutions of mutual benefit and use the Hobbesian analysis as a guide to reforms. But often norm-followers will dismiss the problems of egoists and, importantly, will conclude the institutions fit for egoists would ill suit them. Most obviously, egoists will stress an instrumentalist approach to compliance, seeking to show how legal punishment regimes can channel self-interested individuals into compliance, and so may erect extensive enforcement procedures that would be counterproductive for norm-followers. At the same time, the Hobbesian theorist—not taking the prior moral norms as constraints on solutions (and on the viability of legal regulations)—is apt to be overly optimistic about the range of institutional schemes that could produce effective social cooperation. The Hobbesian thus will overlook both resources (regarding compliance) and constraints (about the fit with preexisting norms), rendering any proposals of limited value.

BUCHANAN'S RECOGNITION OF THE MORAL ORDER

Most readers of Buchanan's better-known works, I would venture, would see the previous analysis as applying to his Hobbesian project. "The Hobbesian jungle," he wrote in 1977,

> is something to be avoided and something that people with rational self-interest will seek to avoid through general agreement on law along with the requisite enforcement institutions. . . . The contractarian seeks "*ordered anarchy*"; that is, a situation described as one which offers maximal freedom for individuals within a minimal set of *formalized rules* and constraints on behavior. (Buchanan 2001a, 26; emphasis added)

And indeed, he sometimes identifies "rules" with "law," suggesting that all order is formal order (Buchanan 2001a, 23).

That, however, is not his considered view. "Life in society, as we know it, would probably be intolerable if formal rules should be required for each and every area where interpersonal conflict might arise" (Buchanan [1975] 2000, 118). "A society," he tells us, "is held together by some combination of moral community and moral order. Its cohesion is reduced by the extent to which moral anarchy exists among its members" (Buchanan 2001b, 188). A moral community, then, "exists among a set of persons to the extent that individual members of the group identify with the collective unit." In contrast:

> A moral order exists when participants in social institutions treat each other as moral reciprocals, but do so without any sense of shared loyalties to a group or community. Each person treats other persons with moral indifference, but at the same time respects their equal freedoms with his own. Mutual respect, which is an alternative way of stating the relationship here, does not require moral community in any sense of personal identification with a collective or community. . . . In a moral order, it is possible for a person to deal with other persons who are not members of his community if both persons have agreed, explicitly or implicitly, to abide by the behavior precepts required for reciprocal trust and confidence.
>
> The emergence of the abstract rules of behavior describing moral order had the effect of expanding dramatically the range of possible interpersonal dealings. Once rules embodying reciprocal trust came to be established, it was no longer necessary that both parties to a contract identify themselves with the same moral community of shared values and loyalties. (Buchanan 2001b, 189)

True moral anarchy is thus the absence of moral community *and* of moral order. Individuals treat each other simply strategically: "Each person treats other persons exclusively as a means to further his own ends and advantage" (Buchanan 2001b, 190). With these richer concepts in play, Buchanan now is able to offer a moralized understanding of the idea of "ordered anarchy" as "universal adherence to the rules of mutual respect among persons"—that is, moral order (Buchanan 2001b, 191).

Buchanan manifestly views the moral order as necessary to a functioning and free politico-legal order. He says: "For several decades, however, our moral order has been in the process of erosion. Larger and larger numbers of persons seem to have become moral anarchists; they seem to be losing mutual respect for one another along with any feeling of obligation to abide by generalizable codes of conduct" (Buchanan 2001b, 197). His "moral order" (an idea equivalent to Hayek's "Great Society") (Buchanan 2001b, 188) is a far-flung moral network extending far beyond particularistic, moral communities:

Indeed, I should argue that it is through the development of the rules of such a "moral order" that humans have successfully confronted the challenge of civilization. The moral order that allows humankind to supersede the effective limits of its expressly revealed moral community is best described as the order of *law*, in which persons abide by abstract rules of law that lay down rights of separate persons and that provide bases for mutual respect, tolerance and, most importantly, for trade and exchange that, in turn, greatly enhances the level of personal well-being for all participants. (Buchanan 2001b, 208)

BUCHANAN'S PREACHING MODEL OF THE ORIGINS OF NORMS

Internalizing Ethical Externalities

One might be tempted to suppose that, given his recognition of the fundamental role of the moral order in supporting an extensive politico-legal order, Buchanan might not, after all, view economic rationality (qua effective promotion of self-interest) as foundational to modeling social life in general, but only to justifying the political and economic orders. Although perhaps the analysis of constitutional rules is grounded on self-interested maximizers, not so the very foundation—the moral order. This, however, would be an error. Buchanan endorses the foundational role of the moral order; he nevertheless seeks to give an economic analysis of the origins of the moral order itself. For Buchanan it is Hobbesian rational choice analyses all the way down.[5]

As with many analyses of social norms and moral rules (Bicchieri 2006, 26–27; Gaus 2011, 53ff.), Buchanan begins with the (all-too) familiar prisoner's dilemma, shown in figure 1.

FIGURE 1: ECONOMICALLY (AND ETHICALLY) RELEVANT EXTERNALITIES (ORDINAL UTILITY, 4 = BEST)

		Betty: C_b	Betty: D_b
Alf	C_a	3, 3	1, 4
	D_a	4, 1	2*, 2*

FIGURE 2: (POTENTIALLY) ETHICALLY RELEVANT EXTERNALITIES

		Betty	
		X_b	Y_b
Alf	X_a	4, 2	3*, 3*
	Y_a	3, 1	2, 4

Of course, as Buchanan points out—and which, in the view of many, Thomas Hobbes did in the 16th century—although $\{D_A, D_B\}$ is the sole equilibrium, Alf and Betty could benefit from a contract that would enforce $\{C_A, C_B\}$. Buchanan observes that a choice of D by either Alf or Betty imposes externalities on the other. "The existence of *externality* is necessary for the initiation of any effort aimed at constraining behavior" (Buchanan 2001b, 216). In this case the economist can point out that a $\{C_A, C_B\}$ contract, despite the constraints it entails, is a Pareto improvement over the $\{D_A, D_B\}$ noncooperative equilibrium, so this is an externality that is economically relevant and with which economics readily deals. Now consider figure 2.[6]

The sole Nash equilibrium in this game is $\{X_A, Y_B\}$. Once the equilibrium has been achieved, no Pareto improvements are possible. Still, when Alf plays X_A he imposes an externality on Betty: if he had played Y_A Betty would have been better off.[7] A shift on the part of Alf from X_A to Y_A will have significant "spillover benefits on B[etty]" (Buchanan 2001b, 219). This externality, Buchanan argues, is economically irrelevant (because there are no mutual gains to be had) but is potentially ethically relevant. Betty may hold that Alf is defecting from the best rule of "everyone plays Y," and the costs he imposes on her by defecting to X are ethically important. There may be an ethical case for, say, $\{Y_A, Y_B\}$, which eliminates the externalities that Betty imposes on Alf. Thus, while for economics the externalities modeled in figures 1 and 2 are categorically different, this is not so for ethics.

Suppose, then, that Betty seeks to eliminate the externality Alf imposes on her in figure 2: she seeks to get him also to play Y. Of course, given the payoffs in figure 2, this would be irrational for Alf: Y_A is not his best response to her Y_B. As with many accounts of norms, Betty must induce a change in Alf's payoffs so that he is playing a different game, as in figure 3.

In this transformation, Betty induces a preference change in Alf that eliminates the externality he imposed on her; in game 2 he comes to see playing Y when

FIGURE 3: BETTY MORALIZES ALF, AND EACH (SORT OF) GAINS IN THE PROCESS

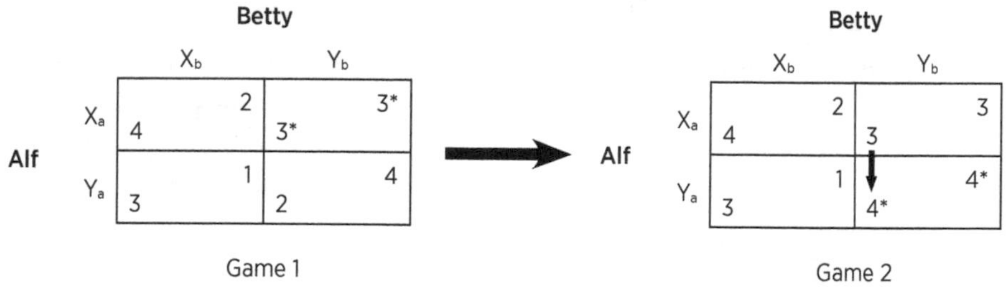

she plays Y as the best thing to do. As Buchanan notes, we cannot say that the move from game 1 to game 2 is Paretian: because the preferences are different, they are strictly noncomparable games. Yet it is also true that in game 2 both parties have an equilibrium outcome $\{Y_A, Y_B\}$ that each prefers to the $\{X_A, Y_B\}$ outcome that was in equilibrium in game 1. So, at least after the fact, both parties may judge themselves to be in a preferred state (Buchanan 2001b, 225).

In Buchanan's model, then, Betty has an incentive to invest in changing Alf's preferences; we can think of this as her efforts to induce Alf to internalize the "act on Y" rule. She has an incentive to preach to Alf that Y is the thing to do.

> To be productive, investments in the promulgation of moral norms must change the behavior through a shift in the utility function. . . . The analysis here does not require that persons seek to change *their own* preferences. While it may be empirically descriptive to say, with Frank Knight, that persons really "want better wants," we do not need to take this additional step here. We need no such bootstrap ethics. My model suggests, much more restrictively, that persons rationally will "want others to have better wants," or, specifically, that others will behave more cooperatively toward them in social discourse. (Buchanan 2001b, 223)

More of a Convention than a Norm

Note that, in this analysis, for Alf to internalize the "Y norm" does not imply that he accepts that he ought to play Y even though he would benefit by defecting, or that he is committed to following the Y norm despite his self-interested X-inclining preferences. "Individuals behave in accordance with norms of cooperation in social interaction because of the dictates of their preference orderings. They 'do not want to steal,' even when opportunities exist" (Buchanan 2001b, 230). Such a view of internalization reflects the thought expressed by Lincoln: "When I do good, I feel good. When I do bad, I feel bad" (Bowles and Gintis 2011, 169). Although this certainly picks up on a feature of moralization, if that is the entire story we have something closer to a convention than a moral norm.[8] Given the preference change in game 2, coordination on Y is secured through entirely "self-serving" action; each has no other concern than securing his or her best outcome, given the choices of the other. Once empirical expectations about the Y rule are secured, the underlying incentive to comply is the same as a convention: the "Y rule" would be entirely self-enforcing (without threats of punishment) because neither Alf nor Betty would have any incentive to defect—they are each doing what they most want to do.

What is missing from Buchanan's account of moral norms is the sense of "internal ought" that we find in moral philosophers such as Hobbes, David Hume, and Francis Hutcheson (Darwall 1995). A capacity for normative guidance is not simply a disposition to form a prosocial cooperative attitude such as "I don't like to harm people" but is a rational preference to follow rules even when one sees that such following does not yield what, on the basis of one's core interests and goals, one wants. Interestingly, Hartmut Kliemt (1990)—in a way similar to social theorists such as Amartya Sen (1982) and Kurt Baier 1995, chap. 5)—extends Buchanan's framework so that moralized individuals possess both self-interested and "moral" suborderings, such that the power of an individual's normative guidance can be modeled in terms of the meta-ordering (or trade-off rate) between the two suborderings. The moral individual will defer to the moralized preference ordering over the self-interested one. This approach provides a more promising way of modeling guilt: an individual who gives into temptation and acts on self-interested, rather than moralized, preferences experiences guilt. In the basic model introduced by Buchanan, there is no reason why Alf should feel guilty if he fails to play Y in game 2—he simply failed to maximize his own preference satisfaction.

Preaching and Attitude Change

A deeper worry about Buchanan's model of the origin of moral norms stems from the proposed mechanism of moralization: preaching. It seems a dubious origin for norms. Studies indicate that "preaching" or "exhorting" others to, say, donate to charity has relatively little effect on behavior. On the other hand, when others observe people *being* charitable, they are much more likely to engage in charitable acts (Henrich and Henrich 2007, 29–30). Subjects who experience inconsistency between what a person preaches (the person's stated normative expectations) and what that person actually does, tend to have a harder time recalling the content of the exhortation; those who witness conformity of preaching and action better recall the content of the preaching message. This suggests that statements of normative expectations that do not mesh with observed behavior are washed out, whereas the congruence of normative expectations with action increases the subjects' awareness of the normative expectations. So, as in our example, it is critical that Betty acts on the Y norm before she preaches to Alf.[9] Normative behavior must precede effective preaching. In an important experiment, Bicchieri and Erte Xiao (2009) studied the role of empirical expectations—what people *do*, rather than what they say *should* be done. They found that, indeed, expectations about what others will do are crucial for norm-following. In dictator games, normative ideas about what others think *ought to be done* do not have a significant impact when they run counter to empirical expectations about *the expected behavior of others.* In their experimental work on public goods games among two small-scale societies (the Machiguenga and the Mapuche), Joseph Henrich and Natalie Smith (2004, 13) also found that "the primary indicator of what a subject will do is what the subject thinks the rest of the group will do." There thus seems good evidence to support the claim that people often act on social and moral norms when they expect that a sufficiently large subset of others will. Unless people form the empirical expectation that cooperation is the "done thing" in a group, individuals do not have sufficient reason to comply with the normative exhortations of their fellows. Consequently, simply being preached to that I should adopt a rule—even with others reporting that they endorse it—does not tell me what I really need to know: Do people actually follow the rule?

Attitude change is, moreover, often costly—imbuing people with new attitudes typically requires sustained persuasion, and to be effective we often need to know something about the target's preexisting beliefs and attitudes. Not only is this often costly but, even if attitudes are changed, it is also uncertain whether behavior will be changed. As we saw earlier, attitudes often do not directly induce behavior. Given that attitude change tends to be a rather costly activity that is of dubious reliability, investing in it is generally rational only if one will have sustained relations with the target and if inducing the target's cooperative actions will have fairly significant payoffs to the preacher. In small group settings where the interests of the participants are tightly bound, the investment may be rational. Knowledge of the other's preexisting attitudes may be readily available, and sustained interaction is apt to provide many opportunities for preaching. In this case, some of the conditions for direct reciprocity and iterated games can employ preaching; when others fail to act on the cooperative norm, we respond by preaching internalization (Kliemt 1990). But, as the size of the cooperative network expands to include many strangers, this dynamic becomes impossible to sustain. The number of interactions increases rapidly, and opportunities for effective preaching to any one individual are drastically reduced. Moreover, as networks become heterogeneous, it becomes more difficult to know for any given target what an effective sermon would be. In these cases, preaching takes on the features of a public good: let others devote themselves to inculcating pro-social attitudes, while I devote myself to maximizing my gains within the existing attitude parameters. If, as most have argued in the social-moral norm literature, the evolution of social norms is a key factor in scaling up human cooperation beyond the small band (Gaus 2015), then the attitude change model seems unable to do precisely what is required of a norm-focused account. The rational strategy in large groups is to refrain from investing in norm change.[10]

It is important that, in the Hayekian "Great Society" (which Buchanan takes as equivalent to his "moral order"), individuals interact with strangers, whom they often do not expect to meet again. Thus, the rule network of the moral order is not simply an outcome of the interaction of many small-scale norm networks in which preaching may be efficient. Indeed, a recurring finding is that small-scale norm networks ("moral communities") are based on a strong distinction between "Us" and "Them." It seems that the evolution of humans as norm-followers may be at the root of this distinction: in learning to follow norms it was important to know who was one of "Us" so that one knew what norms and behaviors to comply with—ours, not the outsiders (Henrich 2016, 204; Boyd and Richerson 1985, 113–17). But this very sensitivity to "Us-ness" is one of the most serious challenges to truly mass moral orders—it all too easily produces the sort of "tribalism" against which Hayek fought (Greene 2013). The breakout from small-scale to large-scale norm networks is a fundamental moment in the evolution of the free society, and it was not accomplished simply through the interaction of small-scale networks.

Preaching and Norm Stabilization

Although of course they no doubt have some role, preaching and attitude change are, I think, inadequate grounds for an account of the origin of norms in large-scale settings, especially without a centralized "norm change agent." Until people expect others to follow a norm N, most preaching will have little effect. However, because preaching is more effective when behavior and sermon are consistent, preaching can have a significant role in stabilizing existing norms. This hypothesis is implied in Bicchieri's most recent statement of her theory of social norms. In her account, individuals are tempted to defect from norms to secure opportunistic self-interested gains. For any norm N and any given individual, that individual will have a certain "sensitivity," k_n, to the norm, which determines how much weight that norm receives in conflicts with opportunistic gains.

> Sensitivity in this case refers to how much a person adheres to what the norm stands for [see here Bicchieri 2006, 52]. Norm sensitivity embodies one's personal reasons for adhering to the norm. A highly sensitive individual could list several good, important reasons for why a particular norm should be enforced, whereas a low-sensitivity individual, who doesn't care much about what the norm stands for, may only list the fact that, since the norm is widespread, it makes sense for her to obey it (to avoid the sanctions that transgressions incur). Let's call a person's sensitivity to a particular norm, N, k_n. For example, a person who is not very convinced of the advisability of child marriage will have very low sensitivity to that norm (in other words, a very low k_n), whereas a person who is convinced that child marriage is the best way to protect a child's honor will be highly sensitive to such a norm (Bicchieri 2016, 165).

Although preaching is unlikely to be sufficient to get the target to adopt a norm, it does increase people's sensitivity to current norms.[11] In contrast to norm adoption, which has significant threshold properties (one must be "convinced enough" to adopt a norm), sensitivity is a continuous variable; even if preaching is not terribly powerful, we can expect marginal increases in preaching to have some marginal effects in increasing sensitivity to a norm. And, when a person's sensitivity to a norm is increased, that person is less tempted by opportunistic cheating.[12]

Normative Expectations (and Expressing Them)

Buchanan's model tends to collapse two functions of preaching: (a) changing the attitudes of others, which we have thus far been examining, and (b) alerting others to our normative expectations of them. When Betty preaches to Alf about why he should comply with the norm and not set back her interests, she is expressing her normative expectations to him. As Geoffrey Brennan and Loren Lomasky (1993) have famously argued, expressive action is very low cost (indeed, we usually positively enjoy it) and is apt to occur in many-person interactions when the agent is very unlikely to be significant in securing a consequential result. When Betty observes Alf inflicting "moral externalities" on her—in the sense that she observes him flouting a current norm in a way that sets back her interests—she certainly is apt to convey to him that he has disappointed her normative expectations, and this can matter. People's norm-based behavior is driven by both their empirical expectations and their beliefs about what others normatively expect of them.

One of the most striking "social experiments" based on this insight about the importance of expressing normative expectations was that of Antanas Mockus, mayor of Bogotá in the late 1990s and early 2000s (Mockus 2012; Tognato 2017). Bogotá was characterized by a very high rate of traffic fatalities in the mid-1990s, with widespread disregard for traffic regulations. Mockus distributed 350,000 "Thumbs Up/Thumbs Down" cards that drivers could display when another driver violated the formal rule, to emphasize the message that such behavior violated their normative expectations. As a result of this and other programs, Bogotá witnessed a 63 percent decrease in traffic fatalities between 1995 and 2003. The normative expectations of others do matter to us; signaling that we have them can stabilize compliance and reduce opportunistic cheating.

THE IMPLAUSIBILITY OF A COMPREHENSIVE HOBBESIAN ACCOUNT OF THE EMERGENCE OF THE MORAL ORDER

That Buchanan's preaching model of the origin of moral norms fails does not, of course, show that the Comprehensive Hobbesian project fails. Perhaps other essentially Hobbesian accounts, such as those of Ken Binmore (2005) or Moehler (2014, 2016), succeed in showing that the origins of informal norms lie simply in self-interest. Obviously, we cannot go into the details of these interesting accounts here. Yet we have good reason to suspect that any account of the origin of norms that presupposes only Hobbesian maximizers will fail to result in the emergence of large-scale moral norms. A generalized argument for the implausibility of any Hobbesian account of the origins of large-scale moral norms is suggested by an early essay of Buchanan's (1965), in which he explores the special difficulties of rule-following in large populations. I alter, and extend, his presentation.

We now suppose that Alf has a choice between two rules of behavior and that a rule "commits"[13] to certain actions (Buchanan 1965). Alf's two choices are (a) a moral norm N that secures the benefits of cooperation and social order (for example, by securing Paretian gains in mixed motive games) and (b) R, which is Alf's personal maxim of behavior that allows him to secure what he sees as the best results in an unconstrained way (Buchanan 1965).[14] True Kantian-inclined agents are willing to follow N even in the face of large-scale defections; at a limit, the true Kantian would commit to N regardless of the behavior of others.[15] However, for Hobbesian agents the decision to follow a moral norm involves securing for themselves the benefits of social cooperation, and these benefits can generally be secured only if enough others are acting on it. Let $m_a(\text{N}_x)$ be the utility Alf receives if X number of others act on the cooperative norm N, and $m_a(R_X)$ be the utility Alf would receive if, instead, he acted on his own personal rule (where X remains the number of others acting on N). Now what the Hobbesian would likely say is that Alf should act on N if $m_a(N_X) > m_a(R_X)$. Obviously, the Hobbesian would say, Alf should not act on N if most others do not (X is low) because only a few acting on N will at best secure meager cooperative benefits; therefore, it would be better for Alf to act on his own personal rule. Alf and a few others cannot bring about social cooperation. But if the number of cooperators begins to rise, Alf might find that the benefits of acting on N exceed that of acting on his personal rule, R, which allows unconstrained behavior.

The attraction of this set-up is that it opens a way for the Hobbesian to explain the emergence of norms through appeal to cascades, based on sensitivity to empirical expectations of the behavior of others. Suppose that we have a population of diverse Hobbesian agents, who place a wide range of value on the benefits of social cooperation as well as the value of acting on personal unconstrained rules and who vary in their estimates of how many people need to act on the norm to secure significant cooperative benefits.[16] Consider group a, composed of people who deem the benefits of cooperation great, the number needed to produce it modest, and the costs in terms of forgone opportunities to act on personal rules low. Thus, for even low values of X, they will tend to hold that $m_a(N_X) > m_a(R_X)$, and so act on N. Suppose that a "moral entrepreneur" (Buchanan 2001b, 442) or a "trendsetter" (Bicchieri 2016, chap. 5) in the a group decides that there are enough as to get the norm going, and succeeds in gaining allegiance to N in this pronorm group. This will change the calculations of group b, who, say, were slightly more skeptical that sufficient others were willing to join in, or who believed a somewhat greater number is needed to secure significant cooperative benefits. Now that group a has adopted N, those in group b might revise their judgments and conclude that for them, given this new level of participation Y, $m_b(N_Y) > m_b(R_Y)$. We can see how a cascade might get underway, as each group slightly less inclined toward N comes to the conclusions that its "threshold" for participation has been reached (Gaus, forthcoming).

The unstated assumption of the above cascade model—which is truly a model of norm emergence—is that Alf can secure the cooperative benefits of the norm only if he acts on N himself. So Alf keeps on looking at the cooperative gains of acting on N, given the number of others doing so, and switches at some point to secure these gains when they have surpassed his threshold value (i.e., they are greater than $m_a[R_X]$). However, none of this applies if Alf receives $m_a(N_X)$ whether or not he acts on N himself. In that case, his choice is between acting on N and receiving $m_a(N_X) - m_a(R_X)$ or acting on R and receiving $m_a(R_X) + m_a(N_X)$—hardly a difficult choice. As Buchanan ([1975] 2000) argues, in this case for any level of participation x, the latter strictly dominates the former. Recall further that the gains to Alf of x others acting on N comes from eliminating the ethical externalities they impose *on him*. His own acting on N provides him with no direct benefits whatsoever and thus does not in any way increase $m_a(\text{N}_\text{X})$.

Unless, that is, others make their acting on N *toward Alf conditional upon his acting on it.* As Buchanan ([1975] 2000) stresses, if others can withhold from Alf the benefits of their norm following (say, by continuing to impose externalities on him if he fails to act on N), then this conditionality imposes on Alf a necessary cost for receiving $m_a(\text{N}_\text{X})$: he must forgo $m_a(\text{R}_\text{X})$. This is by now the familiar lesson of the folk theorem in repeated games (Binmore 2005). If one can deny the benefits of cooperation to defectors, then a stable cooperative equilibrium can be achieved. The folk theorem formalizes this idea of "direct reciprocity." Suppose Alf and Betty are playing a series of games where cooperation yields mutual benefits but unilateral defection is the best payoff in any single play (e.g., a series of prisoner's dilemmas as in figure 1). Alf may be tempted to defect in game 1 to gain the unilateral defection payoff, $\{\text{D}_\text{A}, \text{C}_\text{B}\}$; but, if (given certain constraints about payoffs, expectations for future games and discounting the future) Betty threatens to respond with her own defection in game(s) 2 (or onwards), pushing Alf's payoff to $\{\text{D}_\text{A}, \text{D}_\text{B}\}$ (i.e., his "maximin payoff") in those subsequent games, it will be rational for Alf to cooperate rather than defect in game 1.[17] In small-scale settings (dyads, triads, etc.) with long histories of play, direct reciprocity can sustain cooperation, but it has severe problems scaling up to even medium-sized groups (Henrich and Henrich 2007, 48ff; Bowles and Gintis 2011, 63–68). The "bookkeeping" costs become excessive because both must keep track of the history of all their dyadic interactions, and of the costs and benefits of each. These demands are so excessive that there is increased skepticism about whether direct reciprocity is more than a minor basis for human cooperation (Boehm 2012, 60ff.).

Much more plausible is "indirect reciprocity," or generalized reputation. Indirect reciprocity does not require detailed information on the history of Alf's play with Betty but requires more general information, which can be shared among norm compliers, as to whether Alf is in general a norm complier or a noncomplier. This information is much easier to secure and disseminate. The problem, as I have pointed out elsewhere (Gaus 2011, 90–96), is that the information is rather blunt, subject to strategic manipulation, and sensitive to being degraded by false gossip. It is blunt because, given the number of norms a person may or may not be following at any given time, reputational information tends to sum up whether the person "is a good group member" or a "reliable person." But this can be distorting. As Henrich and Henrich (2007, chap. 4) discovered in their ethnographic studies, a person can secure a reputation as "unreliable" if he has flouted an important group norm that is not really indicative of his cooperativeness—such as marrying into a different ethnic group. When general reputations are important, people come to strategize over gaining reputations, where this may not cohere with genuine conditional cooperation. Again, as Henrich and Henrich (2007) discovered, when general reputations are critically important, people are very reluctant to withdraw cooperation from anyone because third parties might falsely interpret this as a defection rather than a reply to another's defection. The costs of being mistakenly branded a defector are high; thus one tends to cooperate with anyone who is not already widely known as a defector. This, then, undermines the effectiveness of reputations because many opportunistic defectors can, after all, gain the benefits of cooperation. Moreover, if the aim is to secure reputations, people invest significant resources in broadcasting—and overemphasizing or simply lying about—their cooperative accomplishments. Last, malicious gossip can quickly undermine the reputations of cooperators (Vanderschraaf 2006). Again, all these problems become debilitating when the moral order is one among strangers for whom any reputational information is, at best, scant.

In some models, withholding the benefits of cooperation is understood as a sort of punishment, but in the present model we should recall that, if Alf is not complying with N, he is imposing ethical externalities on others; if they withdraw they impose externalities on him. This need not be costly to them given his current noncompliance. Whether or not we deem this to be "punishment," we should distinguish it from acts where Betty, at a positive additional cost to herself, imposes sanctions on Alf with the aim of reducing or eliminating his gains from noncompliance. Although, as I have pointed out, punishment is necessary to stabilize norms, it is very difficult to plausibly model how it can arise in large populations of Hobbesian agents. When x, the number complying with the norm, is large, the benefits to any one individual noncomplier from defection are apt to be high. Alf receives $m_a(N_x)$, the benefits of x individuals not imposing ethical externalities on him as he goes about his business. For Betty alone to effectively punish him, she would essentially have to impose negative (punishment) utility that would drive his utility below what he would have received if he complied with the norm, so erasing all his gains from defection. That is apt to be very costly to her, and it would seem irrational for her to do so. More plausible is to model punishers as forming a quorum—a number that is sufficient to punish without high costs to any member (Bowles and Gintis 2011, 150–63). But in extensive societies the punishing group also would have to be extensive to minimize punishing costs on any individual. Among Hobbesian agents this would require group norms about punishing to ensure that each punisher does his or her part. This, however, would be to suppose the presence of a norm to explain the emergence of punishers. Generally, it is extraordinarily difficult to model Hobbesian agents acting as punishers in large groups.[18]

After reviewing this general model, Buchanan ([1975] 2000, 8) concludes that there is "elemental truth" in "the old adage, 'Never trust a stranger.'" If, however, the aim was to provide a Comprehensive Hobbesian account of the origins of moral order, which was to undergird the constitutional political economy project, this admission is unsettling. Hobbesian models probably can yield the emergence of norms in small groups, but Buchanan's account of the origins of the moral order was meant to push beyond the limits of "moral community" (and, we might say, tribalism) to account for a large-scale moral order among strangers. It seems very doubtful that he succeeded.

RETHINKING THE CONSTITUTIONAL POLITICAL ECONOMY PROJECT

Rule-Following versus Best Response

Whatever their differences, the disciplines of economics and philosophy embrace *Homo rationalis* as their basic model. *Homo economicus* is one articulation, depicting the rational individual as a maximizer, making the best response to the maximizing choices of others. Hayek refused to endorse *Homo ecomonicus* and best response as the mainstay of his analysis. Explicitly drawing on cultural anthropology, he argued that our reasoning abilities were an adaptive, evolutionary response to the challenges of human group life and that norm-following and purpose seeking are equally basic to rationality (Hayek 1973, 74–81). Hayek repeatedly stressed that humans are learners—we learn to follow rules, the functions of which we do not fully understand. This feature of our rationality is fundamental to Vernon Smith's (2008, 13–42) inquiry into ecological rationality and Douglass North's ([1993] 2016) learning-based institutionalism. The last 20 years have witnessed an increasing recognition of the importance to economic analysis of humans as cultural beings (Storr 2013). Indeed, there has been an explosion of work in cultural anthropology and cultural evolution supporting the Hayekian insight (Boyd and Richerson1985, 2005; Richerson and Boyd 2005; Henrich and Henrich 2007; Boehm 2012). Henrich (2016) summarizes a large body of these findings, stressing that in a wide variety of contexts those who rely on cultural norms radically outperform those who seek to individually judge their best option for themselves.

Once we view humans as fundamentally cultural beings, individual maximizing rationality no longer uniquely defines us. Indeed, there is reason to think that our true excellence may be in copying and imitating. In a fascinating series of experiments, Josep Call, Malinda Carpenter, and Michael Tomasello (2005), compared learning in chimps (median age 11 and a half years) and two-year-old human children. Chimps were found to be better at emulating a successful process: observing what worked, they reproduced it; observing what did not, they ignored it. Humans, in contrast, simply copied the actions of the "teacher." Victoria Horner and Andrew Whiten (2005) arrived at similar conclusions, providing evidence that chimps rely more on causal reasoning (the glory of *Homo economicus*) whereas children basically copied whatever they observed, causally efficacious or not. A child, some have said, is essentially a "cultural sponge" (Mesoudi 2011, 15). Other experiments indicate that adult humans excel at copying (Henrich 2016, 112). We tend to copy those who strike us as especially successful or who have high prestige: seeing the way they do things, most of us easily imitate their actions—without much causal understanding of what is going on. Henrich (2016, 165) echoes Hayek: "In many cases people don't understand how or why their norms work or that their norms are even 'doing' anything."

Being rule-guided follows from being cultural copiers. Children seeing a bit of behavior by a person judged to be competent must form a rule: in situations like *C*, do such-and-such. As Hayek ([1952] 1976) recognized, categorization of behavior implies rules. To copy we must categorize, and so form behavioral rules. And children automatically convert these categorizations into norms: seeing that doing such-and-such in circumstances is associated with good results, children convert this into a rule "Do such-and such in these circumstances!" and "It is wrong not to" (Schmidt and Tomasello 2012) Whereas imitation is inherently classification and rule-governed, best-response maximizing is inherently act-focused: What should I do right now that gives me the best results, given what others are doing? The attractions of best-response reasoning are so powerful that they have led generations of philosophers and economists down the garden path of seeking to reduce rule-governed behavior to enlightened best response. The results have been impressive displays of creativity and ingenuity, but, I would venture, there is no adequate solution to the puzzle of how maximizers can use maximizing reasoning to get themselves not to maximize (Gaus 2011, chap. 2).

Economists and philosophers typically resist (to understate matters) this line of thinking: it severely limits the scope of "rational choice reductionism" (Buchanan 2001b, 439) as well as the aspiration for thoroughgoing rational justification of our moral and social practices (Gaus 2017). As Hayek so often stressed, rational constructivist social contracts are replaced by evolutionary mechanisms and self-organizing systems. Political philosophy no longer can give comprehensive blueprints for social and political orders. However, what we have seen here is that acknowledging these limits allows us to ground politico-legal orders in a powerful account of the underlying moral order. And as our insight into the moral order deepens, best-response reasoning will have only a subsidiary role in its explanation.

Reimaging Constitutional Political Economy

Constitutional political economy thus confronts a fundamental dilemma. To stay true to Comprehensive Hobbesianism's commitment to rational choice all the way down, it would have to embrace the fatal lacuna (see the Introduction and the section titled "The Fatal Lacuna")—seeing government and law arising out of a thoroughly disordered state of nature populated by egoists, who manage to see that their true best response to the strategies of others is to agree to the rule of laws and their enforcement. It is perhaps not surprising that so many see Buchanan's constitutional political economy project in this light—it is the natural way to understand Comprehensive Hobbesianism. Yet, I have argued, it is an unattractive option that runs counter to our increasing knowledge of the normative basis of order. And, despite the popular impression, Buchanan did not take this route but consistently explored ways to ground the state in a moral order that was itself grounded in Comprehensive Hobbesianism. This more sophisticated Hobbesian project, I have argued, also fails. In the end, Buchanan's constitutional political economy project is torn between its commitment to Comprehensive Hobbesianism and its acceptance of a large-scale moral order. It cannot have both.

In reimagining constitutional political economy without Comprehensive Hobbesianism we might identify two visions. A modest modification would more fully recognize that the appropriate baseline for political negotiation is often the moral order, not simply a clash of individual interests. In this reimagining the distinction between the protective and productive state (Buchanan [1975] 2000, 95–98) becomes even sharper. Because the protective state focuses on basic individual rights, its baseline will be the norms in the moral order about, say, harm to others and various jurisdictional rights, including some contours of property rights (Gaus 2017, chap. 6). These norms define the accepted moral baseline, and the formal state apparatus would seek Pareto improvements on it. Individual rights would not be solely—and perhaps not even primarily—the outcome of individual interest-based bargaining but would be critically about interpretations of the demands of the moral order; however, as Hobbes ([1651] 1994) recognized, these disputes are always affected by interests. Much of this, I think, is nascent in Buchanan's work (see, for example, Buchanan [1975] 2000, chapter 1), but it has often not been well integrated into the constitutional political economy project, which so often supposes an amoral baseline. In contrast, because the productive state's concern is supplying public goods that are in the interests of individuals to supply, Buchanan's ([1986] 2016) fundamental insights about a Wicksellian-inspired politics as exchange endures as the core of this part of constitutional political economy.

However, when we reflect not simply on the fact that a preexisting moral order obtains but also on the theory of rationality that accounts for it, a more radical reimagining seems called for. *Homo economicus* and its assumption of self-interest are no longer general accounts of rational action (Buchanan [1986] 2016) but become domain-specific. The rational basis of individual action is complex, and only sometimes can it be best understood as maximizing self-interest. That, however, calls into question the import of Buchanan's key "argument from symmetry," which insists that "it is illegitimate to restrict *Homo economicus* to the domain of market behavior while employing widely different models of behavior in non-market settings, without any coherent explanation of how such a behavioral shift comes about" (Brennan and Buchanan 1985, 50).[19] If *Homo economicus* is inherently domain-specific, we ought not to begin with the supposition that it is a general model and that we need an explanation why *not* to apply it; rather, we should endeavor to better understand its legitimate domain. When, say, do people maximize by playing subgame perfect equilibria, and when do they trust others even when doing so fails to make the best (i.e., equilibrium) response? (Smith [2003] 2016) When do they bargain about interests, and when will they sacrifice interests for ideologies? And when will they act selfishly, and when will they act fairly and contribute to public goods? (Henrich and Smith 2004; Smith 2008, chapters 10–11). I certainly do not believe that in the face of these types of questions the constitutional political economy project withers, but it becomes much more complex. It demands a more nuanced model of individual action, individual learning, and their relation to the overall decision-making context or, we might say, its ecology (Smith 2008). The upshot is perhaps closer to Elinor Ostrom and Vincent Ostrom's (2004) institutional analysis and development (IAD) model rather than the more elegant version we have learned from Buchanan.

Constitutional political economy is not a completed artifice to be admired and defended, but an ongoing project, constantly refining its assumptions and analysis. Such is the nature of science. Discovering tensions moves us forward, pointing us toward the next step—and a better account of social cooperation and public choice. James Buchanan got us on our way. It is up to us to move further.

NOTES

A version of this essay was delivered to the symposium on "Tensions in the Political Economy Project of James M. Buchanan," held in Fairfax, Virginia, on December 14–15, 2016. The author thanks the participants and an anonymous reviewer for valuable comments and suggestions.

1. I say "commonly understood," but it is debatable whether this is Hobbes's considered view (Gaus 2013). In this essay, I assume this common view of the Hobbesian project.

2. These games can be combined. See Vanderschraaf (2006).

3. I do not distinguish here between social and moral norms, though distinctions certainly can be drawn (Brennan et al. 2013, 57ff.; Platteau 2000, 291ff.) As Bicchieri observes (2006, 21), her notion of social norms is essentially what Hume means by "justice." I have employed the term "social morality" to refer to rule-based moral claims, and to distinguish such claims for personal moral claims that do not suppose social uptake (Gaus 2011, 2ff., 163ff.)

4. In ultimatum games one person has the role of proposer, and the other is responder. In a common version proposer is given an amount of money; he can propose any division he wants. Responder then can either accept or reject. If responder accepts, both parties get what the proposer offered; if responder rejects, no one gets anything. Offers in which the responder gets less than 20 percent are routinely rejected. The typical offer gives the responder between 40 and 50 percent. In dictator games, the proposer simply divides the money any way she wants, and the game's over—not really much of a game.

5. Although he allows that there may be more than one type of explanation of the basis of the moral order (Buchanan 2001b, 231).

6. I am simplifying Buchanan's presentation. In his paper on "Moral Externalities" (which Buchanan cites in Buchanan 2001b, 215n, as providing a more detailed analysis), Kliemt (1990, 37) develops an account of moral externalities in which the "moral externality" arises out of an agent *seeking to impose a moral rule* on another. In the paper discussed here ("The Economic Origins of Ethical Constraints"), however, Buchanan (2001b, 216) sees moral rules as attempts to limit damages to one caused by "nonconstrained behavior" of others. So in Kliemt's interpretation, the moralist imposes an externality, whereas, in this essay by Buchanan, ethical rules are responses to externalities engendered by unconstrained pursuit of self-interest. I am analyzing the latter idea here.

7. I assume that there is no inducement Betty would be willing to offer that would get Alf to contract to play Y_A. Note that Betty also imposes an externality on Alf by playing Y_B rather than X_B. I shall simply focus on Alf's externality here. In Buchanan's more complex model, which involves an assumption of symmetry, both Alf and Betty must change their move to secure the "ethical equilibrium."

8. Although it does not pick out one equilibrium in a multiple equilibria game, as do standard conventions. But the compliance dynamic is the same.

9. This was not the case in Buchanan's (2001b, 219–24) example, where both switch play, from the $\{Y_A, Y_B\}$ equilibrium to a new $\{X_A, X_B\}$ equilibrium. The simpler case considered here is actually a more plausible account of norm emergence because here Betty is already acting on the Y rule, so her preaching would have more effect. But that asymmetry is only for the sake of simplicity of presentation.

10. This is not to deny that some forms of preaching are effective once a central agency takes over the task of supplying the "public good." Norm-change technologies in large-scale societies, such as media campaigns and "edutainment" of well-designed soap operas, may well transform attitudes. For example, students of large-scale norm change have recently focused on so-called "edutainment" like soap operas produced in Latin America, seeking to change gender and workplace norms (see Bicchieri 2006, chapter 5).

11. "Persistence can thus be explained without explaining emergence" (Brennan et al. 2013, 150).

12. For similar reasons preaching is no doubt important in the process of norm abandonment by reducing sensitivity. But without a change in the empirical expectations—which preaching alone cannot accomplish—norm change will not occur. See Bicchieri (2016, 119–27).

13. In this model, then, Buchanan is supposing that ethical rule following involves a weak type of commitment strategy; but we shall also see that he allows constant reevaluation of the choice of which commitment strategy to adopt.

14. Buchanan insists that the choice should be between two rules, not between a rule and simply unconstrained behavior. In the present context nothing rides on the distinction.

15. I have modeled populations composed of such quasi-Kantian agents and agents who have stronger conditional preferences for norm following. Under a surprising range of parameters, even the quasi-Kantians opt for norms that are followed by all (Gaus, forthcoming)

16. As Hobbes ([1651] 1994, 23) points out, individuals not only have divergent interests but also have divergent judgments.

17. Buchanan (2000) draws on iterated game results to argue that Hayekian cultural evolution is not necessary to explain rule-following behavior.

18. Not to say that many do not try (see Hampton 1986, 176ff.).

19. See also my earlier essay (Gaus 2010), which has, alas, often miffed followers of Buchanan. I hope the present effort will prove to be less irritating.

REFERENCES

Andrighetto, Giulia, Daniel Villatoro, and Rosaria Conte. 2010. "Norm Internalization in Artificial Societies." *AI Communications* 23 (4): 325–39.

Baier, Kurt. 1995. *The Rational and the Moral Order: The Social Roots of Reason and Morality*. La Salle, IL: Open Court.

Bicchieri, Cristina. 2006. *The Grammar of Society: The Nature and Dynamics of Norms*. Cambridge, U.K.: Cambridge University Press.

———. 2016. *Norms in the Wild: How to Diagnose, Measure, and Change Social Norms.* New York: Oxford University Press.

Bicchieri, Cristina, and Alex Chavez. 2010. "Behaving as Expected: Public Information and Fairness Norms." *Journal of Behavioral Decision Making* 23 (2): 191–208.

Bicchieri, Cristina, and Erte Xiao. 2009. "Do the Right Thing: But Only if Others Do So." *Journal of Behavioral Decision Making* 22 (2): 191–208.

Binmore, Ken. 2005. *Natural Justice.* Oxford, U.K.: Oxford University Press.

Boehm, Christopher. 2012. *Moral Origins: The Evolution of Virtue, Altruism and Shame.* New York: Basic Books.

Bowles, Samuel, and Herbert Gintis. 2011. *A Cooperative Species: Human Reciprocity and Its Evolution.* Princeton, NJ: Princeton University Press.

Boyd, Robert, and Peter J. Richerson. 1985. *Culture and the Evolutionary Process.* Chicago: University of Chicago Press.

———. 2005. *The Origin and Evolution of Cultures.* New York: Oxford University Press.

Brennan, Geoffrey, and James Buchanan. 1985. *The Reason of Rules: Constitutional Political Economy.* Cambridge, U.K.: Cambridge University Press.

Brennan, Geoffrey, Lina Eriksson, Robert E. Goodin, and Nicholas Southwood. 2013. *Explaining Norms.* Oxford, U.K.: Oxford University Press.

Brennan, Geoffrey, and Loren Lomasky. 1993. *Democracy and Decision.* Cambridge, U.K.: Cambridge University Press.

Buchanan, James M. 1965. "Ethical Rules, Expected Values and Large Numbers." *Ethics* 76 (1): 1–13.

———. (1975) 2000. *The Limits of Liberty: Between Anarchy and Leviathan.* Vol. 7 of *The Collected Works of James M. Buchanan.* Indianapolis, IN: Liberty Fund.

———. 2000. "The Legacy of Friedrich von Hayek: Vol. 7 Morality and Community in the Extended Market Order." (Audio). Indianapolis, IN: Liberty Fund. http://oll.libertyfund.org/titles/2153.

———. 2001a. *Choice, Contract, and Constitutions.* Vol. 16 in *The Collected Works of James M. Buchanan.* Indianapolis, IN: Liberty Fund.

———. 2001b. *Moral Science and Moral Order.* Vol. 17 in *The Collected Works of James M. Buchanan.* Indianapolis, IN: Liberty Fund.

———. (1986) 2016. "The Constitution of Economic Policy." In *Mainline Economics: Six Nobel Lectures in the Tradition of Adam Smith*, edited by Peter J. Boettke, Stefanie Haeffele-Balch, and Virgil Henry Storr, 43–59. Arlington, VA: Mercatus Center.

Buchanan, James M., and Gordon Tullock. (1962) 1999. *The Calculus of Consent: Logical Foundations of Constitutional Democracy.* Vol. 3 of *The Collected Works of James M. Buchanan.* Indianapolis, IN: Liberty Fund.

Call, Josep, Malinda Carpenter, and Michael Tomasello. 2005. "Copying Results and Copying Actions in the Process of Social Learning: Chimpanzees (*Pan Troglodytes*) and Human Children (*Homo Sapiens*)." *Animal Cognition* 8 (3): 151–63.

Darwall, Stephen. 1995. *The British Moralists and the Internal "Ought."* Cambridge, U.K.: Cambridge University Press.

Friedman, Daniel. 2008. *Morals and Markets: An Evolutionary Account of the Modern World.* New York: Routledge.

Gaus, Gerald. 2008. *On Philosophy, Politics, and Economics*. Belmont, CA: Thomson-Wadsworth.

———. 2010. "The Limits of *Homo Economicus*." In *Essays on Philosophy, Politics & Economics*, edited by Christi Favor, Julian Lamont, and Gerald Gaus, 14–37. Stanford, CA: Stanford University Press.

———. 2011. *The Order of Public Reason: A Theory of Freedom and Morality in a Diverse and Bounded World.* Cambridge, U.K.: Cambridge University Press.

———. 2013. "Hobbesian Contractarianism, Orthodox and Revisionist." In *The Bloomsbury Companion to Hobbes,* edited by S.A. Lloyd, 263–78. New York: Bloomsbury.

———. 2015. "The Egalitarian Species." *Social Philosophy and Policy* 31 (2): 1–27.

———. 2017. "Hayekian 'Classical' Liberalism." In *The Routledge Handbook of Libertarianism,* edited by Jason Brennan, David Schmidtz, and Bas van der Vossen. New York: Routledge.

———. Forthcoming. "Self-Organizing Moral Systems: Beyond the Social Contract." *Politics, Philosophy and Economics.*

Green, T. H. (1889) 1986. *Lectures on the Principles of Political Obligation.* In *Lectures on the Principles of Political Obligation and Other Writings*, edited by Paul Harris and John Morrow, 13–193. Cambridge, U.K.: Cambridge University Press.

Greene, Joshua. 2013. *Moral Tribes: Emotion, Reason, and the Gap Between Them and Us.* New York: Penguin.

Hampton, Jean. 1986. *Hobbes and the Social Contract Tradition*. Cambridge, U.K.: Cambridge University Press.

Hayek, F. A. 1973. *Rules and Order*. Chicago: University of Chicago Press.

———. (1952) 1976. *The Sensory Order: An Inquiry into the Foundations of Theoretical Psychology*. Chicago: University of Chicago Press.

———. 1988. *The Fatal Conceit: The Errors of Socialism*, edited by W. W. Bartley. Chicago: University of Chicago Press.

Henrich, Joseph. 2016. *The Secret of Our Success*. Princeton, NJ: Princeton University Press.

Henrich, Joseph, and Natalie Smith. 2004. "Comparative Evidence from Machiguenga, Mapuche, and American Populations." In *Foundations of Human Sociality: Economic Experiments and Ethnographic Evidence from Fifteen Small-Scale Societies*, edited by Joseph Henrich, Robert

Boyd, Samuel Bowles, Colin Camerer, Ernst Fehr, and Herbert Gintis, 125–67. Oxford, U.K.: Oxford University Press.

Henrich, Natalie, and Joseph Henrich. 2007. *Why Humans Cooperate: A Cultural and Evolutionary Explanation.* Oxford, U.K.: Oxford University Press.

Hobbes, Thomas. (1651) 1994. *Leviathan*, edited by Edwin Curley. Indianapolis, IN: Hackett.

Hopfensitz, Astrid, and Ernesto Reuben. 2009. "The Importance of Emotions for the Effectiveness of Social Punishment." *Economic Journal* 119 (540): 1534–59.

Horner, Victoria, and Andrew Whiten. 2005. "Causal Knowledge and Imitation/Emulation Switching in Chimpanzees (*Pan Troglodytes*) and Children (*Homo Sapiens*)." *Animal Cognition* 8 (3): 164–81.

Kitcher, Philip. 2011. *The Ethical Project.* Cambridge, MA: Harvard University Press.

Kliemt, Hartmut. 1990. "Moral Externalities." In *Papers on Buchanan and Related Subjects*, 37–60. Munich: Accedo Verlagsgesellschaft.

———. 2009. *Philosophy and Economics I: Methods and Models.* Munich: Oldenburg.

Mackie, Gerry. Forthcoming. "Effective Rule of Law Requires Construction of a Social Norm of Legal Obedience." In *Cultural Agents Reloaded: The Legacy of Antanas Mockus*, edited by Carlo Tognato. Cambridge, MA: The Cultural Agents Initiative at Harvard University.

Mesoudi, Alex. 2011. *Cultural Evolution.* Chicago: University of Chicago Press.

Mockus, Antanas. 2012. "Building 'Citizenship Culture' in Bogotá." *Journal of International Affairs* 65: 143–46.

Moehler, Michael. 2014. "The Scope of Instrumental Morality." *Philosophical Studies* 167 (2): 431–51.

———. 2016. "Orthodox Rational Choice Contractarianism before and after Gauthier." *Politics, Philosophy and Economics* 15 (2): 113–31.

Montesquieu, Baron De. (1748) 1949. *The Spirit of the Laws.* Translated by Franz Neumann. New York: Hafner Press.

North, Douglass C. (1993) 2016. "Economic Performance through Time." In *Mainline Economics: Six Nobel Lectures in the Tradition of Adam Smith*, edited by Peter J. Boettke, Stefanie Haeffele-Balch, and Virgil Henry Storr, 81–99. Arlington, VA: Mercatus Center.

Ostrom, Elinor, and Vincent Ostrom. 2004. "The Quest for Meaning in Public Choice." Special issue on the "Production and Diffusion of Public Choice Political Economy: Reflections in the VPI Center." *American Journal of Economics and Sociology* 63 (1): 105–47.

Platteau, Jean-Philippe. 2000. *Institutions, Social Norms and Economic Development.* Amsterdam: Harwood Academic Publishers.

Richerson, Peter J., and Robert Boyd. 2005. *Not by Genes Alone: How Culture Transformed Human Evolution.* Chicago: University of Chicago Press.

———. 2008. "The Evolution of Free Enterprise Values." In *Moral Markets: The Critical Role of Values in the Economy,* edited by Paul Zak, 107–41. Princeton, NJ: Princeton University Press.

Robinson, Paul. 2000. "Why Does the Criminal Law Care What the Layperson Thinks Is Just? Coercive versus Normative Crime Control." *Virginia Law Review* 86 (8) "Symposium: The Legal Construction of Norms": 1839–69.

Rose, David C. 2011. *The Moral Foundations of Economic Behavior.* New York: Oxford University Press.

Schmidt, Marco F. H., and Michael Tomasello. 2012. "Young Children Enforce Social Norms." *Current Directions in Psychological Science* 21 (4) 232–36.

Schwab, David, and Elinor Ostrom. 2008. "The Vital Role of Norms and Rules in Maintaining Open Public and Private Economies." In *Moral Markets: The Critical Role of Values in the Economy,* edited by Paul Zak, 204–27. Princeton, NJ: Princeton University Press.

Sen, Amartya. 1982. "Rational Fools." In *Choice, Welfare and Measurement,* 84–106. Cambridge, MA: Harvard University Press.

Smith, Vernon. 2008. *Rationality in Economics: Constructivist and Ecological Forms*. Cambridge, U.K.: Cambridge University Press.

———. (2003) 2016. "Constructivist and Ecological Rationality in Economics." In *Mainline Economics: Six Nobel Lectures in the Tradition of Adam Smith,* edited by Peter J. Boettke, Stefanie Haeffele-Balch, and Virgil Henry Storr, 103–90. Arlington, VA: Mercatus Center.

Storr, Virgil Henry. 2013. *Understanding the Culture of Markets*. New York: Routledge.

Stuntz, William J. 2000. "Self-Defeating Crimes." *Virginia Law Review* 86 (8) "Symposium: The Legal Construction of Norms": 1871–99.

Thrasher, John, and Gerald Gaus. Forthcoming. "Calculus of Consent." In the *Oxford Handbook of Classics in Contemporary Political Theory*, edited by Jacob Levy. Oxford, U.K.: Oxford University Press.

Tognato, Carlo, ed. 2017. *Cultural Agents Reloaded: The Legacy of Antanas Mockus.* Cambridge, MA: The Cultural Agents Initiative at Harvard University.

Tyler, Tom R. 1990. *Why People Obey the Law*. New Haven, CT: Yale University Press.

Vanderschraaf, Peter. 2006. "War or Peace? A Dynamical Analysis of Anarchy." *Economics and Philosophy* 22 (2): 243–79.

———. 2007. "Covenants and Reputations." Synthese 157 (2): 167–95.

Young, Iris Marion. 2011. *Responsibility for Justice.* Oxford, U.K.: Oxford University Press.

CHAPTER SEVEN

THE PROTECTIVE STATE

A GRAVE THREAT TO LIBERTY

CHRISTOPHER J. COYNE

Can government simultaneously be empowered and constrained? This paradox of government is the central question of constitutional political economy (see Buchanan 1975; Brennan and Buchanan [1985] 2000; Weingast 1995; Gordon 2002). The power possessed by government can produce outcomes deemed beneficial by citizens. There is no guarantee of these beneficial outcomes, however, because government can instead use its power to abuse, exploit, and plunder citizens. The Madisonian project of addressing this paradox was a central focus of James M. Buchanan's writings in the area of constitutional political economy. His solution involved creating appropriate governance structures to empower government to engage in beneficial behaviors while constraining its ability to engage in predation.

In *The Limits of Liberty*, Buchanan ([1975] 2000, 95–97) develops his notion of the *protective state*, which emerges at the constitutional level and is tasked with protecting the core rights of citizens via internal security, contract enforcement, and defense against external threats. The purpose of the protective state is to guard people from the perils of anarchy on the one hand and the threat of coercion by the state on the other. Within Buchanan's framework, the protective state is a purely liberty-enhancing apparatus. The purpose of this chapter is to analyze how the operations of the protective state can undermine the liberties it is meant to uphold.

I identify five specific channels through which the activities of the protective state may yield anti-liberty outcomes. They include (a) interpretation in an open-ended system, (b) institutional changes within constraints, (c) the centralization of state power, (d) the emergence of coercion-enabling human capital, and (e) the emergence of coercion-enabling physical capital. These channels are endogenous to the operation of the protective state and do not require any nefarious motivations on the part of those involved. As such, they appreciate and reflect the insight of Justice Frank Murphy (1943) who noted, "Few indeed have been the invasions upon essential liberties which have not been accompanied by pleas of urgent necessity advanced in good faith by responsible men."

My argument is a straightforward extension of two ideas. The first is that rarely are government actions limited to doing just one thing. Government actions have unintended repercussions, which have subsequent repercussions, and so on (see Mises [1929] 1977; Jervis 1997; Ikeda 1997; Coyne 2008, 2013). These unintended consequences can occur even when the government's initial actions are within the confines of the ideal protective state. The second is an extension of Buchanan's (1979) insistence on "politics without romance," which entails modeling the realities of politics instead of assuming some idealized notion of political action. These realities entail purposive action by fallible people responding to the incentives generated by political institutions. Extending this idea, this chapter is an attempt at constitutional political economy without romance. Rather than simply assuming an idealized protective state, one must realize that activities intended to protect liberties can generate anti-liberty outcomes.

The potential for the protective state to produce anti-liberty outcomes is not a new idea. For example, James Madison ([1795] 1865) provided the following warning regarding the state's war-making abilities:

> Of all the enemies to public liberty, war is perhaps the most to be dreaded, because it comprises and develops the germ of every other. War is the parent of armies; from these proceed debts and taxes; and armies, and debts, and taxes are the known instruments for bringing the many under the domination of the few. In war, too, the discretionary power of the Executive is extended; its influence in dealing out offices, honors, and emoluments is multiplied; and all the means of seducing the minds, are added to those of subduing the force, of the people. . . . No nation could preserve its freedom in the midst of continual warfare.

It is possible that the state will employ its war-making power in a manner that upholds the rights of citizens, as per Buchanan's ideal protective state. As Madison cautions, however, this power also has the potential to bring about a number of undesirable consequences. Some of these consequences, such as the fiscal burden, deal with the scale or size of the state. Other consequences, such as expansions in the discretionary power of the state, affect the scope or range of state activities. Both scale and scope are important aspects of the state and do not necessarily correlate—as recognized by Buchanan (1975, 163), who notes, "An interfering federal judiciary, along with an irresponsible executive, could exist even when budget sizes remain relatively small."

Alexis de Tocqueville also recognized the potentially deleterious effects of war on domestic political institutions. Specifically, he warned:

> War does not always give over democratic communities to military government, but it must invariably and immeasurably increase the powers of civil government; it must almost compulsorily concentrate the direction of all men and the management of all things in the hands of the administration. If it does not lead to despotism by sudden violence, it prepares men for it more gently by their habits. All those who seek to destroy the liberties of a democratic nation ought to know that war is the surest and the shortest means to accomplish it. (Tocqueville 1840, 285)

Like Madison, Tocqueville recognized that the fundamental powers of the state could potentially have perverse effects on domestic political institutions through expansions in state power and through changes in the fundamental relationship between citizens and their government. War might protect the rights of citizens, but war-making powers can have long-term effects that undermine the very liberties the protective state supposedly upholds.

One potential solution to this tension is constitutional constraints that limit the powers of government as they pertain to its protective function. Ideally, the protective state would undertake only those activities that uphold and defend the rights of its citizens. Appropriate constraints would exist to mitigate any unforeseen consequences that emerged in future periods, avoiding the concerns raised by Madison and Tocqueville. The historical record, however, suggests that this ideal protective state rarely, if ever, exists because "[f]oreign affairs, and its close relation national security, have been a graveyard for civil liberties" (Dorsen 1989). An existing literature documents instances across time and space in which state-led security and war activities result in significant, and often permanent, expansions in state power over the lives of domestic citizens (see Corwin 1947; Higgs 1987, 2004, 2007, 2012; Linfield 1990; Porter 1994; Rehnquist 1998; Cole and Dempsey 2006; Cole 2008; Cole and Lobel 2009; Herman 2011; Coyne and Hall 2018).

The possibility that the activities of the protective state can endogenously produce anti-liberty outcomes highlights a fundamental tension in constitutional political economy. Namely, even in cases in which a government is performing its protective activities within the boundaries specified by the constitution, there is still the potential that these actions will undermine the freedoms it purportedly guards.

I proceed as follows. The next section considers how the activities of the protective state require government to possess a significant amount of coercive force. I discuss how this force may undermine freedom through the indirect erosion of citizens' liberties. I then identify five channels through which the activities of the protective state can generate anti-liberty outcomes in an indirect manner. Each subsection discusses a theoretical channel and provides examples from the U.S. experience to illustrate the conceptual point. I conclude with a discussion of the implications.

THE NATURE OF PROTECTIVE STATE ACTIVITIES

Two characteristics of the protective state are central to understanding how its activities can produce anti-liberty outcomes. First, at the core of the protective state's activities is the threat or use of coercive force. As Brennan and Buchanan ([1985] 2000, 31) write, "Of course, in the establishment of the political entity, powers of coercion are granted to governments, powers that are designed to prevent criminal trespass and exploitation of rights by internal and external aggressors." The state is a mechanism for enforcing rules over the population of a geographic space. Backstopping these rules is the threat of coercive force that, in the present day, includes state-of-the-art policing, military, and surveillance capabilities. This monopoly on the use of force can potentially produce pro-liberty outcomes, but one cannot assume this outcome because governments can, and have, abused their power throughout history. Brennan and Buchanan ([1985] 2000, 31) recognize this distinct possibility when noting that "[i]n the assignment of these powers, problems of control may arise, problems that are not amenable to easy solution. Once established as sovereign, government may not willingly remain within the limits of its initially delegated authority."

Second, in practice, the activities of the protective state influence and affect almost all areas—economic, political, and social—of domestic life. In its ideal form, the protective state enforces contracts, provides internal security to protect property rights, and supplies national defense against external threats. When viewed in terms of these general categories, the functions of the protective state seem quite limited. In reality, however, these functions create the potential for the emergence of a wide scope of government activities both in the immediate and future terms. The state's power to engage in national security policy making is a "master key" because it "opens all doors, including the doors that might otherwise obstruct the government's invasion of our most cherished rights to life, liberty, and property" (Higgs 2015, 276).

One need only consider the revelations about the U.S. surveillance state in the aftermath of the September 11 attacks to understand how the security-related activities of government can bleed into almost all aspects of private life. These revelations made clear that, among other things, the government was monitoring the communications, financial transactions, and travel of U.S. and non-U.S. persons; and surveillance is but one aspect of the overall portfolio of government activities related to its protective function.

The conventional terminology employed when discussing the activities of the protective state contributes to obscuring the wide range of powers possessed by government in the name of guarding the rights of citizens. The terms "defense" and "security" suggest passive acts of protection from internal and external threats. They imply that the state employs defense and security in a purely responsive manner to mitigate threats and resist attacks. However, what actually constitutes defense and security—for example, weapons, arms, equipment, surveillance and intelligence, and all of the related subcomponents of these activities—are all technologies that lower the cost to governments of controlling and harming people both at home and abroad.

One implication of this semantic issue is that the language typically used to describe the activities of the night watchman state overemphasizes its pro-liberty aspects while downplaying its potential anti-liberty aspects. Although it is true that government can employ force for purely defensive and protective purposes, it is equally true that it can also use that same force for offensive purposes—actively engaging in activities that undermine the life, liberty, and property of ordinary people. Indeed, historically, many governments use their monopoly on force not to defend the person and property of their domestic populations but rather as a tool of direct and indirect social control. This has occurred both under authoritarian regimes and under constitutionally constrained states. As Bruce Porter (1994, 10) writes, "Wars throughout modern history have fostered authoritarian rule, undermined the civic order of traditional states, perverted consensual political processes within constitutional states, and threatened or destroyed established rights and liberties." From the perspective of constitutional political economy, this raises an important issue because the activities of the protective state can lead to the erosion of domestic liberties, cutting against the protective state's fundamental purpose for existing. These erosions can be either direct or indirect.

Direct erosions occur when governments use blunt and observable force to control and oppress citizens. Recent civil conflicts in Libya (under Muammar

Gaddafi) and Syria (under Bashar al-Assad) provide examples of the direct scenario: the respective governments of these countries deployed blunt coercive force to attempt to repress citizens. Under the direct scenario constitutional constraints demarcating the functions of the protective state are either ineffective or altogether absent. From the standpoint of constitutional political economy, the direct scenario is of little interest because it suggests that when governments are unconstrained they will abuse their powers, which is exactly what one would expect. Indeed, the very purpose of constitutions is to prevent the direct scenario from occurring.

The bigger concern, from the perspective of constitutional political economy, is *indirect erosion*, which occurs when a constitutionally constrained government slowly expands the scope of its powers over the lives of the citizenry. Supreme Court Justice William O. Douglas (1987, 162) captured the essence of this indirect process when he observed:

> As nightfall does not come all at once, neither does oppression. In both instances there is a twilight when everything remains seemingly unchanged. And it is in such twilight that we all must be most aware of change in the air—however slight—lest we become unwitting victims of the dark.

Under this scenario, expansions in government power occur slowly, and often in a concealed manner, so that they are not readily observable to nondiscerning citizens who are still under the belief that they are living under a constitutionally constrained government. When this happens, it creates a genuine tension for constitutions intended to limit, if not altogether avoid, expansions in state power that undermine the rights of citizens.

HOW THE PROTECTIVE STATE CAN PRODUCE ANTI-LIBERTY OUTCOMES

There are five channels through which the activities of the constitutionally constrained protective state can erode the liberties of citizens.

Interpretation in an Open-Ended System

Constitutions contain significant space for interpreting the appropriate role of the protective state. As Charles Beard (1936, 30) writes, each word or phrase in the U.S. Constitution

> covers some core of the reality and practice on which a general consensus can be reached. But around this core is a huge shadow in which the good and wise can wander indefinitely without ever coming to any agreement respecting the command made by the "law." Ever since the Constitution was framed or particular amendments added, dispute has raged among men of strong minds and pure hearts over the meaning of these cloud covered words and phrases.

The necessity of interpretation is a result of the fact that constitutional designers have limited information regarding future states of the world at the time they author rules.

Constitutions establish rules for an open-ended system characterized by creativity, genuine surprise, and shifting interests (Devins et al. 2015). As the future unfolds in unknown and unanticipated ways, constitutional rules require interpretation and reinterpretation. For example, no one at the Constitutional Convention in 1787 could have imagined or anticipated the nature of the surveillance tools available to the members of the U.S. government today. As a result, the constitutional rules written over two centuries ago require interpretation in light of these technological advances and the power that they grant to government. The specific nature of these interpretations, which may be pro- or anti-liberty, are influenced by the beliefs and views of key decision makers—for example, the public, elected officials, and members of the court—involved in selecting interpreters and actually interpreting the constitution.

The interpretative space in constitutions is especially evident in U.S. history during times of national emergencies (see Higgs 1987, 2004, 2007; Congleton 2005; Coyne 2011). Despite the fact that the U.S. Constitution does not contain any specific delineation of emergency powers, the government has undertaken a wide range of crisis-related activities (Higgs 1987, 2004). Courts have often stepped aside during periods of perceived or real emergency, granting the other branches of government near free reign to do as they please (see Fraenkel 1946; Dorsen 1989; Rehnquist 1998). For example, during World War II the Supreme Court "gave judicial sanction to whatever powers and actions the President and Congress found necessary to the prosecution of the war" (Rossiter [1948] 2002, 265). In general, "when critical trade-offs must be made, war will override all other concerns, and as the ancient maxim aptly warns us, *inter armas silent leges* [in the midst of arms, the laws are silent]" (Higgs 2015, 276).

The Supreme Court's subsequent interpretation of the legality of government behaviors during times of emergency varies greatly (see Higgs 2004, 201–18; Rossiter [1948] 2002). To provide one illustration of how these interpretations can be anti-liberty, consider the case of the internment of Japanese-American citizens during World War II. During the war, the U.S. government forcibly relocated over 110,000 Japanese Americans, an estimated two-thirds of them U.S. citizens, into internment camps (Higgs 2004, 203). Absent an explicit provision to carry out this forced relocation, the Supreme Court needed to interpret the constitutionality of the government's actions. It did so in two cases in 1943 and 1944.

In *Hirabayashi v. United States*, 320 U.S. 81 (1943), the Court upheld the curfew set by General John DeWitt, indicating that restrictions against a group of U.S. citizens were constitutional when the United States was at war with the group's country of origin. In *Korematsu v. United States*, 323 U.S. 214 (1944), the Court heard the case of Fred Korematsu, a U.S. citizen arrested after staying in his home in California despite the government's order compelling Japanese Americans to report to relocation camps. The Court upheld the relocation order as constitutional. According to Clinton Rossiter ([1948] 2002, 282), "The punishment of this loyal citizen [Korematsu] of the United States was sanctioned by the highest court of the land; his crime: sitting in his own home." He goes on to summarize the broader implications of these two Supreme Court decisions as follows:

> The important lessons for the problem of constitutional dictatorship in the United States are these: that the President's unlimited range of dictatorial crisis power was again exerted without legislative, judicial, or popular contradiction; that the Supreme Court demonstrated its continued unwillingness to get in the way of the war power of the United States; and that the most basic rights of a large group of American citizens were grossly flouted under conditions considerably less than desperate, and can be again. (Rossiter [1948] 2002, 283)

As this example makes clear, the activities of the protective state can, and have, produced anti-liberty results within the confines of existing constitutional rules. During the war, the government expanded the scope of its activities over the lives of American persons, reducing their liberties. The Court upheld the government's actions, which institutionalized the widened scope of state power over both current and future persons.

Institutional Changes within Constraints

Rules determined at the constitutional stage frame subsequent post-constitutional activity, including processes for making changes to political institutions. Given the uncertainty of the future, however, changes to political institutions that might make sense at one point in time may lead to unforeseeable outcomes in future periods. Even *if* initial institutional changes are pro-liberty, they can generate an array of possibilities for anti-liberty outcomes in the future.

To provide a concrete illustration of this channel, consider the National Security Act of 1947 (and its subsequent 1949 amendments). In the wake of World War II, the national security ideology in the United States was one of global war driven by the perceived Soviet threat. As Hogan (1998, 14) notes,

> In the national security ideology, then, the nature of the Soviet regime put a premium on military preparedness, the immediacy of the Soviet threat made preparedness a matter of urgency, the long term nature of that threat required a permanent program of preparedness, and the danger of total war dictated a comprehensive program that integrated civilian and military resources and obliterated the line between citizen and soldier, peace and war.

This set of beliefs led to a massive reorganization of the U.S. government's military and intelligence agencies through the National Security Act.

The act followed the constitutional process for implementing a public law, including congressional hearings, debate, and approval, as well as the signature of President Harry Truman. It created the National Military Establishment (later the Department of Defense), unified the military under a new position (the Secretary of Defense), and established the Central Intelligence Agency, the Joint Chiefs of Staff, the National Security Council, and the Armed Forces Security Agency (later the National Security Agency). The goal was to centralize the state's defense and security operations to reduce waste and duplication, and to improve capacity and efficiency for the realities of perceived global total war. In this regard, the National Security Act of 1947 did exactly what its designers intended it to do: create "all of the leading institutions of the U.S. national security bureaucracy, except for the Department of State" (Stuart 2008, 1). These reforms, however, had real, long-term effects on the structure of government and the relationship between citizens and the state.

In the wake of the passage of the National Security Act, "there was a growing militarization of the American government and an increase of presidential and Executive Branch power normally associated with wartime" (Jablonsky 2002/03, 9). This expansion in authority included increases in the power of the new national security agencies in influencing and designing foreign policy. Over time, this shift eroded the checks and balances on potential abuses of government power.

In tracing the long-term implications of the National Security Act of 1947, Michael Glennon (2015) has identified a "double government" with two distinct sets of institutions. The first set of institutions consists of the "dignified institutions," including the executive, legislative, and judicial branches. These are the institutions that most people have in mind when they think of the constitutionally constrained protective state. The foundations of the dignified institutions are the Madisonian structure of dispersed power across the three branches of government intended to address the paradox of government.

The National Security Act of 1947 eroded these Madisonian checks and balances on the national security state. Centralizing power and granting the security agencies significant independence weakened existing checks, lowering the barriers to expansions in both the scale and scope of government over time. Ultimately, the reforms created an environment within which national security institutions could expand given the significant slack in the constraints they faced.

The result was that the dignified institutions were joined by a new set of government institutions—the "efficient institutions"—that exert significant influence over foreign policy (Glennon 2015, 6–7). This deep state consists of the complex network of government agencies and departments—military, intelligence, law enforcement, diplomatic—as well as the private contractors and consultants that constitute the national security state. They are efficient in that those operating within these institutions are largely relieved of the full burdens created by the original Madisonian checks and balances intended to prevent abuses of power. As a result, those operating within the security state have greater freedom to shape and pursue their own agendas in an unconstrained manner.

The implications of the increased autonomy possessed by the security state are troubling for those concerned with the paradox of government. According to Glennon (2015, 6), "Large segments of the public continue to believe that America's constitutionally established, dignified institutions are the locus of governmental power; by promoting that impression, both sets of institutions maintain public support." And, although the "dignified" institutions still maintain some control over protective state activities, the efficient institutions exert significant influence. Each of the three branches constituting the dignified institutions has limited power to constrain the efficient institutions, leaving space for expansions in the scope of state power over the lives of citizens (for examples of expansions in state power in a variety of contexts, see Bamford 1983, 2008; Higgs 1987, 2004, 2007, 2012; Cole and Dempsey 2006; Cole 2008; Cole and Lobel 2009; Herman 2011; Priest and Arkin 2011; Greenwald 2014; Risen 2014; Coyne and Hall 2018).

Elected officials—both in the executive branch and in Congress—face several realities limiting their ability to monitor and constrain the deep state. The first is sheer information overload due to the array of issues—both domestically and internationally—that these officials must understand in order to make policy.

There is simply no way to understand or monitor all of the activities of the complex security state. This leaves scope for those in the efficient institutions to control and influence those aspects of foreign policy not highly prioritized. Second, those in the efficient institutions can control the information available to elected officials, thereby affording them the opportunity to shape policy. Third, members of Congress are constrained by classified information that they cannot obtain. Even when this classified information is available to members of oversight committees, they typically cannot share it with nonmembers. This secrecy limits the effectiveness of nonmember representatives as a check on the security state. Fourth, the electorate tends to suffer from rational ignorance regarding foreign affairs and the complexities of the security state. The result is that people tend not to pressure their representatives to understand and check the activities of the national security state. This lack of voter oversight reinforces the ineffectiveness of monitoring by elected officials.

The judiciary is also limited as a check on the security state. As Edward Corwin (1947, 177) argues, during "war the Court necessarily loses some part of its normal freedom of decision and becomes assimilated, like the rest of society, to the mechanism of national defense." This alignment and integration of the courts with the other branches of government weakens the checks created by the separation of powers, leaving space for those in the deep state to exert a range of influence over security policy in an unchecked manner.

The abuse of surveillance powers by the U.S. government is but one example of the slack in constraints on the protective state, as illustrated by the six-volume Church Committee report released in the wake of the public revelation of the government's domestic surveillance activities in the 1970s. Among other things, the report indicated that the unchecked surveillance apparatus unleashed an unconstrained leviathan, as "virtually every element of our [U.S.] society has been subjected to excessive government-ordered intelligence inquiries" and that "this extreme breadth of intelligence activity is inconsistent with the principles of our Constitution which protect the rights of speech, political activity, and privacy against unjustified governmental intrusion" (Senate Select Committee 1976, 169). Despite the implementation of reforms—for example, the U.S. Foreign Intelligence Surveillance Court—to check the U.S. government, the revelations by Edward Snowden in 2013 regarding the activities of the U.S. surveillance state indicate the persistence, and expansion, of the status quo (Greenwald 2014). The Snowden revelations demonstrate not only the independence of the national security state, but also its tendency to perpetuate and grow.

The National Security Act of 1947, initially passed with the intention of empowering the government to protect the rights of private persons from the perceived global threat of the Soviet Union, facilitated these expansions and violations of domestic liberties. As this historical experience illustrates, changes made within constitutional constraints in the name of national security can have long-lasting anti-liberty effects by undermining the effectiveness of checks and balances over time. In the face of uncertainty, those who design and implement institutional reforms cannot fully anticipate the long-term effects of their decisions in the future; those effects may entail increased state power and concomitant reductions in liberty.

Centralization of State Power

Different levels of government can execute the functions of the protective state. For example, policing activities take place at a variety of different levels of government operation. The federal government, however, plays a central role in protective state activities, especially as they pertain to the large portfolio of activities falling under the broad category of national security. Moreover, activities at the national level often spill over and influence governments at lower levels. This has important implications because, in carrying out its protective activities, the national government can increase its power relative to lower levels of government and to citizens. This shift in relative power occurs because conducting national-level security and defense activities requires the federal government to increase its discretionary decision-making powers as well as its control over resources. Porter (1994, xv) captures the essence of this dynamic when he notes:

> A government at war is a juggernaut of centralization determined to crush any internal opposition that impedes the mobilization of militarily vital resources. This centralizing tendency of war has made the rise of the state throughout much of history a disaster for human liberty and rights.

The consolidation of control and power at the national level takes place through two main subchannels. The first is through bureaucratization, whereby existing federal government agencies gain more power and resources and, simultaneously, new bureaus emerge. Corwin (1947, 181) captures this logic when, discussing the effects of World War II on American society, he argues that "on the plea of war necessity we have assembled the most numerous bureaucracy since the Roman Empire, and now that the war is over, appear to be unable or unwilling to reduce it materially."

Second, national security and defense activities provide a focal point for rallying citizens around a common external cause. This common cause diverts citizens' attention to external matters and away from the paradox of government they face domestically. During a war, for example, citizens and the government unify in the common effort against an external threat. The result is twofold. First, national government activities that previously would have been intolerable become acceptable sacrifices necessary to achieve "the country's" foreign policy goals. Second, there is an increasing centralization of power in the hands of those in the national government relative to the subunits as the central government seeks to combat the external threat.

Among the main consequences of the centralization associated with the activities of the protective state is the erosion of federalist checks. Federalism divides power between a central political unit and subunits in order to disperse power and limit what any unit is able to do. By doing so, federalism serves as one potential solution to the paradox of government.

There is no assurance, however, of the pro-liberty benefits of federalism. As Richard Wagner (2014, 4) argues, "Whether federalism is favorable or hostile to liberty depends on whether the governments within the system must compete with one another for citizen support or whether those governments are able to collude with one another, and thus expand political power relative to citizen liberty" (see also Greve 2012). As the national government consolidates its power, the activities of the protective state shift the relative balance of power toward the center of political power, weakening the ability of subunits to serve as a check against potential abuses.

To provide an illustration of this phenomenon, consider Section 1208 of the National Defense Authorization Act of 1990, which authorized the Department of Defense to transfer military equipment to federal, state, and local agencies. In 1997, this initiative became the 1033 Program, which allowed the Department of Defense to transfer military equipment such as aircraft, armor, riot gear, surveillance equipment, watercraft, and weapons to state and local police. These programs have had two effects. First, they led to the militarization of police, whereby domestic police forces have increasingly adopted military equipment and tactics (see Hall and Coyne 2013; Balko 2013; Boettke, Lemke, and Palagashvili 2016; Coyne and Hall 2018). Second, these programs linked lower-level governments to the central government through resource flows, increasing their connection to, and dependence on, the political center. The result is the erosion of the separation of government units that is necessary to ensure the pro-liberty aspects of federalism.

Writing in 1816, Thomas Jefferson (1854, 543) asked, "What has destroyed liberty and the rights of man in every government which has ever existed under the sun?" His answer was that it was "generalizing and concentrating all cares and powers into one body, no matter whether of the autocrats of Russia or France, or of the aristocrats of a Venetian Senate." An appreciation for Jefferson's insight highlights a tension regarding the protective state. The activities of the protective state purportedly protect the rights and liberties of citizens. Carrying out these activities, however, often requires the national government to increase the scope and scale of its power. This expansion increases the discretionary power of the political center while eroding the checks and balances on that power offered by the subunits in the political periphery. When this shift occurs, the protective state expands as a threat to the very liberties it is supposed to safeguard.

Coercion-Enabling Human Capital

The operations of the protective state require certain skills or human capital. As discussed, the threat and use of force are the foundation of the activities of the protective state. In order to operate effectively, the protective state requires those it employs to possess coercion-enabling human capital (Coyne and Hall Blanco 2016). For example, members of the military must be willing to follow the directives of superiors in an unquestioning manner to adopt certain coercive techniques against those deemed threats by decision makers in government. In the case of the U.S. government, these coercive techniques have historically included some mix of occupation, monitoring and surveillance, segregation, bribery, censorship and suppression, policing and imprisonment, torture, and violence of varying kinds.

Those who enter the employment of the protective state and wish to succeed in this environment either will already possess the requisite human capital or will acquire it as part of the system (Coyne and Hall Blanco 2016, 243–47). Returning again to the case of the military as an illustration, Colonel James Donovan (1970, 33) notes, "It takes only a matter of months for each of the services to remold the average young American and turn him into a skilled, indoctrinated and motivated member of the armed forces." The coercion-enabling human capital required for success in the protective state can generate pro-liberty outcomes by protecting the rights and liberties of citizens. The same human capital, however, can have longer-term effects resulting in anti-liberty outcomes.

To understand why this is the case, consider that the coercion-enabling human capital required for success in the protective state becomes a fundamental part of the people involved. These people often reallocate their talents to other areas of life after leaving the operations of the protective state. In some cases, people move from the public sector to the private sector—for example, from the Department of Defense to a private defense contractor. In other instances, they move across the functions of the protective state—for example, from active military duty to the domestic police force. In still other cases, people move from the protective state to other areas of public life—for example, from the military to elected office.

In each of these, and other, cases, those involved take their specialized human capital with them, becoming key political decision makers, security analysts and consultants, executives at private defense firms, police officers, and so on. As this process unfolds, the skills necessary for success in the protective state—a comparative advantage in the use of force—bleed into civilian life, and the nature of domestic institutions and the relationship between the state and citizens change.

Godfrey Hodgson (1990, 384–85) captures these dynamics when discussing the effects of World War II on U.S. society:

> Government service in World War II—in the War Department or other civilian departments for the slightly older men, in the Office of Strategic Services or elite military units for the younger ones—gave a whole generation of ambitious and educated Americans a taste for power, as opposed to business success, and an orientation toward government service which they never lost. When they went back to their law offices or their classrooms, they took with them contacts, attitudes and beliefs they had learned in war services.

Similarly, Donovan (1970, 32) emphasizes, "The indoctrination with military codes and creeds experienced by millions of men and women [during World War II] who move in and out of the services has a continuing and prolonged and even regenerative effect upon the ideas, attitudes, and martial fiber of the nation as whole." He goes on to note, "The lives, the attitudes, and the beliefs of America's war veterans have been influenced by their military service; and because they represent such a large share of the adult male population their degree of militarism creates a strong imprint on the national character" (Donovan 1970, 37). Those involved in the protective state develop specific traits and skills that they carry with them throughout their lives and subsequent careers. As these passages suggest, the activities of the protective state can have anti-liberty effects on domestic political and social institutions by influencing the attitudes, beliefs, and skills of the people staffing and shaping those institutions.

One illustration of this channel is the U.S. surveillance state. The origins of the modern surveillance state can be traced back to the Philippine–American War (1899–1902) and its aftermath, when the U.S. government established a surveillance state to combat potential and actual insurgents. At the end of the war, those involved in operating the surveillance state abroad returned home, bringing their unique human capital for state-produced social control with them. These individuals worked to establish a similar apparatus domestically, which served as the foundation of today's surveillance state (see McCoy 2009; Coyne and Hall 2018).

In general, the operation of the human capital channel creates the possibility for the protective state to expand beyond its role as an external referee limited to protecting the rights of citizens. This occurs because of the accumulation of coercive-enabling human capital as well as the change in the perceived relationship between citizens and the state at home that often follows in the wake of crises (Higgs 1987). Thus, the scope of state activity expands over domestic life at the expense of the freedoms of private individuals.

Coercion-Enabling Physical Capital

In order to carry out its operations, the protective state requires coercion-enabling physical capital—for example, weapons, prisons, and surveillance technologies. Governments invest a significant amount of resources developing coercion-enabling physical capital. For example, in fiscal year 2014 the U.S. Department of Defense spent $63.1 billion on research and development and $100.7 billion on procurement (U.S. Department of Defense 2014). In principle, these investments in physical capital enable the members of the protective state to effectively project force in order to neutralize any threats to the liberties of citizens. At the same time, however, innovations in coercive-enabling physical capital threaten to contribute to anti-liberty outcomes.

Technological advances are one key factor behind the growth of government because improved technology lowers the cost of operating a larger government (Cowen 2009). For example, it is easier to collect taxes with electronic banking than it is to send a tax collector door to door to collect taxes in person. This same logic extends to the scale and scope of protective state activities. For example, advances in surveillance and weapon technologies for efficiently monitoring and killing threats allow the protective state to uphold the rights of citizens. These same technological advances, however, also enable the state to undermine the liberties of citizens in a more efficient manner. Technological advances in coercion-enabling physical capital enable governments not only to more efficiently project force over a greater geographic space, but also to more easily conceal their activities so that citizens are unable to recognize expansions in the scope of state power.

Consider, for example, the use of "Stingrays," or "cell site simulators." This technology enables the user to surreptitiously redirect cell phones into transmitting information, such as location and other identifiers. Originally developed for use by the military and intelligence communities, Stingrays have expanded in availability as part of the U.S. government's War on Terror. These devices are now in use within the United States by members of local law enforcement agents, who are able to surveil domestic people with little to no oversight (see Wessler 2014; ACLU 2015; Waddell 2015; Bates 2017). This example highlights how the physical capital of the protective state can turn inward to threaten the liberties of citizens. It also illustrates how technological advances enable the members of the protective state to conceal the true cost of their activities because citizens are unaware of the extent of the state's surveillance activities.

Ideally, constitutional rules would limit the protective state's use of coercion-enabling physical capital to only those activities that uphold the rights of citizens. For the three reasons discussed in previous subsections, however, rules may fail to be effective constraints. First, there is room for interpretation of laws regarding the appropriate scope of protective state activities. This includes the proper use of physical capital by members of the protective state.

Second, previous institutional changes within existing constitutional rules create significant space for the protective state to engage in unchecked activities in the name of protecting U.S. citizens. Technological advances allow the state to conduct a greater range of activities in a more efficient and covert manner, enabling it to take better advantage of a large unconstrained space.

Finally, there are synergies between the coercion-enabling human capital developed by those in the protective state and coercion-enabling physical capital. The unique human capital developed by those working in the protective state includes the skillful use of physical capital to make force more effective and efficient. Just as human capital can influence domestic life through changes in attitudes and beliefs regarding the relationship between the citizen and the state, so too can the coercion-enabling physical capital of the protective state.

CONCLUSION

As envisioned by James Buchanan, the ideal protective state performs a limited range of tasks to uphold the rights of the citizenry established at the constitutional stage. To the extent it does so, the protective state produces pro-liberty outcomes. There is no guarantee, however, that this will be the case. Through the channels discussed in this chapter, the activities of the protective state can also generate anti-liberty outcomes. These anti-liberty outcomes are endogenous to the activities of the protective state and do not require any assumption of insidious motivations on the part of the actors involved. Of course, introducing nefarious motivations into the analysis will only exacerbate the threat posed by the protective state to the liberties of citizens. An appreciation of the need for a constitutional political economy without romance opens the door to several areas for future research.

The first area deals with the robustness of the protective state, especially during times of crisis, when calls for urgent government action tend to be strongest (Higgs 1987). Given that the task of the protective state is to defend citizens from threats, this call for action appears logical. As F. A. Hayek (1981, 124) emphasizes, however, national emergencies "have always been the pretext on which the safeguards of individual liberty have been eroded." Recognizing this tension, Rossiter ([1948] 2002, 298–306) offers some potential solutions to limit the damage of a "constitutional dictatorship" invoked in times of crisis, including mechanisms of accountability, limiting abuses of citizens' rights, and a clear and permanent end to the expansion of state powers with provisions to ensure this outcome.

These types of suggestions, however, do not address the fundamental tension regarding the protective state as a threat to liberty. Even if the design and implementation of the mechanisms suggested by Rossiter are effective, they do not change the fact that expansions in state power, even when they retrench, have long-lasting effects on the very fabric of political, social, and economic institutions (Higgs 1987). As William Graham Sumner (1934, 473) warned, "It is not possible to experiment with a society and just drop the experiment whenever we choose." In carrying out its ordinary functions, the protective state influences domestic life in ways that can have permanent, anti-liberty effects. An open issue is whether and how the protective state can respond to crises without undermining the liberties it is supposed to protect.

A second area of further exploration is the role that ideology plays in constraining the scale and scope of protective state activities. As Buchanan (2005, 19) pointed out, when people are "afraid to be free," reliance on the state allows them to "escape, evade and even deny personal responsibilities." This observation suggests that people's beliefs about the relationship between the state and the individual can, in principle, limit the range of acceptable government activities. From this perspective, constraining the state would require people to possess skepticism of the awesome powers of the protective state and a fear of the possibility that those powers can produce anti-liberty outcomes. The specifics of this ideology, as well as its relationship to effective constraints on the protective state, remain a topic for further study.

Another area for future research is alternatives to the formal protective state for upholding the rights and liberties of citizens. An existing literature on the economics of anarchy explores the ability of individuals to identify mechanisms that facilitate cooperation through the protection of basic rights and liberties in the absence of the formal state (see Stringham 2005, 2007, 2015; Powell and Stringham 2009;

Leeson 2014). Exploring the conditions under which these mechanisms function, and their strengths and weaknesses relative to alternative institutional arrangements, including the formal state, in varying contexts requires additional study.

A final area for subsequent scholarship deals with the selection of rules during the process of constitutional formation. An appreciation of the channels discussed above might affect the rules chosen by those behind the veil of uncertainty. Given the uncertainty of future technologies and states of the world, and in light of the potential for the protective state to abuse its powers, what type of rules would people select behind the veil? Exploring the answer to this question deserves further attention.

Appreciating the potential anti-liberty outcomes of the protective state highlights a tension in James Buchanan's constitutional political economy project. The constitutional project envisioning a protective state as a basic element of a liberal political order often overlooks the capacity for that same protective state to erode, if not outright destroy, liberty. Determining potential resolutions to the various aspects of this tension, if any exist, remains a crucial issue in the broader constitutional research program.

NOTE

Earlier versions of this chapter were presented at the Department of Political Economy's Research Seminar at King's College London on February 15, 2017, and at the Free Market Institute at Texas Tech University on March 28, 2018. The author thanks participants for useful comments and feedback. He also thanks Bryan Cutsinger for useful comments and suggestions.

REFERENCES

ACLU (American Civil Liberties Union). 2015. "Stingray Tracking Devices: Who's Got Them?" American Civil Liberties Union. https://www.aclu.org/map/stingray-tracking-devices-whos-got-them.

Balko, Radley. 2013. *Rise of the Warrior Cop: The Militarization of America's Police Forces*. New York: Public Affairs.

Bamford, James. 1983. *The Puzzle Palace: A Report on America's Most Secret Agency*. New York: Penguin Books.

———. 2008. *The Shadow Factory: The Ultra-Secret NSA from 9/11 to the Eavesdropping of America*. New York: Anchor Books.

Bates, Adam. 2017. *Stingray: A New Frontier in Policy Analysis*. Washington, DC: Cato Institute.

Beard, Charles A. 1936. "The Living Constitution." *Annals of the American Academy of Political and Social Science* 185 (1): 29–34.

Boettke, Peter J., Jayme S. Lemke, and Liya Palagashvili. 2016. "Re-evaluating Community Policing in a Polycentric System." *Journal of Institutional Economics* 12 (3): 305–25.

Brennan, Geoffrey, and James M. Buchanan. (1985) 2000. *The Reason of Rules: Constitutional Political Economy*. Vol. 10 of *The Collected Works of James M. Buchanan.* Indianapolis, IN: Liberty Fund, Inc.

Buchanan, James M. (1975) 2000. *The Limits of Liberty: Between Anarchy and Leviathan*. Vol. 7 of *The Collected Works of James M. Buchanan*. Indianapolis, IN: Liberty Fund.

———. 1979. "Politics without Romance: A Sketch of Positive Public Choice Theory and Its Normative Implications." *IHS Journal, Zeitschrift des Instituts für Höhere Studien* 3: B1–B11.

———. 2005. "Afraid to Be Free: Dependency as Desideratum." *Public Choice* 124 (1): 19–31.

Cole, David. 2008. "No Reason to Believe: Radical Skepticism, Emergency Power, and Constitutional Constraint." *University of Chicago Law Review* 75 (3): 1329–64.

Cole, David, and James X. Dempsey. 2006. *Terrorism and the Constitution: Sacrificing Civil Liberties in the Name of National Security*. New York: The New Press.

Cole, David, and Jules Lobel. 2009. *Less Safe, Less Free: Why America Is Losing the War on Terror*. New York: The New Press.

Congleton, Roger D. 2005. "The Political Economy of Crisis Management: Surprise, Urgency, and Mistakes in Political Decision Making." *Advances in Austrian Economics* 8: 183–204.

Corwin, Edward S. 1947. *Total War and the Constitution*. New York: Alfred Knopf.

Cowen, Tyler. 2009. "Does Technology Drive the Growth of Government?," George Mason University, Fairfax, VA, June 22.

Coyne, Christopher J. 2008. *After War: The Political Economy of Exporting Democracy*. Stanford, CA: Stanford University Press.

———. 2011. "Constitutions and Crisis." *Journal of Economic Behavior and Organization* 80 (2): 351–57.

———. 2013. *Doing Bad by Doing Good: Why Humanitarian Action Fails*. Stanford, CA: Stanford University Press.

Coyne, Christopher J., and Abigail R. Hall Blanco. 2016. "Empire State of Mind: The Illiberal Foundations of Liberal Hegemony." *Independent Review: A Journal of Political Economy* 21 (2): 237–50.

Coyne, Christopher J., and Abigail R. Hall. 2018. *Tyranny Comes Home: The Domestic Fate of U.S. Militarism*. Stanford, CA: Stanford University Press.

Devins, Caryn, Roger Koppl, Stuart Kauffman, and Teppo Felin. 2015. "Against Design." *Arizona State Law Journal* 47 (3): 609–81.

Donovan, James A. 1970. *Militarism, U.S.A.* New York: Charles Scribner's Sons.

Dorsen, Norman. 1989. "Foreign Affairs and Civil Liberties." *American Journal of International Law* 83 (4): 840–50.

Douglas, William O. 1987. *The Douglas Letters: Selections from the Private Papers of Justice William O. Douglas*. Edited by Melvin I. Urofsky. Bethesda, MD: Adler & Adler.

Fraenkel, Osmond K. 1946. "War, Civil Liberties, and the Supreme Court." *Yale Law Journal* 55 (4): 715–34.

Glennon, Michael J. 2015. *National Security and Double Government*. New York: Oxford University Press.

Gordon, Scott. 2002. *Controlling the State: Constitutionalism from Ancient Athens to Today*. Cambridge, MA: Harvard University Press.

Greenwald, Glenn. 2014. *No Place to Hide: Edward Snowden, the NSA, and the U.S. Surveillance State*. New York: Metropolitan Books.

Greve, Michael S. 2012. *The Upside-Down Constitution*. Cambridge, MA: Harvard University Press.

Hall, Abigail R., and Christopher J. Coyne. 2013. "The Militarization of U.S. Domestic Policing." *Independent Review: A Journal of Political Economy* 7 (4): 485–504.

Hayek, F. A. 1981. *Law, Legislation, and Liberty, Volume 3: The Political Order of a Free People*. Chicago: University of Chicago Press.

Herman, Susan N. 2011. *Taking Liberties: The War on Terror and the Erosion of American Democracy*. New York: Oxford University Press.

Higgs, Robert. 1987. *Crisis and Leviathan: Critical Episodes in the Growth of American Government*. New York: Oxford University Press.

———. 2004. *Against Leviathan: Government Power and a Free Society*. Oakland, CA: Independent Institute.

———. 2007. *Neither Liberty nor Safety: Fear, Ideology, and the Growth of Government*. Oakland, CA: Independent Institute.

———. 2012. *Delusions of Power: New Explorations of State, War, and Economy*. Oakland, CA: Independent Institute.

———. 2015. *Taking a Stand: Reflections on Life, Liberty, and the Economy*. Oakland, CA: Independent Institute.

Hodgson, Godfrey. 1990. *The Colonel: The Life and Wars of Henry Stimson, 1867–1950*. New York: Alfred A. Knopf.

Hogan, Michael J. 1998. *A Cross of Iron: Harry S. Truman and the National Security State, 1945–1954*. New York: Cambridge University Press.

Ikeda, Sanford. 1997. *Dynamics of the Mixed Economy: Toward a Theory of Interventionism*. New York: Routledge.

Jablonsky, David. 2002/03. "The State of the National Security State." *Parameters* 43 (4): 4–20.

Jefferson, Thomas. 1854. *The Writings of Thomas Jefferson.* Vol. 6, edited by H. A. Washington. Washington, DC: Taylor and Maury.

Jervis, Robert. 1997. *System Effects: Complexity in Political and Social Life*. Princeton, NJ: Princeton University Press.

Leeson, Peter T. 2014. *Anarchy and the Law: Why Self-Governance Works Better Than You Think*. Cambridge, MA: Cambridge University Press.

Linfield, Michael. 1990. *Freedom Under Fire: U.S. Civil Liberties in Times of War*. Boston: South End Press.

Madison, James. (1795) 1865. "Political Observations, April 20, 1795." In *Letters and Other Writings of James Madison*, vol. 4, 485–505. Philadelphia: J.B. Lippincott & Co.

McCoy, Alfred W. 2009. *Policing America's Empire: The United States, the Philippines, and the Rise of the Surveillance State*. Madison: The University of Wisconsin Press.

Mises, Ludwig von. (1929) 1977. *A Critique of Interventionism*. New Rochelle, NY: Arlington House.

Murphy, Frank. 1943. Concurring opinion, Kiyoshi Hirabayashi v. United States, 320 U.S. 81, 113.

Porter, Bruce D. 1994. *War and the Rise of the State: The Military Foundations of Modern Politics*. New York: The Free Press.

Powell, Benjamin, and Edward P. Stringham. 2009. "Public Choice and the Economic Analysis of Anarchy: A Survey." *Public Choice* 140 (3): 503–38.

Priest, Dana, and William M. Arkin. 2011. *Top Secret America: The Rise of the New American Security State*. New York: Little, Brown, and Company.

Rehnquist, William H. 1998. *All the Laws but One: Civil Liberties in Wartime*. New York: Vintage Books.

Risen, James. 2014. *Pay Any Price: Greed, Power, and Endless War*. New York: Houghton Mifflin Harcourt Publishing Company.

Rossiter, Clinton. (1948) 2002. *Constitutional Dictatorship: Crisis Government in the Modern Democracies*. Piscataway, NJ: Transaction Publishers.

Senate Select Committee to Study Governmental Operations with Respect to Intelligence Activities. 1976. *Intelligence Activities and the Rights of Americans, Book II*. Washington, DC: U.S. Government Printing Office.

Stringham, Edward Peter, ed. 2005. *Anarchy, State and Public Choice*. Northampton, MA: Edward Elgar Publishing, Ltd.

———. 2007. *Anarchy and the Law: The Political Economy of Choice*. Oakland, CA: Independent Institute.

Stringham, Edward Peter. 2015. *Private Governance: Creating Order in Economic and Social Life*. New York: Oxford University Press.

Stuart, Douglas T. 2008. *Creating the National Security State: A History of the Law That Transformed America*. Princeton, NJ: Princeton University Press.

Sumner, William Graham. 1934. *Essays of William Graham Sumner*. Edited by Albert G. Keller and Maurice R. Davie. New Haven, CT: Yale University Press.

Tocqueville, Alexis de. 1840. *Democracy in America. Part the Second, The Social Influence of Democracy*, translated by Henry Reeve. New York: J. & H. G. Langley.

U.S. Department of Defense. 2014. "U.S. Department of Defense: Fiscal Year 2015 Budget Request." Under Secretary of Defense (Comptroller) web page, http://comptroller.defense.gov/budget.aspx.

Waddell, Kaveh. 2015. "Who Is Spying on US Cellphones? Lawmakers Demand an Answer." *Defense One*, November 9.

Wagner, Richard E. 2014. *American Federalism: How Well Does It Support Liberty?* Arlington, VA: Mercatus Center.

Weingast, Barry. 1995. "The Economic Role of Political Institutions: Market-Preserving Federalism and Economic Development." *Journal of Law, Economics, and Organization* 11 (1): 1–31.

Wessler, Nathan Fred. 2014. "Trickle Down Surveillance." Al Jazeera America, June 12.

CHAPTER EIGHT

LIMITS ON THE APPLICATION OF MOTIVATIONAL HOMOGENEITY IN THE WORK OF BUCHANAN AND THE VIRGINIA SCHOOL

DAVID M. LEVY AND SANDRA J. PEART

At its founding, the set of ideas that came to be known as Virginia Political Economy originated from the work of Rutledge Vining, James Buchanan, Warren Nutter, Ronald Coase, and Gordon Tullock. In terms of scholarly stature, that short list comprises two Nobel Prize winners (Buchanan and Coase) and a recipient of the American Economic Association Distinguished Fellow award (Tullock). It also includes an economist (Nutter) who, in the midst of the Cold War, described the Soviet economy more accurately than any of the major experts in the field. Virginia Political Economy was characterized by four foundational principles: the endogeneity of group goals, egalitarianism, reciprocity, and trade. By offering an overarching vision of the principles of the Virginia School, we distinguish between tensions that are difficult to reconcile and gaps that are easily addressed.

The four foundational ideas of the Virginia School are interdependent. If the group decides social goals, the question that follows is "By whom in the group?" For a democracy, the Virginia School answer is "By everyone." Thus, the School adheres to a weak form of egalitarianism—what we have called analytical egalitarianism. The next question asks what sort of interaction might characterize decisions related to the group goals. The Virginia School answer is reciprocity. The final question is "Supposing there is disagreement within the group about the several goals of the group, what principle is used to make decisions?" In the main, the Virginia School's answer relies on trade.

The tension that emerged early on within the School, and that continued to characterize Buchanan's thought through the early years of the 21st century, relates to his supposition that everyone is motivationally approximately the same. Another question that arises with this supposition is how far to extend it. Buchanan and the Virginia School economists were eager to push the assumption that decision makers—be they consumers, producers, or policymakers—are roughly the same in terms of private and public motivations. Buchanan, however, was unwilling to suppose that economists, too, were characterized by the same bundle of private and public motivations as everyone else. We shall focus here on this key tension within the School: the question of how far to extend analytical egalitarianism. Without an overview of the connecting principles of the School, one might well think separating the motivations of economists from those of everyone else is a gap that is easy to correct. But that was not Buchanan's attitude.

At least since the 18th century, all major economists have been important reformers, so it comes as no surprise that Buchanan also gave the economist a major role to play in social reform. Buchanan abhorred the idea that no improvements could be found in the world. He insisted by contrast on the potential for significant improvements, and he staked a claim for economists in the potential achievement of such improvements. When he introduced economists into the circle of exchange, he supposed along Popperian lines that economists are truth-seekers. Because truth is a public good, an obvious tension arises if economists, like everyone else, are also motivated to seek the private good of happiness. Karl Popper recognized this tension: his correspondence with Tullock explicitly acknowledged that not all scientists are Popperian truth-seekers (Levy and Peart 2017b).

RUTLEDGE VINING AT THE BEGINNING

In terms of vision and organization, the Virginia School starts from foundations laid by Rutledge Vining. He helped select the two founders of the Thomas Jefferson Center (TJC) at the University of Virginia. His vision of a "free society," which would come into question with TJC's application to the Ford Foundation, supposed the endogeneity of group goals. His decade-spanning disagreement with Tjalling Koopmans focused on the importance of that endogeneity. Vining's defense of National Bureau of Economic Research (NBER) procedures in 1949 focused on what he took to be Koopmans' presuppositions and denied that one could infer group goals by aggregating individual goals.[1]

Two of Vining's 1955/1956 activities are worthy of attention. First, he published a pamphlet for the United Nations Educational, Scientific and Cultural Organization (UNESCO) in which he laid out the differences between classical economics instantiated in the tradition continued by Frank Knight and more recent work of Koopmans and his associates.[2] Unlike the situation in 1949, Vining could point to an exemplar of a Koopmans-type model.[3] Second, Vining wrote to Milton Friedman for assistance with a delicate staffing issue (see letter 1).

A Free Society

Vining begins the 1956 essay by presupposing a world of free agents:[4]

> In brief, to economize is to choose, and the possibility of a choice implies the existence of alternatives. Hence, by economic problem we shall always refer to a problem of choice among alternatives, and the burden of the discussion of a particular economic problem will be the description of alternatives and the designation or discovery of an acceptable criterion by which a selection is made. Three types of choice problems readily come to mind. First, if there is a given end to be attained and if there are alternative means of attaining the end, there is a problem of choosing a particular means. This type includes only conditional problems, the choice being conditioned by a well-defined end. Decisions made by the management of a business firm are examples of choices of this type. Second, each individual as a *free agent* chooses his own ends. A consumer will have made a choice of this type when he decides upon the allocation of his budget. Third, the individuals constituting a group or *society of free agents* jointly choose the constraints and regulations which they impose upon their individual actions. The decisions made by a legislative body in the drafting of legislative acts are examples of choices of this third type.
>
> . . . Economic analysis of the conventional sort, however, does not directly deal with problems of this first type, but is rather concerned primarily with problems of the third type, which are social problems in that social conflict and the seeking for consensus are essential elements. In recent times the discussion of this third type of problem has had to do with the farm problem, the labour problem, the employment problem, the problem of trade restrictions,

> and the like. To name them is to realize that these are problems inherent in the idea of a social organization of free individuals. The touchstone, it is said, of any legislative constraint upon individual action that may be imposed lies in the question whether a rational people could have imposed such a law on itself. Social discussion is always a discussion of this question. It was the question at the base of Adam Smith's and David Ricardo's discussions and analyses, no different in any respect from the essential question involved in any contemporary issue of public policy. In this sense, the third type is the classical economic problem. (Vining 1956, 9)

Vining addresses the meaning of "free agent" next. He provides a Kantian explanation:

> Hence, when we think of a free and rational individual we do not envisage an individual unconstrained by law but rather an individual who acts in accordance with rules of conduct which he has chosen. The statement that a free man enacts his own laws expresses only the principle that he chooses no rule of action which he would not accept as universal law to be acted upon by all individuals. (Vining 1956, 19)

In a footnote to this comment, Vining adds this:

> The discussion of this section will be recognized as a paraphrase of Kant's analysis of the concept of freedom as presented in his *Groundwork of the Metaphysics of Morals*. A remark may be added here regarding political procedure. How does an individual see to it that the laws which he recognizes as binding upon his actions are of his own choosing? Is a majority vote to be interpreted as an expression of "consensus"? The answer to this latter question is clearly no. The majority rule is no more than a device constituting a part of a political procedure which is accepted by the individual. There is no implication that he accepts as right and just a particular law which results from a particular application of this device.[5]

Asking Milton Friedman

Judging by the material at the Hoover Institution archives,[6] the correspondence between Vining and Milton Friedman began with Vining's response to Koopmans' attack on the NBER procedures. The early correspondence begins with letters addressed to Professor Friedman and Professor Vining. By 1955, the correspondents use the more familiar salutations, Milton and Rutledge. The first letter reproduced here contains Vining's request for Friedman's judgment of Nutter and Buchanan as potential staff members. Friedman offers an opinion in the second letter. Vining then thanks Friedman and tells him that he has incorporated Friedman's comments from another letter—which does not appear to be in the Hoover archives—into the UNESCO essay.

LETTER 1: FROM VINING TO FRIEDMAN

University of Virginia
James Wilson Department of Economics
University Station
Charlottesville, Virginia

Wednesday

Dear Milton:

We have an appointment or so to make to our staff, and there are two names now before us—Warren Nutter and James Buchanan. We of course don't know that we could get either of them. Also, from what of knows [sic] of each of them, I would like to have both of them on our staff. But I don't know a great deal about them, and it may be that we can only make a strong bid for one of them. I wonder if you would mind confidentially expressing your judgment regarding the relative merits of these two men. We have had a long letter from your Professor Hamilton which did not include much about Nutter but which was an extraordinarily strong recommendation for Buchanan.

Incidentally, I think our staff would like to think of our next appointment becoming within the next couple of years the chairman of the department so that we would like to have a person with the kind of imagination and ability which goes with such a post.

Sincerely yours,

Rutledge

[Letter reprinted by permission of David Vining.]

LETTER 2: FROM FRIEDMAN TO VINING

10 December 1955

Mr. Rutledge Vining
Department of Economics
University of Virginia
Charlottesville, Virginia

Dear Rutledge:

You ask a very hard question in your letter because both Warren Nutter and James Buchanan are both exceedingly able people and either would be an ornament to your faculty. I am in perhaps a position the reverse of Earl Hamilton in that I know Nutter rather better than Buchanan.

As between the two I would say that Nutter has a better judgement and greater command of empirical materials, whereas Buchanan has perhaps somewhat more interest in the purely analytical. Nutter is, I suspect, the broader in his interests. Both have an absolutely first rate command of economic analysis. I know Nutter's work well enough to know that he has an unusual capacity to apply his economic analysis to particular systematic problems. I do not know Buchanan's work well enough to judge this aspect of it.

On the suitability of the two men for the chairmanship of the department, I have no basis for any opinion about Buchanan. I have great confidence that Nutter would be extraordinarily good. As you know he occupied a fairly high administrative post at the Central Intelligence Agency and I know from quite a number of reports that they thought very highly indeed of him and were anxious to have him stay on in an even more exalted position. He is a person of equitable temperament who gets along very well with others; has good judgement about people; and would apply to the affairs of the department standards of value corresponding with your own.

I am sure you know enough about the different fields of interest of the two men so that there is no point in my commenting much about that. Both men could easily handle work in economic theory. Beyond that; Nutter's special competence and background is largely in the field of industrial organization, Buchanan in public finance.

I hope these comments will be helpful to you. My congratulations on having so good a pair between whom to choose.

Perhaps I shall see you at the meetings. Best regards.

Sincerely yours,
Milton Friedman

MF: pan

[Letter reprinted by permission of Gordon Tullock, David Friedman, and Jan Martel.]

LETTER 3: FROM VINING TO FRIEDMAN

University of Virginia
James Wilson Department of Economics
University Station
Charlottesville, Virginia

Wednesday, Dec. 21

Dear Milton,

Thank you very much for your letter about Nutter and Buchanan. The department wants them, and I hope very much that we can get them to join our staff.

I am sending today to the J. P. E. [*Journal of Political Economy*] a review of Lösch's The Economics of Location. The review is much overdue, and it is also too long—about 8 typed pages. My review is not favorable, but I thought perhaps that the reputation of the book might possibly justify a longer review than is ordinarily the case.

You may recall that several months ago you were good enough to read for me a first Part of an extended review of economic research and discussion in this country that I was doing for Unesco. I completed the other two parts and submitted it. Stigler and Mikesell have read the entire piece for me and have had kind things to say about it. I want to rewrite what I have done into chapters and then to add several chapters more in order to complete a book. In general, I am discussing the nature of an economic problem and of a solution of an economic problem; and I wish to demonstrate in detail how the discussion of a problem of political economy generates the development of theoretical economics. I have pestered you so much with requests to look at what I am doing that I hesitate to ask you again. But if you could find any interest in the sort of thing that I am doing, I could find a great deal more profit from what you might say about it.

I wish you and your family a merry Christmas. Give my friends there my best regards. And thanks again for your letter.

Sincerely,

Rutledge

[Letter reprinted by permission of David Vining.]

THE QUESTION OF IDEOLOGY

The question of ideology arose early in the existence of the TJC. In 1960 the principals of the center sent a grant proposal to the Ford Foundation to support a decade of work. The proposal began:

> The Thomas Jefferson Center for Studies in Political Economy was founded in 1957 as an intellectual center to promote enquiry into the problems of preserving and improving a *free society*. (Levy and Peart 2014a; emphasis added)

The emphasized words were interpreted by officials of the Ford Foundation as a commitment to what might today be labeled neoliberalism, and the grant was rejected—even though Buchanan and Coase objected strenuously that there was no such commitment.[7] Vining's UNESCO essay in which he gives the "free society" a Kantian interpretation was evidently not known to the authorities of the Ford Foundation.

The Ford Foundation's characterization of the center in its rejection of the grant application seems to have cascaded. At one of the critical moments for the fate of Virginia Political Economy, a 1963 "Self-Study" Committee of the University of Virginia characterized the "Virginia School" ideologically with the neoliberal label.[8] Yet, as we have argued elsewhere, an ideological reading of the Virginia School provides little guidance to debates within the School and throughout the economics profession at the time (Levy and Peart 2011, 2017a). For example, Nutter and W. W. Rostow mostly agreed in their analyses of Soviet growth; indeed, Nutter's work for the NBER was central to the empirical case that Rostow (1960) made in his *Stages of Economic Growth*. Focusing on Rostow's service for both the Kennedy and Johnson administrations, in contrast to Nutter's work for President Nixon, obscures that analytical commonality. Ideology there is, but it was not a foundational characteristic of the center.

As noted, one aspect of the Virginia School that *is* foundational, and given pride of place by Vining, is the endogeneity of group goals. If group goals are endogenously determined—a view to which Buchanan, Nutter, and Coase all subscribed—then it follows that different groups, and different democratic societies, may very well be characterized by different mixes of government and private provision of services. This is dramatically evident in Coase's work on broadcasting in the United Kingdom and the United States (Levy and Peart 2014b).

Goal endogeneity speaks to analytical egalitarianism (Peart and Levy 2005, 2008), the presumption that all are equally capable of making political and economic choices. In an analytically egalitarian framework, the modeler does not specify the ends for the group; those are matters for the group to determine. The endogeneity of group goals also speaks to the question of democratic procedure. A central aspect of Buchanan and Tullock's work, one that supports an ideological characterization of privileging markets over politics, is their denial of foundational status for majority rule politics. (Vining's work, of course, foreshadowed this, as previously noted.) The letter from John Rawls to Buchanan and Tullock (reproduced as letter 4) provides a helpful guide to this distinction.[9]

Buchanan and Tullock ([1962] 1999) famously argued in *The Calculus of Consent* that majority rule is one of many plausible rules for ordinary politics but is entirely implausible as a constitutional principle. Rawls supports that argument: "I agree that majority-rule is just a *rule* to be adopted on rational grounds like any other, given experience with it. Majority rule as a principle of justice I agree is absent" (see letter 4). Rawls centers his argument on the principle of reciprocity. He writes: "On my view the principles of justice put constraints in the constitution, & on all political majorities; and majority rule is rational only where it can be supposed that majorities will limit themselves by the principles of justice" (letter 4).

ANALYTICAL EGALITARIANISM

In *A Theory of Justice*, Rawls (1971) expanded on his worry about initial equality in the Buchanan and Tullock formulation. At issue was what constitutes initial equality. If analytical egalitarianism prevails and everyone initially possesses much the same capability for political and economic decision-making, then differences among people are endogenous. The issue that separated Buchanan and Rawls was whether that form of analytical egalitarianism was sufficient for political philosophy.[10] We return to Buchanan's analytical egalitarianism when we discuss a tension in his work.

As he concludes, Rawls recognizes that Tullock was likely correct to worry that the main objections to *Calculus* would be philosophical. All in all, the letter illustrates that the doctrine of majority rule was not foundational in the research community of Buchanan, Tullock, and Rawls. Instead, Rawls, as well as Buchanan and Tullock, supported the idea of a rule conditioned upon a form of egalitarianism, which as Rawls notes still needed to be worked out, as well as the principle of reciprocity.

A stronger form of analytical egalitarianism than that of goal endogeneity plus universal participation, described earlier in the section, denies any difference between the motivations of the modeler and the agents being modeled. Such a formulation would extend Buchanan and Tullock's key insight: those who govern

LETTER 4: FROM RAWLS TO BUCHANAN AND TULLOCK

Dear Profs. Buchanan & Tullock

Enclosed is a copy of the paper on liberty which I mentioned in my letter to you. It was given on Dec 28, 1961 at the meeting of the American Association for Political and Legal Philosophy in Chicago. It will appear in *Nomos,* the periodical of the association, but as in the past it has been notoriously slow coming out[.] I don't know when it will see the light of day. Not certainly for a good while yet. I'm going to try to get in a footnote with a reference to your book.

The paper represents, in somewhat abbreviated form[,] roughly the first half of a chapter on Liberty in a short book which I have been trying to write on justice, but which I never seem able to finish. All parts exist in a handwritten version (several of them by now), but they don't fit together as a whole.

In the second part of the Chapter on Liberty I discuss majority rule and adopt a view in many ways similar to yours, but not I think in all respects. In any case, I agree that majority rule is just a *rule* to be adopted on rational grounds like any other, given experience with it. Majority rule as a principle of justice I agree is absent. On my view the principles of justice put constraints in the constitution, & on all political majorities; and majority rule is rational only where it can be supposed that majorities will limit themselves by the principles of justice, and where reasonable differences of opinion may exist and where the disadvantages & injustice of other rules might be worse. If I ever decide to get this part typed up & it doesn't strike me as too bad, I'll send a copy to you, if you wish.

Thanks for your letters.

Yours sincerely

John Rawls

P.S. Secs 2–3, pp. 3–13 (of the paper included) state the ideas (in even briefer form) of the paper on justice—nothing is lost by skipping them.

P.S.S. I want to read your book again & see if I have any decent objections worth making. I suspect there may be a problem about initial equality & the preservation of it, etc[.], but I'll have to think about it.

I hope the enclosed is of some value in a supplementary in your work. I suspect Tullock is right in thinking the main objections to your book may be philosophical; so perhaps it may be relevant.

[Letter reprinted by permission of the estate of John Rawls.]

are neither more nor less public spirited than those who are governed, those who model or advise, and, in particular, those who are economists. A key question for the early TJC economists, and a consequent tension in their work, was whether they were willing to extend their stated principle of homogeneity of motivations to economists.

Although the principle of analytical egalitarianism never fully characterized the TJC's founding documents, key participants in the TJC occasionally endorsed the foundational equality of persons. One such occasion occurred when Coase presented a paper at the American Economic Association (AEA) in 1974 on the markets for ideas and goods. Coase made the provocative point that, regardless of one's views on regulation, the two markets are symmetrical. That is to say, if one supports a good deal of regulation in one market, then one should consider supporting the same degree of regulation in the other. A reporter for *Time* magazine attended, and Coase's argument received a surprising amount of attention.

At the time, Coase was at the University of Chicago Law School and Tullock was in Blacksburg at the Public Choice Center. Tullock wrote to Coase, teasing him that any economist attacked by both the *New York Times* and the *Blacksburg Sun* must be deeply misunderstood. Coase's response (letter 5) focused directly on the sort of egalitarianism that characterizes the Virginia School.

Tullock's response will not surprise anyone who knew him. He offered to make a list of superior people for Coase. The first two entries were easy, but after that it would be hard going.

Ultimately, the reason we consider ideology as nonfoundational is that the Virginia School economists occasionally relied on dimensions other than the size of government. Rawls' agreement with Buchanan and Tullock and Ayn Rand's disagreement with Coase demonstrate the significance of these other dimensions.

RECIPROCITY

As noted, Vining's statement of free agency relied on Kant's universalization principle. Like Knight before him, Vining supposed free agency to be self-enforcing. The immediate question is whether Tullock's work also relies on reciprocity. Tullock's *Organization of Inquiry* ([1966] 2005) connects reciprocity and his well-known idea of predation via well-founded institutions. He distinguished between real science—in which reported results are replicated—and the "racket" of economics—in which reported results are not replicated (Levy and Peart 2012, 2017a). In his view, replication in economics is testing by others with distinct preferences and presuppositions.

LETTER 5: FROM COASE TO TULLOCK

The Journal of Law & Economics
THE UNIVERSITY OF CHICAGO LAW SCHOOL
1111 EAST 60TH STREET
CHICAGO • ILLINOIS 60637

R. H. Coase *Editor*

October 9, 1974

Professor Gordon Tullock
Virginia Polytechnic Institute
Center for Study of Public Choice
Blacksburg, Virginia 24061

Dear Gordon:

Thank you for attempting to put the *Blacksburg Sun* straight.

I doubt whether you will succeed. Although it is easy for people to perceive the advantages of freedom when it is proposed to regulate their own activities, the argument for freedom seems to be less persuasive when it is thought to apply to others.

I have been attacked on all sides as a result of my paper.

I suppose it would not have been noticed had not a reporter from *Time* been present at the AEA [American Economic Association] meetings. The most savage attack has, however, come from the Right. Ayn Rand has devoted two issues of her Newsletter to an attack on my paper. She chooses to assume that I want the government to start regulating the press (really I suppose one should say, to regulate the press more than it does already). She finds the economists' usual arguments for government intervention to be so powerful if applied to the market for ideas that it surely must have been my intention to support government intervention in the market for ideas. But underneath it all she seems to hold the view that philosophers and writers are superior people who should not be treated as others are.

Best wishes

Ronald

Yours ever,

RHC: j

[Letter reprinted by permission of Ning Wang.]

Interesting differences exist here among the Virginia School economists, differences that reveal variations in their willingness to push the motivational homogeneity principle to new domains. At stake was the question of whether economists might take advantage of gaps in institutions to pursue their private interests. Tullock's answer is a variation on the theme, "Wouldn't anyone?" Buchanan's (and Vining's and Knight's) answer is usually different. Here, as noted previously, it becomes evident that some members of the Virginia School were willing to advance analytical egalitarianism further than others. Buchanan was unwilling to recognize that economists, like politicians, are motivated by private as well as public goals. The same tension between what Popper's model supposes and what Popper himself knew about the world thus exists in Buchanan.

GOAL ENDOGENEITY: THREE CASES

Perhaps goal endogeneity is the most distinctive principle of the Virginia School. Certainly, this principle separates the Virginia School from the 20th-century Austrian School and the late-20th-century Chicago School. Knight expressed the principle most pungently in the slogan he attributed to Lord Bryce, that democracy is government by discussion. That might be where the foundational idea began but is certainly not where it ends, as the goal of endogeneity was applied to the great nondemocracy of the 20th century, the Soviet Union.

Discussion

Buchanan responded to what became known as Arrow's ([1951] 1963) Impossibility Theorem in the first wave of responses with his 1954 *Journal of Political Economy* article. As is well known, Arrow had argued that, without restrictions strong enough to violate plausibility, a polity with a democratic decision-making process—even when its members possess coherent desires—will be incoherent and will cycle through policy alternatives without convergence. To make light of a technical issue, Buchanan's 1954 response was akin to "You say that as if there was something wrong with it."

It took more than 40 years for the profession at large to catch Buchanan's point. Amartya Sen's 1995 presidential address for the AEA was the breakthrough. In it, Sen recognized that Arrow had constructed a polity without a mechanism by which consensus might emerge. Arrow assumed that individuals possessed goals that were independent of the decision-making process. That assumption ruled out a Knightian process of democratic deliberation. Buchanan's opposition to the assumption of fixed preferences, a continuing theme in his work, reflects his concern for the endogeneity of goals via discussion. Many of those influenced by Buchanan have, unsurprisingly, been instrumental in bringing language back into economics. Elinor Ostrom's work has been critical here, and experimental economists have further established that, when participants in an experiment communicate, the resulting equilibrium changes (Peart and Levy 2015).

Soviet Growth

Professionally, the most controversial aspect of the Virginia School was Nutter's study of Soviet growth (see, for example, Nutter 1962). His results differed dramatically from the mainstream view that the Soviet economy would shortly overtake the American. Nutter's analysis found no signs of a systematic catching-up. Two easy explanations for the divergent results were Nutter's ideology and his inability to read Russian. After the Soviet Union collapsed, scholars looking back on the episode were quick to suggest that those who were overly favorable to the Soviets were biased by ideology. Paul Samuelson's (1948) textbook was singled out for having confused ideology and analysis (Skousen 1997).

Ideology, however, fails to explain the positions laid out in the textbooks: some authors to the left of Samuelson did not overstate Soviet growth rates, whereas others to the right of Samuelson did. What Samuelson pioneered in his textbook was the use of the production possibility frontier in modeling economies and the idea of efficiency in terms of the frontier. But the supposition that a society was on the frontier was the supposition that no resources were expended for other goals. Supposing the goods of the frontier to be public goals, there nonetheless also exist private goals, the goals of those who run the machinery of government. In Tullock's formulation, those private goals are rents. Samuelson's textbook, and those whose treatment was similar, assumed that no resources were expended for rent-seeking.

We pause to notice the difference between the Virginia School analysis of the Soviet economy with the earlier analysis by Ludwig von Mises and F. A. Hayek. Hayek, uniquely responsible for the Mont Pelerin Society, modestly claimed that Mises and Knight were the society's ideological centers, so they are certainly from the same ideological camp as the founders of the Virginia School (Levy and Peart 2008). Both Mises and Hayek assumed away the problem of rent-seeking. In retrospect, Mises and Hayek were simply doing what Samuelson and other orthodox economists did—assuming that group goals were exogenous and that the norm of reciprocity is self-enforcing. Here again, ideology is not helpful for explanatory purposes; orthodox economic scholars of all ideologies were comfortable with the supposition that group goals are exogenous.

Stigler's Coase Theorem and Coase's Coase Theorem

In the third edition of *The Theory of Price*, George Stigler (1966, 110–14) gave a dramatic presentation of the argument in Coase's (1960) "The Problem of Social Cost." Stigler, along with all his colleagues at Chicago, was initially skeptical about Coase's argument that a divergence between private and social costs motivated some external correction to the terms of trade. The reader could not have known that this skepticism was overcome at an after-dinner discussion at Aaron Director's home. In his autobiography, Stigler ([1988] 2003) remembered how Coase laid out the argument: Imagine a world without transaction costs. Then consider a typical problem of the Pigovian divergence—a railroad generating sparks that start a fire on a wheat field near the tracks. It is important that separate individuals own the railroad and the farm because otherwise the "externalities" would be "internalized."

In a world with zero transaction costs, the fact that different people own the railroad and the wheat farm would be irrelevant to the final outcome. Negotiations—assumed at zero cost—would produce the solution that was an overall maximum output of net costs. The solution might well be that the wheat would not be grown so close to the tracks. And, critically, for the question of output, it would not matter on whom the liability was placed. Liability rules would of course influence who paid but not what was produced.

Coase (1992) protested—in his Nobel prize lecture!—that Stigler had assumed away what interested him, the actual impact of liability rules. Suppose, he argued, that negotiation was prohibitively expensive at the other extreme of transaction costs. If the farmer were liable for the damage, then the profit-maximizing solution might well be to remove some wheat production. But what if the railroad were liable? Perhaps the railroad would run less frequently, perhaps not at all in dry seasons. Obviously, liability assignment matters to output.

This is another instance in which group goals are endogenous for the Virginia School. Thinking in terms of commodities, the question was whether the group wants more wheat or more railroad movement. Alternatively, does the group make the decision on the basis of principles, as, for example, the status quo's tacit assignment of rights? (Levy and Peart 2017b) The choice of liability rules will make a difference. The zero transaction cost assumption emphasized by Stigler has the remarkable property of making goals exogenous. Under this condition, the maximum value of output will be forthcoming irrespective of liability. The group output is exogenous. Coase's disagreement with Stigler has been long relegated to the attention of specialists in the economics of externalities. It is, however, central to the distinction between the Virginia and the Chicago schools.[11]

POLITICS AS TRADE

It is unlikely that group goal endogeneity would be the answer to a quiz on how to characterize the Virginia School; the answer might well be "politics as exchange." There are so many dimensions of that principle in the work of Buchanan and Tullock that we will mention only a few. This principle was a source of tension within the Virginia School because it was sharply disputed by Nutter, who held with politics as power. We start with the most famous examples and then look backward.

Log-rolling was a largely disreputable activity until *The Calculus of Consent* made the useful point that this was how exchange was made in legislatures: A votes for B's bill if B votes for A's (Buchanan and Tullock [1962] 1999).[12] To make trades, one probably needs more than one dimension, so one needs to be very careful about extending one-dimensional insight summarized in the median voter theorem to higher dimensions. The great early statement of that problem is the Plott (1967) conditions for high-dimensional median voter theorem. Charles Plott, a graduate student at the University of Virginia who studied with Buchanan and Coase, established a sufficient condition of "ordinal pairwise symmetry of all voters along any vector passing through the status quo" (Hinick and Munger 1997, 65).

Buchanan often wrote about how, lingering at Chicago between dissertation and employment, he chanced upon a book by Knut Wicksell (*Finanztheoretische Untersuchungen*) in which Wicksell described the principle that a vote for governmental services ought to be simultaneously a vote for the taxes to pay for them. Buchanan regarded this insight as the fundamental principle of exchange. Aware of the ideological interpretation that such a procedure might generate, Buchanan emphasized that Wicksell himself believed it would increase, rather than reduce, the size of government because people would be more confident that their taxes would be directed to the activities they desired.

Late in his life Buchanan wrote a series of papers with Yong Yoon in which rotating majorities allowed individuals to take turns in the majority (Buchanan and Yoon 2015). He and Yoon relied on trade of another sort, trade across time: one person is in charge first, another in charge later. In an important sense the Buchanan–Yoon analysis speaks to the problem of representation that worried Lani Guinier (1994) when there are permanent majorities and permanent minorities. The permanent majority/minority situation involves no intertemporal exchange; there is just politics as power. Buchanan's larger concern was to put welfare economics in the circle of exchange. His idea was that a welfare economist proposes a Pareto-improving reform and then sits down. If the reform is adopted, it is true that the proposal was a Pareto-improvement. If not, then it is false. But this supposes motivation by truth considerations, which as we have noted raises a tension in Buchanan's worldview. We shall return to that tension in our final section. The principle of politics as exchange does not begin and end with Buchanan and coauthors Tullock and Yoon.[13] It is central to Coase's proposal in the early 1950s to reform British Broadcasting from a monopoly offering programs the middle and upper classes thought "good" for the lower classes to a competitive system in which everyone can choose programs. By competitive, Coase did not mean private; instead, he meant competition among government providers.

TENSION

Buchanan's teacher Frank Knight seems to have been of two minds about the motivation of economists. Generally speaking, he supposed economists were truth-seekers, just as he supposed that legislation was a form of truth-seeking. In one instance, however, Knight (1933) dropped the truth-seeking assumption and asked what the real motivation of economists is (see also Levy and Peart 2017b). His answer sounded much like that of Gordon Tullock in *Organization of Inquiry.* This essay of Knight's was not included in *Ethics of Competition* but only (as far as we know) as the new addition to the London School of Economics reprint of *Risk, Uncertainty and Profit.*

Buchanan's position on the truth-seeking motivation of economists seems never to have wavered.[14] In a marvelous 1959 article, he offered a Popperian gloss of welfare economics (Buchanan 1959).[15] A proposed policy is Pareto-improving if and only if the public adopts an economist's proposal. But that supposes that economists are motivated only by the truth. Because truth is presumed to be a public good, Buchanan thus induced a motivational difference between the economist and those who pursue happiness. Knight and Vining also relied on this exception to analytical egalitarianism. We have proposed that treating economists as influenced by institutions and ethics would resolve the tension between analytical egalitarianism and the desire to find a role for the economist as reformer. Even Tullock noted that the institution of replication made scientists act as if they were truth-seekers.

NOTES

The authors thank Peter Boettke, Virgil Storr, Roger Congleton, John Nye, Trey Dudley, David Coker, and other participants for helpful suggestions. They thank David Vining for permission to print Rutledge Vining's letters to Milton Friedman, the estate of John Rawls for permission to print his letter to James Buchanan and Gordon Tullock, David Friedman and Jan Martel for permission to print Milton Friedman's letter to Rutledge Vining, and Ning Wang for permission to print Ronald Coase's letter to Gordon Tullock. This essay is the initial chapter of the authors' proposed history of the Virginia School.

1. "Koopmans presumably does not like the unit of analysis used in the Burns and Mitchell study—the 'business cycle' of a given category of economic activity. I too feel that this unit of analysis is limited and, at least, should be regarded as strictly tentative—as it undoubtedly is regarded by these users; but I think that Koopmans' alternative unit—the individual economizing agent—is possibly even more fundamentally limited in the study of many aspects of aggregate trade fluctuations. . . . I think that we need not take for granted that the behavior and functioning of this entity can be exhaustively explained in terms of the motivated behavior of individuals who are particles within the whole. It is conceivable— and it would hardly be doubted in other fields of study — that the aggregate has an existence apart from its constituent particles and behavior characteristics of its own not deducible from the behavior characteristics of the particles" (Vining 1949, 79). "I think that in a positive sense the aggregate has an existence over and above the existence of Koopmans' individual units and behavior characteristics that may not be deducible from the behavior of these component parts" (Vining 1949, 81).

2. Buchanan cites this essay as standing for Vining's influence over "hundreds of hours of informal discussion" (Buchanan 2004, 59).

3. Vining's essay begins: "The critical review by T. C. Koopmans of the recent study by Burns and Mitchell would apparently cast doubt on the efficiency of almost any method of analysis that is not essentially identical with the methods adopted and developed by Koopmans and his associates. While these methods are intriguing and the results of their application will be awaited with keen interest, they are as yet untested" (Vining 1949, 77). Vining discussed the episode at some length in the UNESCO essay, citing Carl Christ's testing of the first of macroeconomic model constructed along Koopmans's lines (Vining 1956, 42–3; Hammond 1996, 40–3). Koopman's (1947) famous technical point, that the NBER approach does not consider identification problems when implemented in early macroeconometric models, supposed that government policy was exogenous. Theil (1971, 476) lays out in detail how the Klein–Goldberger model takes tax rates, as well as government expenditure, as exogenous and, on that basis, identifies the system of equations.

4. Excerpts from Vining (1956) used by permission of United Nations Educational, Scientific and Cultural Orgnanization.

5. From this, the tenor of *The Calculus of Consent* should come as no surprise. We return to this later.

6. See Friedman (2012), the "Collected Works of Milton Friedman."

7. Coase's anger at such a characterization can be (partly) explained by his role in guiding the Fabian Society proposal for the reform of British Broadcasting (Levy and Peart 2014a, 2014b).

8. "It does not need to be emphasized here that the Economics Department has associated itself firmly with an outlook now known as that of the 'Virginia School,' an outlook described by its friends as 'Neo-Liberalism' and its critics as 'Nineteenth-Century Ultra-Conservatism.'"

9. This letter is located in Box 25 of the W. H. Hutt Papers at the Hoover Institution Archive, Stanford University. Hutt was visiting the Thomas Jefferson Center and was perhaps "lent" a file of the correspondence, never to be returned. Hutt and Rawls have in common a deep appreciation for the work of Frank Knight.

10. This is not to suggest that analytical egalitarianism is sufficient. The issue will enter Virginia School controversy when we ask whether economists need better motivation than other people do.

11. "I can justify my classification of Wicksell, Hutt and Coase in the same gains-from-trade category by recalling, autobiographically, my own initial reactions to the Coasian proposition, when first presented among faculty colleagues at the University of Virginia in the late 1950s. Coming at the Coase theorem from a Wicksellian perspective, I found the theorem almost self-evident, and I specifically recall the surprise felt when Coase reported back to us about the controversial reaction to his presentation of the theorem at the University of Chicago" (Buchanan 1988, 11–12)

12. Buchanan (1973, 592–93) considers the general issue of the rights held by "incorruptible" governmental decision makers: "Such rights may, however, be considered to be inalienable; that is, the holder is not entitled to sell them or to exploit his possession of them through collection of personal rewards, either directly or indirectly. It would be inappropriate in this paper to examine in detail the validity of such ethical presuppositions, although this opens up many interesting and highly controversial topics for analysis. The existence of such presuppositions can scarcely be denied. The pejorative content of such terms as 'vote-trading,' 'logrolling,' 'political favoritism,' 'spoils system,' 'pork barrel legislation'—these attest to the pervasiveness of negative attitudes toward even minor attempts on the part of possessors of political decision-making rights to increase rental returns."

13. We have written about this doctrine's roots in Richard Whately and J. S. Mill's exercises in politics as exchange. Wicksell was very well informed about British economic discussions, which suggests a linkage to be explored.

14. We have memories of decades of arguments with Jim on this! We would like to believe that the behavior of economists in the period that preceded the 2007–2008 financial crisis was causing him to waver.

15. Although Popper's official theory of progress by falsification supposes truth-seeking, his letter to Tullock on receipt of *Organization of Inquiry* reveals that Popper, like Tullock, knows about faction in science (Levy and Peart 2017b).

REFERENCES

Arrow, Kenneth J. (1951) 1963. *Social Choice and Individual Values.* New York: John Wiley.

Buchanan, James M. 1954. "Social Choice, Democracy, and Free Markets." *Journal of Political Economy* 62 (2): 114–23.

———. 1959. "Positive Economics, Welfare Economics, and Political Economy." *Journal of Law and Economics* 2: 124–38.

———. 1973. "The Coase Theorem and the Theory of the State." *Natural Resource Journal* 13: 579–94.

———. 1988. "Economists and the Gains from Trade." *Managerial and Decision Economics* 9 (5): 5–12.

———. 2004. "10x10: James M. Buchanan." *Politik* 7: 50–2.

Buchanan, James M., and Gordon Tullock. (1962) 1999. *The Calculus of Consent: Logical Foundations of Constitutional Democracy*. Vol. 3 of *The Collected Works of James M. Buchanan*. Indianapolis, IN: Liberty Fund.

Buchanan, James M. and Yong Yoon. 2015. *Individualism and Political Disorder*. Cheltenham, U.K.: Edward Elgar.

Coase, Ronald H. 1960. "The Problem of Social Cost." *Journal of Law & Economics* 3 (October): 1–44.

———. 1992. "The Institutional Structure of Production." *American Economic Review* 82 (4): 713–19.

Friedman, Milton. 2012. "Collected Works of Milton Friedman" website. Hoover Institution Archives. Stanford, CA: Stanford University. Available at https://miltonfriedman.hoover.org/collections;jsessionid=EA2B9804668BD5A1BA823B1FE28AA655.

Guinier, Lani. 1994. *Tyranny of the Majority: Fundamental Fairness in Representative Democracy.* New York: Free Press.

Hammond, J. Daniel. 1996. *Theory and Measurement: Causality Issues in Milton Friedman's Monetary Economics.* New York: Cambridge University Press.

Hinick, Melvin, J. and Michael C. Munger. 1997. *Analytical Politics*. Cambridge, U.K.: Cambridge University Press.

Knight, Frank H. 1933. "Preface to the Re-Issue." In *Risk, Uncertainty, and Profit*. London: London School of Economics and Political Science.

Koopmans, Tjalling C. 1947. "Measurement without Theory." *Review of Economics and Statistics* 29 (3): 161–72.

Levy, David M., and Sandra J. Peart. 2008. "Socialist Calculation Debate." In *The New Palgrave Dictionary of Economics*, edited by Steven N. Durlauf and Lawrence E. Blume. London: Palgrave Macmillan.

———. 2011. "Soviet Growth and American Textbooks: An Endogenous Past." *Journal of Economic Behavior and Organization* 78 (1): 110–25.

———. 2012. "Tullock on Motivated Inquiry: Expert-Induced Uncertainty Disguised as Risk." *Public Choice* 152 (1): 163–80.

———. 2014a. "'Almost Wholly Negative': The Ford Foundation's Appraisal of the Virginia School." https://papers.ssrn.com/sol3/papers.cfm?abstract_id=2485695.

———. 2014b. "Ronald Coase and the Fabian Society: Competitive Discussion in Liberal Ideology." https://papers.ssrn.com/sol3/papers.cfm?abstract_id=2472130.

———. 2017a. "Gordon Tullock's Ill-Fated Appendix 'Flatland Revisited.'" *Constitutional Political Economy* 28 (1): 18–34

———. 2017b. *Escape from Democracy: The Role of Experts and the Public in Economic Policy*. Cambridge, U.K.: Cambridge University Press.

Lösch, August. 1954. *The Economics of Location*. New Haven, CT: Yale University Press.

Nutter, G. Warren. 1962. *The Growth of Industrial Production in the Soviet Union.* Princeton, NJ: Princeton University Press.

Peart, Sandra J., and David M. Levy. 2005. *The "Vanity of the Philosopher": From Equality to Hierarchy in Post-Classical Economics.* Ann Arbor: University of Michigan Press.

———. 2008. "The Buchanan-Rawls Correspondence." In *The Street Porter & the Philosopher: Conversations on Analytical Egalitarianism*, edited by Sandra J. Peart and David M. Levy, 397–415. Ann Arbor: University of Michigan Press.

———. 2015. "On 'Strongly Fortified Minds': Self-Restraint and Cooperation in the Discussion Tradition." In *Liberal Learning and the Art of Self-Governance*, edited by Emily Chamlee-Wright, 35–49. New York: Routledge.

Plott, Charles R. 1967. "A Notion of Equilibrium and Its Possibility under Majority Rule." *American Economic Review* 57 (4): 787–806.

Rawls, John. 1971. *A Theory of Justice*. Cambridge, MA: Harvard University Press.

Rostow, W. W. 1960. *The Stages of Economic Growth: A Non-Communist Manifesto*. Cambridge, UK: Cambridge University Press.

Samuelson, Paul A. 1948. *Economics: An Introductory Analysis*. New York: McGraw-Hill.

Sen, Amartya. 1995. "Rationality and Social Choice." *American Economic Review* 85 (1): 1–24.

Skousen, Mark. 1997. "The Perseverance of Paul Samuelson's Economics." *Journal of Economic Perspectives* 11 (2): 137–52.

Stigler, George J. 1966. *The Theory of Price*, 3rd ed. New York: Macmillan.

———. (1988) 2003. *Memoirs of an Unregulated Economist.* Chicago: University of Chicago Press.

Theil, Henri. 1971. *Principles of Econometrics*. New York: John Wiley and Sons.

Tullock, Gordon. (1966) 2005. *Organization of Inquiry: The Selected Works of Gordon Tullock, Vol. 3.* Indianapolis, IN: Liberty Fund.

Vining, Rutledge. 1949. "Koopmans on the Choice of Variables to Be Studied and the Methods of Measurement." *Review of Economics and Statistics* 31 (2): 77–86.

———. 1956. *Economics in the United States of America: A Review and Interpretation of Research.* Paris: United Nations Educational, Scientific and Cultural Organization.

CONTRIBUTORS

ABOUT THE EDITORS

Peter J. Boettke is University Professor of Economics and Philosophy at George Mason University and director of the F. A. Hayek Program for Advanced Study in Philosophy, Politics, and Economics at the Mercatus Center at George Mason University.

Solomon Stein is a research fellow in the F. A. Hayek Program for Advanced Study in Philosophy, Politics, and Economics at the Mercatus Center at George Mason University.

ABOUT THE AUTHORS

Roger D. Congleton is BB&T Distinguished Chair of Free Market Thought and professor of economics at West Virginia University.

Christopher J. Coyne is associate professor of economics at George Mason University and associate director of the F. A. Hayek Program for Advanced Study in Philosophy, Politics, and Economics at the Mercatus Center at George Mason University.

Gerald Gaus is James E. Rogers Professor of Philosophy at the University of Arizona.

Stefanie Haeffele is a senior fellow in the F. A. Hayek Program for Advanced Study in Philosophy, Politics, and Economics at the Mercatus Center at George Mason University.

Randall G. Holcombe is DeVoe Moore Professor of Economics at Florida State University.

Jayme S. Lemke is a senior fellow in the F. A. Hayek Program for Advanced Study in Philosophy, Politics, and Economics at the Mercatus Center at George Mason University.

David M. Levy is professor of economics at George Mason University.

Sandra J. Peart is dean of the Jepson School of Leadership Studies at the University of Richmond.

Virgil Henry Storr is Don C. Lavoie Senior Fellow in the F. A. Hayek Program for Advanced Study in Philosophy, Politics, and Economics at the Mercatus Center at George Mason University and research associate professor in economics at George Mason University.

Richard E. Wagner is Hobart R. Harris Professor of Economics at George Mason University and Distinguished Senior Fellow in the F. A. Hayek Program for Advanced Study in Philosophy, Politics, and Economics at the Mercatus Center at George Mason University.

INDEX

Note: Information in figures, notes, and tables is indicated by f, n, and t.

CPSIA information can be obtained
at www.ICGtesting.com
Printed in the USA
FFHW02n2224211018

9 781942 951421